THE CAMBRIDGE COMPANION TO
WALLACE STEVENS

Wallace Stevens is a major American poet and a central figure in modernist studies and twentieth-century poetry. This *Companion* introduces students to his work. An international team of distinguished contributors presents a unified picture of Stevens' poetic achievement. The Introduction explains why Stevens is among the world's great poets and offers specific guidance on how to read and appreciate his poetry. A brief biographical sketch anchors Stevens in the real world and illuminates important personal and intellectual influences. The essays following chart Stevens' poetic career and his affinities with both earlier and contemporary writers, artists, and philosophers. Other essays introduce students to the peculiarity and distinctiveness of Stevens' voice and style. They explain prominent themes in his work and explore the nuances of his aesthetic theory. With a detailed chronology and a guide to further reading, this *Companion* provides all the information a student or scholar of Stevens will need.

JOHN N. SERIO is Professor of Humanities at Clarkson University, New York, and editor of the *Wallace Stevens Journal*.

T0328432

THE CAMBRIDGE
COMPANION TO
WALLACE STEVENS

EDITED BY
JOHN N. SERIO

CAMBRIDGE
UNIVERSITY PRESS

CAMBRIDGE UNIVERSITY PRESS
Cambridge, New York, Melbourne, Madrid, Cape Town, Singapore,
São Paulo, Delhi, Dubai, Tokyo

Cambridge University Press
The Edinburgh Building, Cambridge CB2 8RU, UK

Published in the United States of America by Cambridge University Press, New York

www.cambridge.org
Information on this title: www.cambridge.org/9780521614825

© Cambridge University Press 2007

First published 2007

A catalogue record for this publication is available from the British Library

ISBN 978-0-521-84956-2 Hardback
ISBN 978-0-521-61482-5 Paperback

Transferred to digital printing 2009

CONTENTS

CONTENTS

CONTRIBUTORS

MILTON J. BATES is the author of *Wallace Stevens: A Mythology of Self* (1985) and *The Wars We Took to Vietnam: Cultural Conflict and Storytelling* (1996). He has edited the revised edition of Stevens' *Opus Posthumous* (1989) and *Sur Plusieurs Beaux Sujects: Wallace Stevens' Commonplace Book* (1989). He teaches at Marquette University.

JACQUELINE VAUGHT BROGAN has published several books on twentieth-century poetry, including *Stevens and Simile: A Theory of Language* (1986), *Part of the Climate: American Cubist Poetry* (1991), *Women Poets of the Americas* (co-edited with Cordelia Chávez Candelaria, 1999), and *The Violence Within/The Violence Without: Wallace Stevens and the Emergence of a Revolutionary Poetics* (2003). She teaches at the University of Notre Dame.

JOSEPH CARROLL is the author of *The Cultural Theory of Matthew Arnold* (1982), *Wallace Stevens' Supreme Fiction: A New Romanticism* (1987), *Evolution and Literary Theory* (1995), and *Literary Darwinism: Evolution, Human Nature, and Literature* (2004). He has also published a contextualized, annotated edition of Darwin's *On the Origin of Species* (2003). He teaches at the University of Missouri-St. Louis.

BONNIE COSTELLO is Professor of English at Boston University specializing in modern and contemporary poetry. She is the author of *Marianne Moore: Imaginary Possessions* (1981), *Elizabeth Bishop: Questions of Mastery* (1991), and *Shifting Ground: Reinventing Landscape in Modern American Poetry* (2003). She is General Editor of *The Selected Letters of Marianne Moore* (1997).

BART EECKHOUT is the author of *Wallace Stevens and the Limits of Reading and Writing* (2002). He has guest-edited two special issues of the *Wallace Stevens Journal*, one on 'International Perspectives' (2001) and the other, with Edward Ragg, on 'Wallace Stevens and British Literature' (2006). He teaches at the University of Antwerp in Belgium.

ALAN FILREIS is Kelly Professor, Faculty Director of the Kelly Writers House, and Director of the Center for Programs in Contemporary Writing at the University of Pennsylvania. His books include *Wallace Stevens and the Actual World* (1991), *Modernism from Right to Left: Wallace Stevens, the Thirties and Literary Radicalism* (1994), and a new edition of Ira Wolfert's *Tucker's People* (1997). He has just completed a new book, entitled *The Fifties' Thirties: The Conservative Attack on Modern Poetry, 1945–60.*

DAVID R. JARRAWAY is Professor of American Literature at the University of Ottawa and is the author of *Wallace Stevens and the Question of Belief: Metaphysician in the Dark* (1993), *Going the Distance: Dissident Subjectivity in Modernist American Literature* (2003), and many essays on American literature and culture.

B. J. LEGGETT is Distinguished Professor of Humanities at the University of Tennessee. His books on Stevens include *Wallace Stevens and Poetic Theory: Conceiving the Supreme Fiction* (1987), *Early Stevens: The Nietzschean Intertext* (1992), and *Late Stevens: The Final Fiction* (2005).

GEORGE S. LENSING is Bowman and Gordon Gray Professor of English at the University of North Carolina at Chapel Hill. He is the author of *Wallace Stevens: A Poet's Growth* (1986) and *Wallace Stevens and the Seasons* (2001).

JAMES LONGENBACH is the Joseph H. Gilmore Professor of English at the University of Rochester. He is the author of three books of poems, including *Fleet River* (2003) and *Draft of a Letter* (2007), as well as five critical books, including *Wallace Stevens: The Plain Sense of Things* (1991) and *The Resistance to Poetry* (2004).

BEVERLY MAEDER teaches at the University of Lausanne in Switzerland. She is the author of *Wallace Stevens' Experimental Language: The Lion in the Lute* (1999).

ROBERT REHDER's books include *Wordsworth and the Beginnings of Modern Poetry* (1981), *The Poetry of Wallace Stevens* (1988), *Stevens, Williams, Crane and the Motive for Metaphor* (2004), and he has edited *A Narrative of the Life of Mrs. Charlotte Charke* (1999). He is the author of two books of poems: *The Compromises Will Be Different* (1995) and *First Things When* (2007). He holds the chair of English and American Literature at the University of Fribourg, Switzerland.

JOAN RICHARDSON is the author of *Wallace Stevens: The Early Years, 1879–1923* (1986), *Wallace Stevens: The Later Years, 1923–1955* (1988), and co-editor, with Frank Kermode, of the Library of America's edition of Stevens' *Collected Poetry and Prose* (1997). She has just published *A Natural History of Pragmatism: The Fact of Feeling from Jonathan Edwards to Gertrude Stein* (2006). She teaches at The Graduate Center, CUNY.

JOHN N. SERIO has been editor of the *Wallace Stevens Journal* since 1983. He has published *Wallace Stevens: An Annotated Secondary Bibliography* (1994) and, with B. J. Leggett, *Teaching Wallace Stevens: Practical Essays* (1994). He has also edited *Poetry for Young People: Wallace Stevens* (2004) and created, with Greg Foster, an *Online Concordance to Wallace Stevens' Poetry* (2004). He is Professor of Humanities at Clarkson University.

HELEN VENDLER is the A. Kingsley Porter University Professor at Harvard. She has written extensively on Stevens, including *On Extended Wings: Wallace Stevens' Longer Poems* (1969) and *Wallace Stevens: Words Chosen Out of Desire* (1984). Her recent books include *Poets Thinking: Pope, Dickinson, Whitman, Yeats* (2004) and *Invisible Listeners: Intimacy in Herbert, Whitman, and Ashbery* (2005). She is at work on a study of Yeats's lyric forms.

CHRONOLOGY

1879   Born October 2 in Reading, Pennsylvania, the second son of
            Margaretha (Kate), a former teacher, and Garrett Stevens, a
            lawyer and businessman, whose other children included
            Garrett, Jr., born December 19, 1877; John, born December
            9, 1880; Elizabeth, born July 19, 1885; and Mary Katharine,
            born April 25, 1889.

1885–1891   Although raised Presbyterian, attends Lutheran grammar
            schools and studies, among other subjects, French and
            German, which he continues to read throughout his life.

1892–1897   Takes classical curriculum at Reading Boys' High School and,
            after being held back one year due to illness and low grades,
            graduates with merit, having won prizes for writing and
            public speaking.

1897–1900   Attends Harvard College as a special student in a three-year,
            non-degree program, taking most of his coursework in
            English, French, and German languages and literature.
            Publishes over thirty poems, short stories, and sketches in
            the *Harvard Advocate* and *Harvard Monthly*, often under
            pseudonyms, and serves as secretary of the Signet Society
            and president of the *Harvard Advocate*.

1900–1901   Tries his hand as a reporter in New York, working for the
            New York Tribune and *World's Work*, a monthly magazine,
            but finds journalism unfulfilling.

1901–1903   Persuaded by his father, enrolls in New York Law School; clerks for W. G. Peckham, a New York attorney, during the summer of 1902; graduates in June 1903.

1903–1904   Works as a law clerk for Peckham, who befriends him and takes him in late summer 1903 on a seven-week hunting trip to British Columbia.

1904–1908   Admitted to the New York bar in June 1904, visits Reading and meets Elsie Kachel, born in Reading June 5, 1886; begins a five-year courtship, carried on mostly in correspondence. Struggles as a lawyer in New York, moving from firm to firm.

1908   In January, secures a position with American Bonding Co., initiating his lifelong legal specialty in the insurance business. In June, sends Elsie "A Book of Verses," composed for her twenty-second birthday. Becomes engaged to Elsie at Christmas, despite family objections to her lower social status.

1909   Composes "The Little June Book," a collection of poems for Elsie's twenty-third birthday; marries Elsie on September 21 in Reading, with no family members in attendance; resides in New York with Elsie until their move to Hartford, Connecticut, in 1916.

1911   Father dies in Reading on July 14, and Stevens attends the funeral.

1912   Mother dies in Reading on July 16, and Stevens attends the funeral.

1914   Joins the New York office of Equitable Surety Company in February as a vice president. Publishes minor poems, including two poetic sequences, "Carnet de Voyage" and "Phases." His return to poetry stimulated in part by his financial stability and by the company of writers, artists, and musicians – including William Carlos Williams and Marcel Duchamp – who gathered regularly at the New York apartment of Walter Arensberg.

1915   Publishes first mature poems such as "Peter Quince at the Clavier" and "Sunday Morning."

1916   Joins the Hartford Accident and Indemnity Company and moves permanently to Hartford. Specializing in surety bonds, travels extensively throughout the United States, visiting places such as Florida, Oklahoma, and Minnesota, which often form backdrops to his poetry. Wins $100 *Poetry* prize for verse drama *Three Travelers Watch a Sunrise*. Wife's profile serves as image of Mercury on the American dime through mid-1940s.

1917   Does not attend sole performance in October of verse play *Carlos among the Candles* in an off-Broadway theater in New York.

1919   In May, Mary Katharine, his youngest sister, dies in France while serving as a Red Cross volunteer during World War I.

1920   Does not attend the only performance of *Three Travelers Watch a Sunrise* by the Provincetown Players in New York in February. Wins Levinson Prize from *Poetry* for group of poems, "Pecksniffiana," in November.

1921   Submits "From the Journal of Crispin" for the Blindman Prize, sponsored by the Poetry Society of South Carolina, and receives first honorable mention from judge Amy Lowell. Revises the poem as "The Comedian as the Letter C."

1923   In September, shortly before his forty-fourth birthday, publishes first book, *Harmonium*, with Alfred A. Knopf. Takes first extended vacation with Elsie, traveling to Havana, the Panama Canal, the Gulf of Tehuantepec, California, and overland back to Hartford.

1924   Holly Bright Stevens, his only child, born on August 10 in Hartford.

1925–33   Claiming the new baby and work consume his energies, virtually gives up writing poetry.

1931   *Harmonium* reissued by Knopf in a revised edition (three poems were deleted and fourteen – most composed before 1924 – added). Initiates lifelong relationship with Parisian bookseller, from whom he also purchases paintings.

1932   In September, moves to 118 Westerly Terrace in Hartford, the only home he owned, located near Elizabeth Park.

1934   Named vice president of Hartford Accident and Indemnity Company in February, earning, during this year of the Depression, $17,500 (based on the Consumer Price Index, equivalent to $264,500 in 2006 dollars).

1935   *Ideas of Order* published in a limited edition by Alcestis Press in August.

1936   In February in Key West, gets into a fistfight with Ernest Hemingway and breaks his hand on Hemingway's jaw (the two make amends and conceal the cause of the injury). In October, Knopf publishes trade edition of *Ideas of Order*. Awarded *The Nation*'s Poetry Prize for "The Men That Are Falling." Alcestis Press issues a limited edition of *Owl's Clover* in November. Delivers lecture "The Irrational Element in Poetry" at Harvard in December.

1937   *The Man with the Blue Guitar and Other Poems* published by Knopf in October. Older brother Garrett Stevens, Jr., dies in November in Cleveland, Ohio.

1940   Younger brother John Bergen Stevens dies in July in Philadelphia, Pennsylvania.

1941   Presents lecture "The Noble Rider and the Sound of Words" at Princeton University in May. Initiates genealogical studies that preoccupy him for the rest of his life.

1942   In September, Knopf publishes *Parts of a World*. In October, Cummington Press publishes a limited edition of *Notes toward a Supreme Fiction*.

1943   In February, Elizabeth Stevens MacFarland, his last surviving sibling, dies in Philadelphia. Delivers lecture "The Figure of the Youth as Virile Poet" at Mount Holyoke College in August.

1944   In August, against Stevens' objections, Holly marries John Hanchak, a repairman.

1945   Presents lecture "Description Without Place" as the Phi Beta Kappa poem at Harvard in June. *Esthétique du Mal* published by Cummington Press in a limited edition in November. Elected to the National Institute of Arts and Letters in December; inducted the next year in May.

1947   Reads essay "Three Academic Pieces" at Harvard in February. *Transport to Summer* published by Knopf in March. His only grandchild, Peter Reed Hanchak, born on April 26. Receives an honorary doctorate from Wesleyan University in June. *Three Academic Pieces* published by Cummington Press in December.

1948   Presents lecture "Effects of Analogy" at Yale University in March and at Mount Holyoke in April. Reads paper "Imagination as Value" at Columbia University in September.

1949   In September, receives *Still Life* by Pierre Tal-Coat from Parisian art dealer, inspiring him to write "Angel Surrounded by Paysans." In November, reads "An Ordinary Evening in New Haven" at the 150th celebration of the Connecticut Academy of Arts and Sciences in New Haven.

1950   Awarded Bollingen Prize in Poetry for 1949 in March. *The Auroras of Autumn* published by Knopf in September.

1951   In January, delivers lecture "The Relations Between Poetry and Painting" at the Museum of Modern Art in New York; later that month, awarded Gold Medal of the Poetry Society of America in New York. In March, wins 1950 National Book Award in Poetry for *The Auroras of Autumn*. Awarded an honorary doctorate from Bard College in

March. Reads essay "Two or Three Ideas" at Mount Holyoke in April. Receives an honorary degree from Harvard in June. Holly Stevens granted a divorce from John Hanchak in September. In November, Knopf publishes *The Necessary Angel: Essays on Reality and the Imagination*. Presents lecture "A Collect of Philosophy" at University of Chicago and at City College of New York.

1952   In June, receives honorary doctorates from Mount Holyoke and Columbia.

1953   *Selected Poems* published in England by Faber and Faber in February.

1954   Records reading of poems for Harvard Library. Reads "The Sail of Ulysses" as Phi Beta Kappa poem at Columbia in May. In October, on the occasion of his seventy-fifth birthday, Knopf releases *The Collected Poems of Wallace Stevens*.

1955   In January, receives National Book Award in Poetry for 1954. In April, diagnosed with cancer of the stomach. Awarded Pulitzer Prize in Poetry in May. Receives honorary doctorates from Hartt College of Music in Hartford and Yale in June. Dies of stomach cancer on August 2 at St. Francis Hospital in Hartford.

1963   Elsie Stevens dies on February 19 in Hartford.

1992   Holly Stevens dies on March 4 in Guilford, Connecticut.

ABBREVIATIONS

Unless otherwise noted, quotations from Wallace Stevens are taken from *Wallace Stevens: Collected Poetry and Prose*, edited by Frank Kermode and Joan Richardson (New York: Library of America, 1997) and cited parenthetically in the text with page numbers only. Other works will be cited with the following abbreviations:

L   *Letters of Wallace Stevens*, ed. Holly Stevens. New York: Knopf, 1966; rpt. Berkeley: University of California Press, 1996.

SP   Stevens, Holly. *Souvenirs and Prophecies: The Young Wallace Stevens*. New York: Knopf, 1977.

SPBS   *Sur Plusieurs Beaux Sujects: Wallace Stevens' Commonplace Book. A Facsimile and Transcription*, ed. Milton J. Bates. Stanford: Stanford University Press and Huntington Library, 1989.

Other works by Stevens may be found in the Guide to Further Reading.

JOHN N. SERIO

Introduction

The poetry of Wallace Stevens presents a paradox. On one hand, those who know and love his poetry consider him one of America's finest poets. Some critics have singled out particular poems such as "Sunday Morning" and "The Snow Man" as among the best ever written.[1] Enthusiasts enjoy his comic spirit and delight in the freshness of his unusual subjects – placing a jar in Tennessee, eating ice cream at a funeral, dancing around a dead stump. They marvel at the way his musical lines dazzle one into affirming what is undeniably illogical – "Music is feeling, then, not sound," and "Beauty is momentary in the mind . . . / But in the flesh it is immortal" (72–75). They are moved by his expressions of loss, alienation, and despair. But more than this, they see Stevens as a major poet because he addresses major themes: the relationship between the world and the mind, the beauty of planet Earth as an end in itself, poetry (or art in general) as an affirmation of life, the problem of belief in a secular age, the need for creating a sense of nobility in a crass and violent world. They regard Stevens as a great poet because he infuses these subjects with authentic feeling, so that each becomes "An abstraction blooded, as a man by thought" (333).

On the other hand, most people have never heard of Wallace Stevens. Among those who have, many find his work intimidating and "too difficult" to comprehend. Stevens himself is in part responsible for his lack of a wide readership. Reticent by nature, he was not a self-promoter as were some of his contemporaries such as Ezra Pound, T. S. Eliot, and Robert Frost. Although late in life Stevens did accept a number of accolades, he was uncomfortable at the ceremonies and escaped them as quickly and with as little notice as possible. He cringed at opportunities for publicity, declining both *Life* and *The New Yorker* when they wished to run profiles on him.[2] When he received the Bollingen Prize in Poetry, he curtly declined to be interviewed by a local newspaper reporter. The front-page article in the Hartford *Courant*, carrying a three-year-old photograph of him, noted that he had nothing to say except "hurry."[3]

I

However much Stevens may have shunned it, popular awareness plays a role in general acceptance, especially if a writer is challenging. Such recognition provides the reader with a completely different frame of reference, a completely different set of assumptions from which to begin. Public reaction to the complex fiction of William Faulkner is a case in point. Recently, the American television program host, Oprah Winfrey, selected three novels by Faulkner for Oprah's Book Club – *As I Lay Dying*, *The Sound and the Fury*, and *Light in August*. Calling the endeavor "A Summer of Faulkner," she offered guides on how to approach his fiction on her book club website, among them "How to Read Faulkner," "The Stream of Consciousness," and "Breaking Literary Rules." There were also helpful tips for readers: "Be Patient," "Be Willing to Re-Read," and "Make the Story Your Own."[4] One familiar with Faulkner's style cannot help but smile at these. But more pertinent is a remark by Ulf Linde, a longtime member of the body that awards Nobel Prizes in literature. He commented that Stevens "was one of the big misses of the Academy . . . and now it is, of course, too late."[5] One can only conjecture about the general public's attitude toward, and assumptions about, Stevens had he, like Faulkner, won the Nobel Prize in Literature. Perhaps we could have had a "Summer of Stevens."

There is no doubt that Stevens is hard to understand. But is this unusual? With the exception of Frost (and even he cautioned that he was "not undesigning"[6]), who among Stevens' contemporaries – Pound, Eliot, Marianne Moore, William Carlos Williams – is easy? Eliot's famous observation on modern poetry remains apt. It "must be *difficult*" because the "variety and complexity" of modern society, "playing upon a refined sensibility, must produce various and complex results. The poet must become more and more comprehensive, more allusive, more indirect, in order to force, to dislocate if necessary, language into his meaning."[7] Stevens is no exception. The task at hand, then, is not to dismiss him for being too difficult, but rather to learn how to read him.

How should one approach Stevens' poetry? As with any poet, the first step is to enjoy him, to take pleasure in Stevens' exquisite language, subtle rhythms, arresting images, surprise effects, and distinctive sounds. We have become a little too insistent about meaning in poetry, as if a poem were no more than a vehicle for ideas. We should be mindful of Stevens' observation that "A poem need not have a meaning and like most things in nature often does not have" (914). We should also heed his impassioned advice on how to read a poem: "In poetry, you must love the words, the ideas and images and rhythms with all your capacity to love anything at all" (902). Why? So that we can participate in the process of the poem and share, experientially, in the alteration of feeling, perception, and sense of self that the poem makes possible. The vital center of poetry for Stevens is metamorphosis, the poet's ability "to reconstruct us by his transformations" (670). The poet fulfills himself, says Stevens, "as he sees his imagination become the light in the minds of others" (660–61).

The second step in approaching Stevens' poetry is to concede that he, like Proteus, is slippery. He will not be fixed. If there is a common thread throughout his work, it is that reality and our response to it are in constant flux. We must learn to live with multiple perspectives (not just thirteen but innumerable ways to look at a blackbird); be at home with multiple truths (there is no such thing as "The the" [186]); and accept uncertainty, contra-diction, even chaos, as central to existence. His poems run the gamut from dejection to joy, from doubt to belief, from negation to affirmation. In some poems, "The Snow Man," for example, the speaker is overwhelmed by an overpowering, intractable reality – "the nothing that is" (8). In others, such as "The Idea of Order at Key West" or "Tea at the Palaz of Hoon," the speaker absorbs reality with an imagination that subsumes all – "I was the world . . . and what I saw / Or heard or felt came not but from myself" (51). One might say these instances represent the poles of Stevens' notorious "reality-imagination complex" (L 792), but they do not yield a dialectic, as if there were a synthesis or resolution to the continual process of adjust-ment. Rather, they constitute discrete moments in a never-ending cycle in the poet's (and in our) response to reality. Change is the essence of poetry for Stevens because change is the essence of life.

There are certain occasions, however – precious, indeed ecstatic ones – when what is felt and what is thought are one with what is perceived. These moments are hard-earned prizes in Stevens' poetry – validated by the recognition of the other moods – and constitute for him an ideal. As he says in one of his essays, "There is, in fact, a world of poetry indistinguish-able from the world in which we live" (662). That is why the poet is such an important figure for Stevens, for "he creates the world to which we turn incessantly and without knowing it" and "he gives to life the supreme fictions without which we are unable to conceive of it" (662). As readers, we share in the feeling of enlightenment achieved in these poems through the imagination's agreement with reality, evoking what Stevens might term a poetic truth or a truth beyond reason. As he says in "Notes Toward a Supreme Fiction," on the occasion of catching a fresh perception of the sunrise or the sea clearing or the moon hanging in the heavens, "These are not things transformed. / Yet we are shaken by them as if they were" (345).

The third step, and perhaps the key adjustment readers must make when approaching Stevens, is to acknowledge that his poems are not about a subject so much as they are about the poetry of the subject, about the way the subject develops through language. The distinction between these two concepts – the subject of the poetry and the poetry of the subject – is crucial, and it is the primary reason for Stevens' legendary difficulty. Although he strikes one as a poet born and not made, as a poetic genius "just blazing away in line after line,"[8] Stevens aimed to compose poems that captured the essence or inner life of the experience. "Although [these poems] are simple to read, when they're done," he confessed to his wife, "it's a deuce of a job (for me) to do them" (*L* 180). In Stevens' view, there is a tension in all poetry between the subject and the poetry of the subject. For the poet for whom the "subject [is] paramount," he observes, "the subject is constant and the development orderly." However, if it is the poetry of the subject that is foremost, "the true subject is not constant nor its development orderly" (785). This explains Stevens' style – the unexpected shifts in syntax that defy logic, the provisional statements whose open-endedness teases, the rhetoric of denial that paradoxically affirms. To invoke Eliot, this may very well be Stevens' method of dislocating language into meaning.

But what exactly is the poetry of the subject that makes Stevens' writing unique and makes Stevens a great poet? It is his belief that the theory of poetry is the theory of life, "that the structure of poetry and the structure of reality are one" (692). This is a grand concept and, if acknowledged, it makes poetry one of the most lofty of human enterprises. More than other poets, Stevens pointedly declares that everything we believe is a fiction, that reality is an invention of the mind. This explains the outrageously abstract beginnings of so many poems: "Begin, ephebe, by perceiving the idea / Of this invention, this invented world" (329; "Notes Toward a Supreme Fiction"); "The eye's plain version is a thing apart" (397; "An Ordinary Evening in New Haven"); "It is possible that to seem – it is to be, / As the sun is something seeming and it is" (296; "Description Without Place"). This stance does not turn Stevens into a solipsist, nor does it imply a denial of reality, which Stevens explicitly affirms as the "ding an sich" (23), or "the Thing Itself" (451). But it is to grant that all we can know of the outer world is our interpretation of it and that the construction of this interpretation is a poetic act. As Stevens observes in "Adagia," "Things seen are things as seen" (902).

All this is easy enough to understand when one considers the realm of cultural values. Today, as always, people around the globe fight and die for their social, political, and religious beliefs – in other words, for their culture's sense of reality. But this notion is also true of our understanding of the physical world, which has been subject to dynamic paradigm shifts over time – so much so, in fact, that the unquestioned truth of one era becomes the laughable error of the next. Albert Einstein and Leopold Infeld elegantly summarize this argument in their book *The Evolution of Physics*: "Physical concepts are free creations of the human mind, and are not, however it may seem, uniquely determined by the external world."[9]

Einstein and Infeld offer an analogy to elucidate this idea. They suggest that our attempt to understand reality is similar to that of a person trying to understand the mechanism of a closed watch. The individual may account for everything seen and heard, may even create a picture of the inner workings of the watch that fits perfectly with all that is observed; "but he has no way of opening the case. . . . [H]e may never be quite sure his picture is the only one which could explain his observations. He will never be able to compare his picture with the real mechanism and he cannot even imagine the possibility or the meaning of such a comparison" (33). This concept is at the heart of many of Stevens' poems, for, like the romantics before him, he is conscious of how much our response to the world actually constructs it.

"The Dove in the Belly" illustrates this perfectly. A frequently overlooked poem, it contains some of the most sensuous evocations of the beauty of nature in all of Stevens. "How is it," he asks, "that / The rivers shine and hold their mirrors up," or that "the wooden trees stand up / And live and heap their panniers of green . . . ?" "Why," he wants to know, "should / These mountains being high be, also, bright, / Fetched up with snow that never falls to earth?" (318). Reading lines such as these, we are reminded of Stevens' observation that "the great poems of heaven and hell have been written and the great poem of the earth remains to be written" (730), a clear indication, no doubt, of one of his own goals. But Stevens' poem is not as simple as it might appear. First, it uses interrogative sentences rather than declarative ones, thus questioning if not subverting all that is expressed. Second, it is framed by the recognition that "The whole of appearance is a toy" (318) and that any splendor or value in the outer world depends on a response from the inner world, from an imagination imbued with feeling – from "the dove in the belly." As Stevens says in one of his essays:

> It is easy to suppose that few people realize on that occasion, which comes to all of us, when we look at the blue sky for the first time, that is to say: not merely see it, but look at it and experience it and for the first time have a sense that we live in the center of a physical poetry, a geography that would be intolerable except for the non-geography that exists there – few people realize that they are looking at the world of their own thoughts and the world of their own feelings. (684)

How, then, do we redeem Stevens from charges of abstraction and solipsism? The answer resides in acknowledging what Stevens achieves with his thinking, his use of figurative language and sound, and his radical rhetorical patterns. In effect, he creates new linguistic structures that attain integrity. Like Emerson before him, Stevens valorizes perception over conception, moments of genuineness and authenticity that, in a world of constant change, lie beyond, or, one might say, above, reason. In the process, what is evoked, tellingly, if only momentarily, is a credible belief in a fiction that discloses reality. Although it may be "False flick, false form," it is, nevertheless, "falseness close to kin" (333). Einstein and Infeld describe a similar process as the scientist's knowledge increases and his picture of reality encompasses a wider range of perceptions. Then, they state, the scientist may also come to "believe in the existence of the ideal limit of knowledge and that it is approached by the human mind. He may call this ideal limit the objective truth" (33). Stevens' "intimidating thesis" (681), as he emphasizes it, is that "the truth that we experience when we are in agreement with reality is the truth of fact" (680).

The essays in this collection, although stemming from different perspectives, elaborate on these and other aspects of Stevens' work. Beginning with a brief biography, they chart his poetic growth through four major decades and then isolate various influences, qualities, and themes central to his poetry. Some discuss Stevens' personal and intellectual development, noting the heritage of nineteenth-century concepts and values. Others present Stevens' engagement with the revolutionary ideas in art, science, and politics of the first half of the twentieth century. A number focus on unique characteristics of his style and voice or explain complexities in his aesthetic theory. Several unravel the knotty problem of belief in a secular age or offer corrective readings more in line with historical context than earlier interpretations. Although the book refracts Stevens into many parts, it serves as a prism to enable us to see what might otherwise be hidden. What emerges from these essays is a full-color portrait of one of the world's great poets.

NOTES

1. Yvor Winters called "Sunday Morning" "the greatest American poem of the twentieth century and . . . certainly one of the greatest contemplative poems in English" (*In Defense of Reason* [Denver: Swallow, 1947]), 433; more recently, Jay Keyser, in a broadcast on National Public Radio, declared "The Snow Man" to be "the best short poem in the English language bar none" ("All Things Considered," NPR [November 29, 2005]).
2. See Peter Brazeau, *Parts of a World: Wallace Stevens Remembered; An Oral Biography* (New York: Random House, 1983), 47, 56.
3. "Wallace Stevens, Hartford Poet, Awarded $1000 Prize for Contributions to Poetry," Hartford *Courant* (March 28, 1950): 1.
4. See http://www.oprah.com/obc_classic/featbook/asof/booksbooks_main.jhtml and http://www.oprah.com/obc_classic/featbook/asof/books/books_tips_01.jhtml.

5. Quoted by Einar Perman, "News and Comments," *Wallace Stevens Journal* 20.2 (1996): 252.
6. Robert Frost, *Selected Letters of Robert Frost*, ed. Lawrance Thompson (New York: Holt, Rinehart and Winston, 1964), 84.
7. T. S. Eliot, "The Metaphysical Poets," *Selected Essays: 1917–1932* (New York: Harcourt, Brace, 1932), 248.
8. Christian Wiman, "Position Paper: Wallace Stevens," *Wallace Stevens Journal* 28.2 (2004): 240.
9. Albert Einstein and Leopold Infeld, *The Evolution of Physics: The Growth of Ideas from Early Concepts to Relativity and Quanta* (New York: Simon and Schuster, 1938), 33.

I

JOAN RICHARDSON

Wallace Stevens: a likeness

His soil is man's intelligence

The countryside around Reading, Pennsylvania, remains today a preserve of the pastoral. A visitor can walk within a half-hour from where Wallace Stevens was born, a handsome three-story brick row house still standing at 323 North Fifth Street, into a dun-colored landscape, patterned by well-tended farms set amid rolling hills and low gray mountains. Amish in their traditional dress, driving horse-drawn carriages, still pass more than occasionally on the narrow roads and lanes outside of the city. Stevens walked again and again into this landscape, from early childhood into young manhood. During summers when he was a boy, he – together with his four siblings and cousins – spent time in the nearby countryside around Ephrata, around Ivyland, and visited his grandparents' farm in Feasterville, where his father had been born. He fished for bass in the same creek, the Perkiomen, where his father had, and played in the same fields, searching for arrowheads and other traces of the native tribes who inhabited this part of western Pennsylvania well into the nineteenth century. "I look back to that farm and the people who lived in it the way American literature used to look back to English literature" (L 732), Stevens wrote in a letter to Thornton Wilder, another who celebrated the earthy, local habitations so quickly vanishing in twentieth-century America. Stevens' sense of this past remained alive, up-pouring images he would shape into memorializing lines: "The wood-doves are singing along the Perkiomen. / The bass lie deep, still afraid of the Indians" (310); "From a Schuylkill in mid-earth there came emerging / Flotillas, willed and wanted, bearing in them / Shadows of friends, of those he knew" (307). The rivers and rock of this particular landscape became the ground of the poet's "fluent mundo" (351) in which he found "a cure beyond forgetfulness" (446).

Who is my father in this world, in this house, at the spirit's base?

Margaretha Catharine Zeller Stevens (known as Kate) gave birth to her second son, Wallace, on October 2, 1879, at home. Reading and the surrounding area were suffering drought and a yellow fever epidemic, but neither directly affected the household of Kate and her husband, Garrett Barcalow Stevens, though both had been understandably concerned. The couple, both now thirty-one, had married three years earlier; their first child, Garrett Barcalow, Jr., was born just over a year later, in December 1877. Kate would bear three more children who would grow into maturity in the house on North Fifth Street: John Bergen (b. 1880), Elizabeth (b. 1885), and Mary Katharine (b. 1889). Garrett, Sr., was a respected citizen, successfully practicing law and active in the local politics of the bustling, newly industrialized city. Kate, who before her marriage had been a schoolteacher in Reading, devoted herself to family and community, translating her experience and values into important practical lessons for her children in how to live, what to do. The couple shared the same good Puritan values of industry, thrift, and sobriety that characterized the lives of their forebears, the original Protestant settlers of the area around Reading. The strong religious attachments of these individuals continued to dominate the lives of their children and grandchildren. Garrett and Kate Stevens also shared an active appreciation of literature, presenting each other and their children with volumes of poetry, essays, and novels as gifts to fill times of leisure. As Stevens once recalled, "At home, our house was rather a curious place, with all of us in different parts of it, reading" (SP 4).

Stevens' mother, whose ancestry was French and German (the original "Selliers" had been changed to "Zeller"), chose as the first school for Stevens one that included both French and German in its curriculum. Stevens' observation in "Adagia" that "French and English constitute a single language" (914), then, is more than a historical reminder of one of the consequences of the Norman Conquest. The migration of families across the great ocean on their errand in search of religious freedom was one of the worlds held in the words of the languages they brought with them: "luminous / Sequences, thought of among spheres," as Stevens describes it in "The Bed of Old John Zeller," "as if one's grandfather lay / In one's heart and wished as he had always wished" (287).

Stevens' ambiguous relationship with religion also had family roots. Stevens' father was to loosen his ties to religion as he left the farm in Feasterville and educated himself first to become a schoolteacher and later a lawyer in Reading; his mother remained an active member of Reading's First Presbyterian Church throughout her life. She included daily religious

JOAN RICHARDSON

practice in the habits of her children. She sent them to parochial elementary schools and to Sunday-school classes; sang hymns with the family as she accompanied herself on the piano on Sunday evenings; and read Bible stories to them at bedtime. Stevens in adolescence participated in the sacred service as an altar boy and, moving toward manhood, sang hymns himself, "soprano and, later, alto" (*L* 126), as he noted, for two years in the choir of Reading's Christ Cathedral. These experiences would remain at the core of his being. Later in life, Stevens used for his bookplates the keystone inscription of the Trinity Tulpehocken Church (near Myerstown, Pennsylvania) that his ancestor, George Zeller, had joined in dedicating: "WER GOTT BERTRAUT HAT WOL ERBAUT [Who trusts in God has built well]. G. Z. 1772." Stevens noted to the printer who was to copy the inscription, "On my mother's side I am Pennsylvania Dutch and this stone was given to the church by a member of her family" (*L* 541). Yet, writing a few years later to Bernard Heringman, who had asked for an explanation of his religion while writing a dissertation on Stevens, the poet replied, "I dismiss your question by saying that I am a dried-up Presbyterian, and let it go at that because my activities are not religious" (*L* 792). The seeming disjunction between his statement of filial identification with his mother's religious background to be emblematized on his bookplates and the clipped description of his withered religious attachment encapsulates the complicated harmony of what Stevens in the same letter to Heringman referred to as his "reality-imagination complex" (*L* 792). This complex was rooted in "the up and down between two elements" (28) he had already begun to perceive while still a young man, moving, as he recorded in his journal, between the imagination, which he felt he had gotten from his mother, and reason, his "practical side," from his father (*SP* 8).

By the time he left for Harvard in the fall of 1897, the strands of what he had absorbed from his mother and father combined with what he had learned on his own to shape his intention "to be a writer" (*L* 13). In spite of a period of falling back because of "too many nights out" (*SP* 10) and another resulting from illness, he had successfully completed the rigorous classical curriculum (including both Latin and Greek) at Reading Boys' High School, worked on the editorial staff of the school's first newspaper, and won prizes for his oratorical skills. Garrett Stevens, himself a prime example of the American self-made man, had urged each of his sons to do well, "just a little slicker" than the "other fellow" (*L* 24), even when the "other fellow" was a brother. The competition Garrett, Jr., Wallace, and John exercised among one another ensured their graduating at the top of their classes and, as a result, Stevens was accepted by Harvard College. Although formally belonging to the class of 1901, he enrolled in a special,

10

three-year non-degree program that allowed him to choose his courses freely. His curriculum consisted mostly of courses in literature, history, and language. That "first year away from home, at Cambridge," Stevens would write to his future wife in 1909, "made an enormous difference in everything" (*SP* 16).

Take the opposing law

In a letter written in 1943 to one of his Harvard classmates, Stevens, commenting on his recently published "Notes Toward a Supreme Fiction," indicated that its motive derived from what had characterized the spirit of the age, "the will to believe" (*L* 443). His borrowing of the phrase identifiable with William James was significant. Although Stevens had not studied with James at Harvard, interest in the concerns established by James's work in psychology as it stretched itself into America's defining philosophy of pragmatism continued to charge the Cambridge air during the young poet's years there as a student. James and his colleagues Josiah Royce and George Santayana were each in his own way pursuing the questions surrounding the nature of human perception and behavior, questions especially pressing in light of Darwin's challenge to the culture's inherited spiritual beliefs. Conversations with Santayana prompted the young Stevens to practice his skills in a sonnet ("Cathedrals are not built along the sea" [486]) framed as a kind of response to one of their discussions around the theme that would preoccupy the poet throughout his career: religion. For Stevens, religion came to mean what it did for James: *"the feelings, acts, and experiences of individual men in their solitude, so far as they apprehend themselves to stand in relation to whatever they may consider the divine."*[1] As Stevens noted to one of his inquiring readers, "it is a habit of mind with me to be thinking of some substitute for religion. . . . My trouble, and the trouble of a great many people, is the loss of belief in the sort of God in Whom we were all brought up to believe" (*L* 348). As Stevens pursued his studies at Harvard, following the rationality his father prized, he had come, like his father, to leave behind orthodox belief and observance. But, like William James, he realized the value of preserving some variety of religious experience in expressing what he came to consider the "divine." The circuits of reception opened by the imaginative richness provided throughout his childhood and adolescence would keep him "hankering for hymns" (47), feeling "'the need of some imperishable bliss'" (55).

Harvard offered the young Stevens "a radiant and productive atmosphere" (678) where he would find new kinds of imaginative and intellectual nourishment to satisfy that need. Charles Eliot Norton gave courses on

Dante, and Plato's shade spoke again at the meetings of the Jowett Club. Although Stevens was not listed as a member of the club, he shared the strong general interest in Benjamin Jowett evidenced during his Cambridge years. He owned Jowett's translations of Plato's *Dialogues*, which he kept throughout his life, and in 1898 read Jowett's letters. Into the journal he had begun to keep during the same year, he copied a passage whose influence on the development of his own work is clear: "True poetry is the remembrance of youth, of love, of the noblest thoughts of man, of the greatest deeds of the past. – The reconciliation of poetry, as of religion, with truth, may still be possible. Neither is the element of pleasure to be excluded. For when we substitute a higher pleasure for a lower we raise men in the scale of existence" (*SP* 20). Stevens also began writing poetry regularly during the same year, sending one of his first poems, "Autumn," to a magazine established the previous year at Reading Boys' High School, as though announcing himself as a poet to those back home.

Another influence that developed during this period was Stevens' interest in the Far East. The pieces gathered by Ernest Fenollosa for the Oriental Collection at the Boston Museum of Fine Arts stimulated curiosity in the Cambridge community about the art, literature, and culture of the East. Conversations with fellow students, especially Witter Bynner (who would later make extended visits to the East and collaborate in translating major Chinese collections of poetry), prompted Stevens to read as much as possible on this subject. In a 1940 letter, he recalled how his interest in the East had developed while at Harvard: "When I was young and reading right and left, Max Müller was the conspicuous Orientalist of the day" (*L* 381). Müller had translated the *Rig-Veda* and *The Sacred Books of the East*. As a student of Friedrich Schelling and Arthur Schopenhauer and translator of Immanuel Kant as well, Müller applied what he had learned from them – especially concerning the root meaning of words – to his philological investigations of Sanskrit and Pali. In his speculative writing, *The Science of Thought* (1887), for example, he postulated a purely linguistic basis for any future philosophy, looking back to the early Greek philosophers who, in their study of *Logos*, made no separation between language and thought. Stevens would follow Müller's lead, carefully reading of the contributions of the pre-Socratics in John Burnet's *Early Greek Philosophy* (1892). Commenting about the significance of these ancient forms of expression and thought, Stevens noted: "The essence of all this, quite apart from . . . hieratic and religious significance, is of the greatest interest in connection with the poetic side of humanism" (*L* 381).

The importance of Müller's contribution was recognized by another whose work would become an abiding source of intellectual and spiritual nourishment for Stevens, Ralph Waldo Emerson. "History never had problems more interesting than those on which you have thrown so much light," Emerson wrote in an 1872 letter to Müller.[2] A quotation from Schelling in Müller's *Introduction to the Science of Religion* (1873) – "A people exists only when it has determined itself with regard to its mythology"[3] – prefigures Stevens' later preoccupation with this concept as phrased paradigmatically in "A mythology reflects its region" (476). Further, Müller's illustration of the "nucleus of language" to be that of religion as well and thereby "form[ing] the foundation of the . . . world"[4] underscored the purpose and power of Emerson's lifelong project "to enjoy," as he offered in opening *Nature* (1836), "an original relation to the universe"[5] through language responsive to the actuality of "this new yet unapproachable America" (*EL* 485). Stevens would continue to further this purpose and project.

Stevens was presented with a twelve-volume set of Emerson's *Works* (1896–98) by his mother on his Christmas 1898 visit home from Harvard. He kept these volumes throughout his life, reading and rereading them over the years, marking passages and translating Emerson's recognition of nature's "ecstatic" method (*EL* 115–32) into "noble accents / And lucid, inescapable rhythms" (75). Following Emerson, Stevens considered the divine not as the idea of eternal or imminent being but as immanent activity. He directed himself in his journal, "Don't . . . look *at* facts, but *through* them" (*L* 32). The whisperings of Emerson's studious ghost – "But wise men pierce this rotten diction and fasten words again to visible things" (*EL* 23) – reminded the young poet to find and shape words adequate to his time and place, the soil of his intelligence. As Stevens phrased it years later: "One has to pierce through the dithyrambic impressions that talk of the gods makes to the reality of what is being said. What is being said must be true and the truth of it must be seen. But the truth about the poet in a time of disbelief is not that he must turn evangelist. After all, he shares the disbelief of his time" (847). He practiced his skills diligently throughout his Cambridge years, recording observations in his journal and contributing poems and stories regularly to Harvard magazines, many under pseudonyms after his appointment during his last year as president of the *Harvard Advocate*. During summers back in the countryside around Reading, he cultivated "the habits of conversation with nature" (*EL* 251) taught by Emerson while also directing his literary talents to more practical ends, working for the *Reading Times* in July and August of 1899. On leaving Harvard he planned a career in journalism, hoping to combine his "power of painting pictures in words" (*L* 14) with what his father reminded him was the first and foremost law of making a living.

This electric town which I adore

After settling in New York in September 1900 to try his hand at journalism, Stevens' Emersonian reflections carried him regularly into nature for long walks on Sundays. On these excursions, "tramping through the fields and woods [beholding] every leaf and blade of grass revealing or rather betokening the Invisible" (*L* 59), he experienced the sacred. "An old argument with me," he recorded in his journal, "is that the true religious force in the world is not the church but the world itself: the mysterious callings of Nature and our responses" (*L* 58). Yet, he would on occasion also find himself stopping in a church to feel "how the glittering altar worked on [his] senses stimulating and consoling them" (*L* 59). He had by this time given up his journalistic aspirations, having been repeatedly overcome by witnessing and attempting to describe the grizzlier events he had been sent out to cover. Following his father's advice – "he seems always to have reason on his side, confound him" (*L* 53) – he enrolled in New York Law School in 1901. Throughout his fifteen years of residence in and around New York City – first as reporter, then as law student and clerk, then as an attorney in various law firms – the one constant was the ritual he began every Sunday morning. He set out early to walk for hours into the New Jersey or Long Island countryside. He returned in late afternoon or early evening and closed his day, as faithfully as any of his Puritan ancestors, by recording in his journal, and later, in letters to his fiancée, Elsie Kachel, the sensations evoked by what he had seen, heard, and felt. The perceptions inscribed in these entries and letters became the template for what would recombine to shape his poems. "Sunday Morning," for example, is among the first to give formal utterance to all he had come to understand about his feelings, acts, and experiences as an individual in solitude as he apprehended himself in relation to what he had come to consider the divine.

By January 1907, Stevens' letters to Elsie almost completely took the place of his journal entries. He had met her during the summer of 1904 while visiting Reading after passing the bar and basking idyllically once again in the surrounding fields and woods. The twenty-five-year-old lawyer was introduced to the beautiful young woman as "a very fine poet" (*SP* 138) from New York. She had just turned eighteen and worked to help support her mother's household by giving piano lessons, selling sheet music, and playing piano in a local department store. Her father, Howard Kachel, who had married her mother, Ida Smith, only a few months before Elsie's birth, had died during her infancy. Her mother remarried when Elsie was eight. Lehman Moll never formally adopted Elsie, who "insisted to her friends that her name was 'Kachel,' though as the years went by she apparently became used to 'Moll'" (*SP* 137). She left high school during her first year because of financial pressures on the family. As Holly Stevens relates, "[O]wing to the brevity of the first marriage, there were apparently a good many questions (and some aspersions cast) about my mother's legitimacy. All her life, at least during the time I knew her, she suffered from a persecution complex which undoubtedly originated during her childhood" (*SP* 137). Stevens' parents never approved of their son's relationship with this young woman who was literally from the wrong side of the tracks. Stevens' quarrels with his father in the months before his engagement to Elsie in Christmas 1908 occasioned a family rupture. His father died almost three years later, on July 14, 1911. Although Stevens returned to Reading for the funeral, he had not spoken with him in the interim. He had married Elsie in the Grace Lutheran Church in Reading on September 21, 1909. No one from his family was present.

It is clear from the letters Stevens wrote to Elsie – often more than one a day – over the course of their five-year courtship that his enchantment with her was framed by what he repeatedly described as the "faery" setting of the woods and glades where they would walk and sit and talk on the visits he made to see her in Reading on weekends and holidays. Like a bower bird, he displayed all his aesthetic skills in his letters, writing her poems, creating a paradisal setting in which to woo her. He addressed her as "Bo" or "Bo-Bo," for "Bo-Peep," and occasionally "Muse." "Let us wear bells together and never grow up and never kiss each other" (*L* 100), he wrote in March 1907. Excerpts from two letters written the following year give a premonition of the underside to the "starry *connaissance*" (11) he projected of what was to come once they left their pastoral setting: "I have always one ally at home – Lady Nature, whose children we are, both of us, so completely"; "Do you know what I would do, if the world were made of wishes? I'd lock you up – in a large enough place, to be sure; a whole valley as big as a country, maybe – and I'd allow only the most unexceptionable people to come there."[6] Although he had earlier been taken by Sybil Gage, a lovely young woman he had met while on vacation in the Adirondacks, he was at the same time intimidated by her. Well-educated and sophisticated, she was unlikely to take on the role of the *femme couverte* he seems to have needed. Indeed, Stevens while in Cambridge was often socially uneasy. Feeling outclassed by those from patrician backgrounds, he began to experience the shyness and reticence that he attempted to camouflage with "' airs' and a Harvard accent" (*SP* 16) or, all too often, to relieve with the culture's social lubricant, alcohol. The affected manner he took on would later be interpreted by many as condescension.

In contrast to Sybil Gage, Elsie, "sweet, / Untasted, in [the] heavenly, orchard air" (11) of his native countryside, would become his Galatea.

In his letters he shaped her to his wishes, suggesting what she should read, what she should do, how she should be.

> It has always been a particular desire of mine to have you join church; and I am very, very glad to know that you are now on the road. – I am not in the least religious. The sun clears my spirit, if I may say that, and an occasional sight of the sea, and thinking of blue valleys, and the odor of the earth, and many things. Such things make a god of a man; but a chapel makes a man of him. Churches are human. – I say my prayers every night – not that I need them now, or that they are anything more than a habit, half-unconscious. But in Spain, in Salamanca, there is a pillar in a church (Santayana told me) worn by the kisses of generations of the devout. One of their kisses are worth all my prayers. Yet the church is a mother for them – and for us. (L 96)

This example concerning the contrasting natures of their spiritual life illustrates the kind of opposition that would unfold into an increasing emotional distance between them once the reality of their married life in a New York City apartment replaced the imagined habitation he had made out of words. Not surprisingly, Elsie became desperately unhappy living in New York. Urged by her husband, she returned to Reading more and more frequently, staying with her mother for extended visits. He had good reason to worry, as he noted to her in the week before their wedding, how well he would be able to take care of "that shadowy Elsie of long ago."[7] By the second year of their marriage Elsie was hoping they could both return to Reading, to their country idylls; she suggested he open a business back home. He dismissed her suggestion: "I fully intend to continue along my present line – because it gives me a living and seems to offer possibilities. I am far from being a genius – and must rely on hard and faithful work" (962). Though he had not spoken with his father since the rupture, he had taken his father's admonitions to heart.

The possibilities offered in New York furthered Stevens' poetic ambitions as well. Through Harvard contacts he had begun publishing in journals and magazines poems that would define his early style in *Harmonium* (1923). Some of these poems he read at salon-like gatherings in the gracious studio apartment of another Harvard colleague and fellow poet, Walter Arensberg. Heir to one of America's industrial fortunes, Arensberg had accumulated by 1914 a major art collection representing the "avant-garde of the avant-garde."[8] Works by Pablo Picasso, Georges Braque, André Derain, Francis Picabia, Joseph Stella, Charles Sheeler, Constantin Brancusi, Henri Rousseau, Paul Cézanne, Henri Matisse, and Marcel Duchamp surrounded the members of the "Arensberg Circle," who gathered to present their work, talk about the latest in music, film, and photography, and discuss readings "assigned" by Arensberg – Freud's *The Interpretation of Dreams* and Stein's *Three Lives*, for example. Members included Duchamp, William Carlos Williams, and Carl Van Vechten, as well as Stevens. On one occasion, when Elsie accompanied him, Stevens read from among his latest work ("Sunday Morning," "Disillusionment of Ten O'Clock," "Peter Quince at the Clavier"), and Elsie commented that she found "Mr. Stevens' things . . . affected."[9] Over the years of their marriage Stevens would continue to cultivate his intellectual and aesthetic interests in the many epistolary and actual friendships he maintained and would learn to appreciate with Elsie homelier satisfactions – culinary delights, varieties of roses in the garden, music she played on the piano.

Project a masque beyond the planets

The passage from the letter quoted above is important to consider as well for what it discloses concerning the still active force of Stevens' religious habit. His declaration of being "not in the least religious," coupled with his continuing to say his prayers every night and feeling the comfort of the church as "human" and "a mother," reveals precisely the lineaments of the problem he would figure as characterizing his age, "the will to believe." These contours gave shape to his work with words. The problem, as he retrospectively described it in 1951, was "for the poet to supply the satisfactions of belief, in his manner and in his style . . . in a time of disbelief" (841–42). The "satisfactions of belief" would have to take the place of "the thought of heaven" (53), be as effective in giving sustenance and solace as "the goodness of lying in a maternal sound" (411), a mother humming hymns at bedtime. As Stevens noted in an essay, "The philosopher intends his integrations to be fateful; the poet intends his to be effective" (862). In the face of a world in constant flux, as described by the new physics and in particular quantum mechanics, these satisfactions would have to celebrate not the perfecting and protecting order of God's creation but rather "the indifferent experience of life [as] the unique experience, the item of ecstasy which we have been isolating and reserving for another time and place, loftier and more secluded" (848). It was under the topic of how poetry must change that Stevens presented these observations. "Poetry / Exceeding music must take the place / Of empty heaven and its hymns, / Ourselves in poetry must take their place, . . . / Ourselves in the tune as if in space, / Yet nothing changed, except the place" (136–37).

The change in actual place that afforded the poet and the "money-making lawyer" (*L* 32) the possibility of combining their talents was the move to Hartford, Connecticut, in 1916. Having already established a specialty in fidelity and surety bonds working for the American Bonding Company and the Equitable Surety Company in New York, Stevens was brought on at the Hartford Accident and Indemnity Company to handle surety claims and oversee legal affairs for the expanding bond department. Within two years, a separate fidelity and surety claims department was established, which Stevens would head for the rest of his life. The relationships Stevens forged with his co-workers reflected the idiosyncrasies of his personality. Although his standoffish manner was initially experienced as snobbishness, those who came to work with him closely, both underlings and other executives, developed deep affection for him. He would often invite colleagues to lunch with him at Hartford's Canoe Club, where the waitress knew that Mr. Stevens' "martini" meant a pitcher. After such occasions, back at the office, his disposition relaxed to reveal his sense of humor. Many who worked with him, as recorded by Peter Brazeau, remarked on his afternoon joke-telling, his wordplay. Younger staff members learned to appreciate that his quizzing them about the meaning of a word was not meant as intimidation, and so would go off, as he sometimes asked them, to the library to look up all the usages of "ellipse" or "curule."

Investigating claims or considering the viability of issuing surety bonds meant, especially in Stevens' early years at the Hartford, frequent extended business trips to various parts of the country. After the move to Connecticut, Stevens was away most of the following year. He established one of his strongest friendships with Arthur Powell, a business contact from Atlanta. He began visiting Florida to spend an annual winter holiday with Powell and other friends, fishing and carousing in expensive roughing-it locales around Biscayne Bay and Long Key, and once crossing to visit Havana. Back in Hartford, images bursting from Florida's venereal soil and dark night skies prinked by stars would color his dreams and the lines he composed, often scribbling them on pieces of paper as he walked to and from the office. These Florida trips, where he could let himself go "with the boys," as it were, shifted in the mid-1930s to Key West's more literary atmosphere, where he met Robert Frost and, on one particularly raucous evening, let himself go a bit too much and provoked a fistfight with Ernest Hemingway. On a postcard to Elsie written with his bandaged right hand, broken on the novelist's jaw, the poet accounted for his barely legible scrawl by noting that he had fallen down a flight of stairs. This was in 1936; Stevens was fifty-six; his second volume, *Ideas of Order*, was about to be published by Knopf after the thirteen-year hiatus since *Harmonium*. In August 1924, his only child, Holly Bright, had been born, nine months after Stevens and Elsie had returned from the only holiday they had taken together since their marriage: "In that November off Tehuantepec / . . . the sea / And heaven rolled as one and from the two / Came fresh transfigurings of freshest blue" (85). His daughter's eyes were, indeed, "freshest blue." As he noted to the increasing number of literary correspondents writing in the years after *Harmonium* to ask for contributions to magazines, the child demanded his full attention for the while. Ensuring continuing financial success was never more important.

The same intellectual and imaginative skills that allowed Stevens to succeed at business – in 1934 he became vice president of the Hartford, earning a healthy $20,000 in the middle of the Depression – proved equally productive for the "ideas of order" he explored in his poetry. Success in the insurance world depended on fashioning a habit of mind befitting to a universe of chance. Statistical projection and the consideration of probability – concepts also underpinning the new physics – were integral to his thinking. In having to compose briefs that would make the case for or against the Hartford's insuring a bond or paying a claim, he had to translate facts into persuasive language. Well-practiced in this manner for the Hartford, Stevens applied its methods to his poetry. To borrow concepts from Ian Hacking's seminal work on probability, Stevens set up "words in their sites" to project "degrees of belief," provide "confidence intervals": "[O]ne conducts the analysis of words in their sites in order to understand how we think and why we seem obliged to think in certain ways."[10] Stevens recognized that "Poetry is nothing if it is not experiment in language" (823), and his work with words was as deliberate as that of any scientist. Informed by "the idea of creating confidence in the world" (864), he plotted "the fluctuations of certainty, the change / Of degrees of perception in the scholar's dark" (342).

Although he was chastised at different moments in his career by high-toned critics of various stripes, first for having no moral purpose (the 1920s), and later, no political purpose (the 1930s), he realized that in order to join the pantheon of those he had called in his youth "man-poets" (*L* 26) – Homer, Dante, Shakespeare, Milton – he had to write poetry that would transcend local and temporal limitation. He had to create a body of work that could provide at least "a momentary existence on an exquisite plane" (786), find a solution to the equation identifying gravity and grace: "Poetry, then, is the only possible heaven" (*L* 360). In doing this, he was answering Emerson's call for a poet who could "see the world to be the mirror of the soul" (*EL* 91–92). As Stevens realized, poetry of this kind "seems, in the last analysis, to have something to do with our self-preservation, and that, no doubt, is why the expression of it, the sound of its words, helps us to live our lives" (665).

Stevens called attention, as had Emerson in his time, to "the universal decay and now almost death of faith in society" and the "need . . . never greater of new revelation than now" (*EL* 83). The "now" for Stevens in December 1936 – with Hitler in Germany, Mussolini in Ethiopia, and a Spanish Civil War – reflected not only the loss of faith but also portended the end of civilization itself. Stevens believed that resistance to the pressure of events could be accomplished only through a secular form of conversion, through the sound of words belonging to "the highest poetry" (*L* 526). Particularizing the difference between the politician and the poet, he stressed that the poet must not, like the politician, be "absorbed" or "sabotaged" by events, but rather "remain individual . . . free" in order "to produce significant poetry" (*L* 526). Stevens remained clear and adamant about the importance of this kind of poetry, the kind that would win him, before he died, a place in his imagined pantheon.

It is the belief and not the god that counts

Stevens' effort to create poetry that could provide "values and beliefs" (*L* 526) intensified through the 1940s as world events worsened. As he announced in "Of Modern Poetry," "The poem of the mind . . . has to think about war / And it has to find what will suffice. It has / To construct a new stage" (218–19). His conception was epitomized in "Notes Toward a Supreme Fiction," composed in the months following the entry of the United States into World War II to give an alternative shape and direction to "the will to believe." The poem's epilogue made its address explicit. Stevens wanted its first lines printed on the back outside cover of the volume (to be published in a limited edition by the Cummington Press) "to state the idea" (*L* 408): "Soldier, there is a war between the mind / And sky, between thought and day and night" (351). "Notes" added pages to the "missal for brooding sight: for an understanding of the world" (*L* 790). The 630 lines of its three sections forcefully illustrated "the imagination pressing back against the pressure of reality" (665), the poet's attempt to make "his imagination become the light in the minds of others" (660–61).

Stevens dedicated "Notes Toward a Supreme Fiction" to Henry Church, a wealthy arts patron and editor of the French magazine *Mesures*, with whom he had developed a deep friendship around their common interest in establishing the essential place of poetry in American culture. Church wanted to set up a trust that would foster the "pure good" of poetry, and in letters and meetings with Stevens discussed a project for a chair of poetry at Harvard. The aspiration embodied in their friendship, as well as the contacts Stevens made with others through his work and through Church – with the French philosopher Jean Wahl, with Guggenheim Museum director James Johnson Sweeney, with Marianne Moore, with Hi Simons, and José Rodríguez Feo, for example – helped sustain the poet through trying personal moments during these years, as did his continuing to indulge himself in things that gave pleasure: the paintings he bought through his French art dealer; varieties of teas, grapes, wine, pears, cheeses; the quality of light falling through the trees in his garden; a bowl of carnations on the table; a new recording of a Bruckner symphony. Nonetheless, family deaths occasioned poignant memories and feelings of loss; in addition, the effects of time passing on what Stevens once called "that monster, the body" (*L* 176) were increasingly matters of concern. But perhaps most unsettling was Holly's somewhat late and protracted rebellion.

Holly refused to complete her studies and left Vassar at the end of 1942. Stevens found her an office job at the Aetna Life Insurance Company, where she met a young repairman named John Hanchak. Thinking him unsuitable for his daughter, Stevens refused to allow him in the house. In spite of heated quarrels with her father concerning her engagement, Holly married Hanchak in August 1944. In April 1947, she gave birth to a son, Peter Reed Hanchak. The following year, with her father's support, she began divorce proceedings that were completed in 1951. The turbulence of this period finally settled down, and a relationship evolved between father and daughter that became a source of emotional nourishment for both. In the last decade of his life, Holly was always there, whether to accompany him as he gave lectures and received the many honors marking his recognition, or to drive him back and forth to New York for lunch with friends. With her father's help she also came to be sympathetic to her mother's situation, as he had over the years. When Elsie suffered a stroke early in 1955, a few months before Stevens was to undergo surgery that revealed advanced stomach cancer, Holly assured her father that she would, in his absence, care for her mother with understanding and tenderness.

Stevens was graced during his last decade by being able to witness that, indeed, his work had helped "people to live their lives" (661). Knopf's invitations for *Transport to Summer* (1947) and *The Auroras of Autumn*, plus the reissuing of all earlier volumes in 1950, the strongly favorable reviews and healthy royalty checks that followed, all bespoke the widening of the poet's audience. His induction as a fellow of the National Institute of Arts and Letters in 1945, his receiving the Harriet Monroe Poetry Award in 1946, an honorary doctorate from Wesleyan University in 1947, the Bollingen Prize for Poetry in 1949 (awarded in 1950), the National Book Award, and another honorary doctorate from Harvard in 1951 officially established his place as one of America's major poets. The publication of his *Collected Poems* in October 1954, to coincide with his seventy-fifth birthday, celebrated the success of his lifelong effort to demonstrate that "the import of poetry is the import of the spirit" (*L* 378). In 1955, Stevens received the National Book Award for the second time, followed, just months before he died, by the Pulitzer Prize. The poet was deeply moved by the public recognition of his success, as he expressed in affectionate letters to the many whose correspondence with him over the years had given him ongoing encouragement. As he wrote in "The Planet on the Table," he was happy he had written his poems, hoping that in the meagerness of their words he was able to convey "Some lineament or character, / Some affluence" (450) of the earth of which they were part.

Reading through the lines Stevens composed as he moved through his time, we come to know the feeling of religious experience naturalized to the "exquisite environment of fact" (904). In cadences remembered from the Psalms, to which he returned again and again, he celebrated the faith of believing "God and the imagination are one" (914), of believing in the "activity of the most august imagination" (471) to provide descriptions of "reality" itself as "heaven-haven" (345). Only the belief in such a reality, "The fiction that results from feeling" (351), can help bring it about, can help transform things as they are into the impossible possible: "It is possible, possible, possible. It must / Be possible" (349).

NOTES

1. William James, *The Variety of Religious Experience* in *Writings: 1902–1910*, ed. Bruce Kuklick (New York: Library of America, 1987), 36.
2. Ralph Waldo Emerson, *The Letters of Ralph Waldo Emerson*, vol. VI, ed. Ralph L. Rusk (New York and London: Columbia University Press, 1966), 200.
3. *Ibid.*, 245 n.
4. *Ibid.*
5. Ralph Waldo Emerson, *Essays and Lectures*, ed. Joel Porte (New York: Library of America, 1983), 7; hereafter *EL*.
6. Wallace Stevens, *The Contemplated Spouse: The Letters of Wallace Stevens to Elsie*, ed. J. Donald Blount (Columbia: University of South Carolina Press, 2006), 46. See also Joan Richardson, *Wallace Stevens, A Biography: The Early Years, 1879–1923* (New York: Beech Tree Books / William Morrow & Co., 1986), 285.
7. Richardson, *Early Years*, 365.
8. Francis Naumann, "Walter Conrad Arensberg: Poet, Patron, and Participant in the New York Avant-Garde, 1914–20," *Philadelphia Museum of Art Bulletin*, 76.328 (Spring 1980): 17. The Arensberg Collection is permanently installed at the Philadelphia Museum.
9. Richardson, *Early Years*, 468.
10. Ian Hacking, *Historical Ontology* (Cambridge, Mass.: Harvard University Press, 2002), 35.

2

ROBERT REHDER

Stevens and *Harmonium*

Harmonium is Wallace Stevens' first book. He had started writing poems seriously when he was a student at Harvard (1897–1900) and made a new start in 1907 when he began composing poems for Elsie Kachel, whom he later married. For *Harmonium* he chose seventy-four poems, but none that he had written before 1914 or 1915 (dates of composition are approximate for Stevens; what we know are the dates of publication). Between 1914 and 1919, Stevens had published thirty-nine poems that he included neither in *Harmonium* (1923) nor in *The Collected Poems* (1954). On December 21, 1922, he wrote to Harriet Monroe concerning the selection he made for *Harmonium*: "I have omitted many things, exercising the most fastidious choice, so far as that was possible among my witherlings. To pick a crisp salad from the garbage of the past is no snap" (*L* 232). Although he waited until he was nearly forty-four to publish his first book, Stevens had been considering collecting his poems for a number of years.

On April 9, 1918, he wrote to William Carlos Williams to congratulate him on the publication of *Al Que Quiere!* (1917), his third book of poems. He had met Williams in 1915 among the group of writers and painters who gathered that summer in Grantwood, New Jersey, on Sunday afternoons and were associated with Alfred Kreymborg's magazine, *Others*. Stevens had hesitated to send the letter, and adds in the upper left corner: "I think, after all, I should rather send this than not, although it is quarrelsomely full of my own ideas of discipline."[1]

The letter survives because Stevens' criticisms irritated Williams and he quotes long passages in the "Prologue to Kora in Hell" (1918) in order to "clash," as he puts it, with Stevens, but also, I suspect, because he was aware that Stevens had read his work carefully and had understood what he was trying to do – and that any praise by Stevens was praise indeed. The letter, five years before *Harmonium*, shows Stevens' worries and scruples about collecting his poems.

> What strikes me most about the poems themselves is their casual character. . . .
> Personally I have a distaste for miscellany. It is one of the reasons I do not
> bother about a book myself.
>
> . . . My idea is that in order to carry a thing to the extreme necessity to convey
> it one has to stick to it; . . . Given a fixed point of view, realistic, imagistic or what
> you will, everything adjusts itself to that point of view; the process of adjustment
> is a world in flux, as it should be for a poet. But to fidget with points of view
> leads always to new beginnings and incessant new beginnings lead to sterility.
>
> (This sounds like Sir Roger de Coverley)
>
>   A single manner or mood thoroughly
> matured and exploited is that fresh thing . . . etc.[2]

Stevens' comments show that he is indeed thinking seriously about a book
and that he wants it to have some kind of coherence. *Harmonium*, the title
that he finally chose, demonstrates the strength of this demand, not simply for
order, but for an order that establishes a peaceful and aesthetically pleasing
concord among the parts of a unified and consistent whole – harmony. This
idea expresses Stevens' feelings about his work so completely that he wanted
to call his collected poems *The Whole of Harmonium* (L 834).

Exactly what he objects to in "miscellany" is not entirely clear, but in
view of his later development, it would appear that he is looking for his
subject and this is what he recommends Williams to do. Jean Prévost in his
book on Stendhal remarks that the artist responds to a vague desire by a
definite work (*"répondre à un désir vague par une oeuvre précise"*).[3]
Stevens writes in "Adagia": "Every poem is a poem within a poem: the
poem of the idea within the poem of the words" (912). He had a need to
state as clearly as he could the idea within the poem. Self-awareness
is a discipline. That he was constantly trying to go further in his analysis is a
major reason for his greatness. Vague desire was never enough. Stevens
restates the idea of the poem within the poem in his lecture "The Irrational
Element in Poetry" (1936), where he distinguishes between "the poetry of
the subject," the specific and precise details of which a poem consists, and
the "true subject" (785), which is what the poem expresses.

Stevens' "true subject" is the relation of reality and the imagination –
terms that constantly recur in all his work but a subject that he is not able to
make fully explicit until *Ideas of Order* (1936). What is remarkable is that
he is looking for it while reading Williams in 1918. Stevens commonly
considers the relationship between reality and the imagination at the
moment of perception. Contact with the world in his poetry is almost
always problematic and, consequently, so is self-definition. The perceiver
has difficulty finding himself in the act of perception.

Stevens finds another way of expressing this true or inner subject in "Of Modern Poetry" (1940) as "The poem of the mind in the act of finding / What will suffice" (218). This is at once self-communication and communication with the other. The poem's "invisible audience" listens "to itself, expressed / In an emotion as of two people" (219). This leads to the clear formulation in "The Auroras of Autumn" (1948): "The mother's face, / The purpose of the poem" (356). Despite his wariness and depreciation of Freud, Stevens has no difficulty in coming to his own psychoanalytic conclusions, and the description of the imagination in "The Auroras of Autumn" resembles that of the father in the poem. The idea that the poem is communion with the mother receives perhaps its fullest statement in "Final Soliloquy of the Interior Paramour" (1951; the title demonstrates Stevens' self-awareness), where "we collect ourselves" in the thought of "the intensest rendezvous," and "being there together is enough" (444). This idea is explicit in a number of the poems of *Harmonium*. "In the Carolinas" (1917) apostrophizes "Timeless mother" (4); "Le Monocle de Mon Oncle" (1918), "'Mother of Heaven'" (11); and "Explanation" (1923), "Ach, Mutter" (58). "A High-Toned Old Christian Woman" and "To the One of Fictive Music" (both published in 1922) are early versions of "Final Soliloquy of the Interior Paramour." Crispin's verse in "The Comedian as the Letter C" (1923) came "like two spirits parleying" (25).

Stevens continues in his letter to Williams:

> Well a book of poems is a damned serious affair. I am only objecting that a book that contains your particular quality should contain anything else and suggesting that if the quality were carried to a communicable extreme, in intensity and volume, etc. . . . But I think your tantrums not half mad enough.[4]

A "communicable extreme" is a nice distinction. Stevens urges Williams to go as far as he can and still be understandable. He says in "Man Carrying Thing" (1946), "The poem must resist the intelligence / Almost successfully" (306). The "almost" sets the limit. James Joyce, in *Finnegan's Wake*, I would say, goes to incommunicable extremes. This rejection of private language with its advice to Williams that his "tantrums" are "not half mad enough" is, nonetheless, a declaration of extravagance.

This is the economy of the spirit in which, as Paul Valéry puts it, the prodigals grow rich, the open-handed generosity and uninhibited playfulness of "The Plot Against the Giant" and "Life Is Motion." The poems of *Harmonium* demonstrate Stevens' ability to let himself go with gusto: "Chieftain Iffucan of Azcan in caftan / Of tan with henna hackles, halt!" (60). The words are strange; the names, invented and far-fetched; and the sound-play, intricate and insistent. The word combinations constantly surprise us. Who else would or could bring together "caftan" and "hackles" in the same stanza, or invent the adjective "turquoise-turbaned" and place it in the same sentence with "saucers," as in "turquoise-turbaned Sambo, neat / At tossing saucers" (85)? Here the double alliteration of *t* and *s* is repeated within the words and played off against the other assonances and consonances. The unlikeliness of Stevens' vocabulary is matched by the unlikeliness of his images: "The hair of my blonde / Is dazzling, / As the spittle of cows / Threading the wind" (50). "[D]azzling" and "threading" make the image dynamic as well as perceptually acute. He is also able to render the fabulousness of the dream world with down-home simplicity – "an old sailor, / Drunk and asleep in his boots, / Catches tigers / In red weather" (53), where the *s*, *e*, and *r* sounds in the final two lines combine perfectly.

Stevens luxuriates in the language and constructs many poems so as to give himself the chance of grand rhetorical gestures, as in:

> Crispin,
> The lutanist of fleas, the knave, the thane,
> The ribboned stick, the bellowing breeches, cloak
> Of China, cap of Spain, imperative haw
> Of hum, inquisitorial botanist,
> And general lexicographer of mute
> And maidenly greenhorns. . . .   (22)

Again the vocabulary and combinations ("lutanist" and "fleas"; "imperative" and "haw"; "inquisitorial" and "botanist"; "lexicographer" and "greenhorns") are one surprise after another. There is no American poet more idiosyncratic than Stevens and with whom the strangeness is so often humorous. He uses the comic to avoid the sentimental. The density of the passage about Crispin is achieved by packing it with long and unusual words, by assonances and consonances repeated across the phrases, and by the grammar. The phrases are all in apposition, hence interchangeable, and allow Stevens to give the impression that he could go on. He was, in 1918 when he writes to Williams, practicing what he hyperbolically preaches. His tantrums are as mad as he can make them and his poems are fantastical in a way that distinguishes him from all his great contemporaries.

Despite Stevens' efforts to find his true subject, there is a certain miscellaneousness about *Harmonium*. Stevens tries out different speaking voices and some poems are presented as more or less formal speeches ("Invective Against Swans," "The Worms at Heaven's Gate," "Of the Manner of Addressing Clouds," "To the One of Fictive Music"), and it is part of his technique to name the person addressed (Remus, 16; Fernando, 18; Vincentine, 42; nuncle, 43), since the explicit and implicit purpose of many (all?) of his poems is to re-create and embody the presence of another person, "an interior paramour." Moreover, Stevens *enjoys* the freedom and virtuosity of rhetoric.

Many poems are small stories. The word "anecdote" recurs among the titles – "Anecdote of Men by the Thousand," "Anecdote of Canna," "Anecdote of the Jar," "Anecdote of the Prince of Peacocks." A few have a mythic quality, such as "Earthy Anecdote" or "Life Is Motion," and seem deliberately constructed to resist interpretation. Others are like fairy tales or fabliaux, such as "The Plot Against the Giant" or "Cy Est Pourtraicte, Madame Ste Ursule, et Les Unze Mille Vierges." Although Stevens entitles one poem "Fabliau of Florida," it does not belong to this group, but is one of the many poems that represent a moment of intense perception ("Nomad Exquisite," "Tea," "Thirteen Ways of Looking at a Blackbird," "Hymn from a Watermelon Pavillon," "Banal Sojourn," and "Indian River").

For the most part, these are short poems that show an effort of condensation and a pressure to move from details of perception and feeling to some kind of summary statement or conclusion, even if it is no more than the hymns, forms, and flaws of "Nomad Exquisite." Most are poems of short stanzas and short lines. Stevens regularly avoids the first person, displacing the action onto an assumed, often mannered and rhetorical voice, as in "Invective Against Swans," or a metaphorical figure, not defined or organized enough to be a persona, such as Hibiscus, the paltry nude, or the Doctor of Geneva. If the experience is ascribed to someone else, he feels freer and can be more analytical.

The data of perception is rendered with verve and accuracy: "the firefly's quick, electric stroke" (12); "warty squashes, streaked and rayed, / . . . splashed with frost, / Distorted by hale fatness, turned grotesque" (13); "A pool shines, / Like a bracelet / Shaken in a dance" (59). Stevens, however, repeatedly cuts the beauty with what he calls "The dreadful sundry of this world" (38). He writes of Williams' *Collected Poems 1921–1931*: "The anti-poetic is his spirit's cure. He needs it as a naked man needs shelter or as an animal needs salt. To a man with a sentimental side the anti-poetic is that truth, the reality to which all of us are forever fleeing" (769). This is also self-description. "To what good, in the alleys of the lilacs," he asks in "Last Looks at the Lilacs," "O caliper, do you scratch your buttocks . . . ?" (39) and begins "Two Figures in Dense Violet Night" by declaring: "I had as lief be embraced by the porter at the hotel" (69). This is the anti-poetic. There are in Stevens many moments rich in beauty, but he does not want them to be too sweet and resists "the bawds of euphony" (76).

Here everything depends on the choice of words. None of Stevens' great contemporaries have such a wide-ranging and varied lexicon with so many rare, archaic, exotic words and idiosyncratic coinages. Marianne Moore and Hart Crane are in some ways comparable, but do not use their vocabulary to vary the tone as Stevens does.

The most famous poem in *Harmonium* and perhaps Stevens' best-known poem is "Sunday Morning" (1915). It announces, for the first time, a great poet in full possession of his powers. Stevens wrote many poems as good as this, but none that are better. Nothing in his earlier work prepares us for "Sunday Morning," and in this respect it is analogous to "Lines Composed a Few Miles above Tintern Abbey" in Wordsworth's development. "Peter Quince at the Clavier" (1915) is a wonderful poem, but it does not have the lyric eloquence, argumentative mastery, or power of statement of "Sunday Morning."

"Sunday Morning" begins in complacencies, with the self-sufficiency of ordinary sensual pleasures. Here "complacency" is the "state of being pleased with a thing," pleasure, delight, what the *OED*2 calls "tranquil . . . satisfaction" and "contented acquiescence," rather than self-satisfaction. The unusual plural needs to be noted, as if every item of sense data brings its own special satisfaction. The poem's protagonist is a woman about whom we know nothing, except that she has gotten up late on a Sunday morning and is sitting in her peignoir in a sunny chair having coffee and oranges for breakfast – and thinking about religion and the changing beauty of the world. Perhaps, because it is Sunday and she has not gone to church, perhaps for other reasons, she thinks about the death of Jesus and the basic tenets of Christianity. She speaks twice in the poem and for the rest of the poem her thoughts and feelings – part meditation, part daydream – are reported in the free indirect discourse of the poem's narrator.

Harmonium is the most sensuous of Stevens' books and the woman's questionings and her answers have their origins in her pleasurable sensations, in "comforts of the sun" (53). The poem is remarkable for its integration of sensuous detail and clear statement. The insistent rhythm of the poem and the sweep of the lines often conceal the delicacy of the action. The complacencies "mingle to dissipate" the "holy hush of ancient sacrifice" (53). They combine in order to scatter the hush. Together the force of her present enjoyments overpowers the reverential silence imposed by the thought of the crucifixion, but the idea returns. "She dreams a little" and then "feels the dark / Encroachment of that old catastrophe, / As a calm darkens among water-lights" (53). The idea of the sacrifice gradually intrudes upon her thoughts the way a calm extinguishes the moving reflections of light upon water. Stevens places heavy, latinate, polysyllabic words – "Complacencies," "Encroachment," "procession," "Dominion" – among the shorter, sharper "oranges," "green," "dark," "pungent," "bright," and "water" that designate the things of the world. "[W]ater-lights," which is not in the *OED2*, appears to be of Stevens' coinage.

Present pleasure set against ancient sacrifice is one of the several antitheses upon which the poem is built: life versus death, change versus stasis, the actual world versus an imaginary one. Delicate and subtle mental action is combined with violence, blood, and death, and the cumulative force of all this causes the woman to ask in the second stanza three questions: Why should she give her good things to the dead? What is divinity if it is only imaginary? Shall she not find in this world things that are as deserving of her care and attention as "the thought of heaven" (53)?

The questions are rhetorical. They are a demand for an alternative to Christianity, for a system of beliefs based on her experience of the natural world. She wants a religion of the earth, not of the supernatural. She does not want divinity to be something exterior, but to "live within herself" (53). As she defines it, in a series of examples, it consists of moments of intense feeling when she is outside: "passions," "moods," "grievings," "elations," "gusty emotions" in the presence of the natural world. Of the second stanza's last eight lines, five are end-stopped, three are enjambed, with a pause after the third or fourth foot to vary the rhythm and emphasize the quality of the emotion. She ends by including "All pleasures and all pains" (54), all feelings good and bad, and specifying that they should be experienced remembering the "bough of summer" and the "winter branch" (54). The branch in full leaf and that without leaves are "the measures destined for her soul" (54). "[D]estined" is an unusual word in this context, as if sooner or later we had no choice but to give up the supernatural and interpret our experiences in terms of the natural world and live according to the rhythm of the seasons. It is the vividness of feelings outdoors that gives measure and significance to our lives. This intensity is the only divinity.

The woman decides that the world would be much friendlier if we could accept that it was "all of paradise that we shall know" (54). Then, out of the blue, Stevens adds a new and unexpected dimension by saying that it will be "next in glory to enduring love" (54). The incredible and sustaining beauty of the natural world is, in a phrase that can be easily overlooked, subordinated to human values. Enduring love suddenly becomes the most glorious of all things, with the implication, perhaps, that its glory is a consequence of its rarity.

Neither the complacencies of Sunday morning nor her memories of beauty are enough. The woman's statement – "But in contentment I still feel / The need of some imperishable bliss" (55) – sums up perfectly the motivation and conclusion of her Sunday-morning reverie. Sacrifice, death, guilt, and sin have no appeal for her. She accepts "all pains" without difficulty, but wishes for some immortal happiness. She trusts her feelings, rather than the beliefs of her culture. Her truth is derived from within herself. This statement is immediately followed by a denial and slight change of subject: "Death is the mother of beauty" (55). "[C]ontentment," "fulfillment," "bliss," "beauty" – Stevens keeps changing the terms to mark the nuances of the argument and to respect the fluidity of his categories.

Beauty resides in "our perishing earth" (55). This is the burden of stanzas V and VI. Things are beautiful because they are finite. "Beauty is momentary in the mind," says Stevens in "Peter Quince at the Clavier," "But in the flesh it is immortal" (74). Change and death are the only sources of fulfillment for whatever we dream or desire. Our paths are strewn with the "leaves / Of sure obliteration" (55). The autumn metaphor is apposite. We are certain to disappear without a trace in the same way that, at the end, the tomb in Palestine is "'the grave of Jesus, where he lay'" (56) – before his body rotted away. Stevens uses the past tense to denote death's finality and is careful to say "Jesus" and not "Christ." There are no "'spirits lingering'" (56). Stevens understands that religion is a denial of reality and an act of wish-fulfillment and that we never escape from our experience. At the end of life, we wish to repeat the beginning and imagine "Our earthly mothers" (55) waiting sleeplessly. The richness of the language and the majestic sweep of the rhetoric gloss over the bleakness of his conclusions, and this, of course, is one of Stevens' purposes.

"Sunday Morning" is a hymn to the earth's beauty, a celebration of its changingness, its finite and transitory nature. It is a poem without existential anguish, comfortable with its doubts and uncertainties – which virtually become values. Stevens is aware of the incommensurability of desire and reality, but, compared to most of the later poems, he does not emphasize the separation of reality and the imagination. He is concerned in "Sunday Morning" with the results rather than the process of perception, with the unanalyzed sensuousness of our vivid awareness of the world.

The psychological maturity of the poem is remarkable. Stevens and his heroine reject the syncretistic bric-a-brac of Christianity and pre-Christian belief systems and accept the solitude and nothingness of the world without self-denial or pathos. There is a certain ring of triumph in that the dew upon the feet of the chanting men "shall manifest" (56) their past and future, "As the immense dew of Florida / Brings forth hymn and hymn / From the beholder" (77) in "Nomad Exquisite." This note of celebration returns again and again in *Harmonium*, in Bonnie and Josie's "'Ohoyaho, / Ohoo'" (65) in "Life Is Motion," in the repeated "hail" (72) of "Hymn from a Watermelon Pavillon."

The poem concludes with an enumeration of different ways of seeing the world, a counter-list to the versions of the afterlife in stanza IV. Considering different perspectives is fundamental to Stevens' way of thinking about the world. Stevens starts with one of the standard scientific hypotheses of his time: that the earth and other planets were formed when they were torn from the sun. Then he sees the earth as dependent on the fact that it rotates on its axis and, therefore, on day and night, and finally, ignoring the rest of the solar system, as an island in space, alone, "unsponsored, free" (56). "[U]nsponsored" means there is no power watching over it; "free" sees its isolation as a liberation, an opportunity – an affirmation.

Stevens has chosen a stanza of fifteen lines so that the argument will always divide unevenly and be asymmetrical. The final sentence is seven lines – of which the deer take less than one; the quail, more than one; the sweet berries, one; and the pigeons, four. Stevens closes the poem with a list of things happening in the present: the deer walk, the quail whistle, the berries ripen, and the pigeons sink. The world continues in its ordinary, everyday course without any of the actions being necessarily connected. The items are chosen at random, but they feel like a whole because they are chosen from the natural world, which is more primitive and more funda-mental than culture. Because it is the given, it is in terms of the natural world that the woman tries to work out what she feels and believes. The pigeons, as they fly down into the darkness of the evening, make "Ambiguous undulations" (56). This motion offers the only hint of meaning at the poem's close, one that is uncertain and, finally, undecipherable. In the context of the poem, the darkness seems like death and the extended wings, a gesture of heroism, but the flocks are "casual" and they are only pigeons. The world does not interpret itself.

Seven years before the publication of "The Waste Land," Stevens offers his own comprehensive analysis of our relations to the world. "Sunday Morning" is a short answer to the question that T. S. Eliot, Ezra Pound, and Hart Crane later answer at greater length in "The Waste Land," *Four Quartets*, *The Cantos*, and *The Bridge*. Stevens has no need of a broken style. His ideas and images are fully integrated in the poem. He has no difficulty in deriving ideas from his feelings and making poetry of his ideas – and stating them clearly: "Death is the mother of beauty"; "until now I never knew / That fluttering things have so distinct a shade" (14); "man is the intelligence of his soil" (22). His summary statements are never final, but points of departure for new distinctions. This constant effort at coher-ence, unity, is one of the reasons for Stevens' power of statement. The best poems in *Harmonium* have a philosophical edge. The details suggest larger wholes, have a bias of interpretation, and are pushed to some kind of conclusion. He collects his thoughts to find out where he is and as a way of going forward. Abstractions accommodate the vagueness of the desire to produce something definite, of sharpening the distinctness of fluttering shades, as they allow for discussions of wholeness and unity as a subject. Effortlessly, he shapes the traditional form of blank verse to his purposes. "The Waste Land" is an urban poem about the difficulty of relations between men and women that echoes with the past. "Sunday Morning" is a poem set in the present about the relations of the poet with himself and concerned with discarding the past in order to enter more fully into the present. Eliot, Pound, and Crane need both a mythic and a historical past. Stevens wants the present.

"Sunday Morning" expresses not skepticism, but the impossibility of believing in Christianity or any established religion and, at the same time, the desire to believe in something. Since Voltaire and Diderot, it has become increasingly difficult for any thoughtful person to believe in established religions. For many this inability to believe is not the result of intellectual argument, but a more or less unconscious process. Charles Darwin says in his *Autobiography* (completed in 1876, three years before Stevens' birth): "disbelief crept over me at a very slow rate, but was at last complete. The rate was so slow that I felt no distress, and have never since doubted even for a single second that my conclusion was correct."[5] The process that brought Stevens to the conclusions of "Sunday Morning" cannot be documented. Stevens feels no need to explain why the world is the way it is; he is concerned with understanding his relationship to it and the act of perception. His poetry is predicated on a residual uncertainty about existence, an inability to believe totally in the reality of reality, which sometimes takes the form of a feeling of separation.

Williams, in his poem "El Hombre," sees a single star in the sunrise and says that, because it takes no part in the sunrise, it gives him "a strange courage." Stevens uses Williams' two stanzas as an epigraph for his poem "Nuances of a Theme by Williams" (1918). He then adds two stanzas of his own. He, too, addresses the star. Both poets in stressing the star's inanimate nature and separateness nonetheless personify it by talking to it. Stevens employs seven imperatives to tell the star to shine and to "Lend no part to any humanity" (15). He wants the star to "shine like bronze, / that reflects neither my face nor any inner part" or "like fire, that mirrors nothing" (14). The star is told to refuse to have anything to do with humans who project their feelings upon it. It is as if there were for the poet some unspoken difficulty or risk about separating one's feelings from the natural world, as if any feeling of involvement or blurring the distinction between them might be a threat to identity, although he insists on their mutual independence.

"Anecdote of the Jar" (1919) is another variation on this theme. The poet imagines placing a jar on top of a hill in Tennessee. The jar, a man-made object, "took dominion everywhere" (61) and causes "the slovenly wilderness" (60) to surround the hill and to cease to be wild. The jar establishes a center and a point of view, but nevertheless has nothing to do with its surroundings: "It did not give of bird or bush, / Like nothing else in Tennessee" (61). It is an idea of order arbitrarily superimposed on the landscape, as independent and separate as Williams' star.

"The Snow Man" (1921) is about what it is to have "a mind of winter" (8). Thinking about the figure that children make, usually out of three large snowballs, Stevens imagines a cold, dispassionate observer at one with his surroundings. Although the conclusion that both the observer and the world are nothing seems bleak, we are consoled by the bright, tactile beauty of the scene: by "junipers shagged with ice," by "spruces rough in the distant glitter," and by the slow unfolding of the single, long, complex sentence of which the poem is composed. Stevens explains what it is to have "a mind of winter," describes the landscape, draws attention to the "misery in the sound of the wind" and, in the final stanza, changes the subject of the sentence from one snowman to another. All the detail of the snow-covered conifers and the fact that the major statements are in the negative – "not to think" and the paradoxical "Nothing that is not there" and "the nothing that is" (8) – mitigate the harshness of the conclusions. The emotion is half-concealed by the length of the sentence, its many clauses, modifiers, and negatives, and by the beauty of the winter, but it is misery on which the poem turns.

Everyone, except someone with "a mind of winter," would hear at least some misery in "the sound of the wind" and "the sound of a few leaves" (8). As none of us are that cold in our feelings, the misery of this bare scene would force itself upon us, and the same sound of the same wind would be heard by the listener who both "listens" and "beholds." This listener is dispassionate in a different way from the snowman. He does not have "a mind of winter" and consequently hears the misery in the sound of a few leaves and the wind blowing over the land; nevertheless, he is able to see the world as it is. This, in Stevens, is always a triumph. He beholds only what is there and "Nothing that is not there." He does not imagine anything. Moreover, he beholds "the nothing that is." This can be understood as a way of saying that the world without the imagination has no value (because value and meaning are products of the imagination), or, more comprehensively, that the world, with or without the imagination, is finally nothing, because men die and things change. As the listener is "nothing himself," Stevens appears to be endorsing the bleaker view of an unhappy people in a world that is neither happy nor unhappy, a bleakness found in "Valley Candle," "Banal Sojourn," and "From the Misery of Don Joost."

The relation of the individual to the world is summarized in "Tea at the Palaz of Hoon" (1921): "I was the world in which I walked, and what I saw / Or heard or felt came not but from myself" (51). This might be understood as a declaration of solipsism, except the mention of the "western day," "you," and the "sea" (51) make it possible to think that there is a reality outside of the speaker's perceptions, even if this is uncertain. However, when the idea is restated in "The Idea of Order at Key West," where the woman singing is "the single artificer of the world / In which she sang" and "there never was a world for her / Except the one she sang and, singing, made" (106), the singing takes place at a particular time and place – at evening on a beach at Key West – and it is clear that the sea, beach, fishing boats, village, stars, Ramon Fernandez, and the speaker exist outside of the woman's song. Stevens believes that there is a real world, but that we perceive it imperfectly. This idea is repeated, in different ways, throughout his poetic career. He shares with Wordsworth the belief that the senses "half-create" what they perceive, a formulation that Wordsworth in a footnote in *Lyrical Ballads* (1798) states that he owes to "an admirable line of [Edward] Young . . . which I cannot recollect." Wordsworth in "Lines Composed a Few Miles Above Tintern Abbey" (1798) declares that he is a lover "of all the mighty world / Of eye and ear, both what they half-create, / And what perceive." Young in *Night Thoughts* (1742–45) says of the senses that they "half-create the wondrous world they see."[6]

The fundamental uncertainty of any act of perception affects our sense of selfhood. If the relation between the individual and the world is uncertain, then any definition of the self is problematic. After recognizing that all his perceptions come only from himself, the speaker in "Tea at the Palaz of Hoon" declares: "And there I found myself more truly and more strange" (51); "More truly," because that he is the world in which he walks is the truth; "more strange," because the consequent separation from everything else, loneliness, and indefiniteness make him feel strange. It is this uncertainty that causes Stevens to return again and again to the same subject and is, in part, responsible for his creativity. One poem is never enough.

The definition of the individual in relation to his surroundings is the explicit subject of the early poem "Theory" (1917): "I am what is around me" (70). Stevens returns to it in "Bantams in Pine-Woods," where he asserts the independence and separateness of each individual: "Your world is you. I am my world" (60). "The Comedian as the Letter C" shows how its protagonist, Crispin, is transformed by his journey from France to the Carolinas by way of Yucatan and Havana, a process that is, among other things, a struggle with the imagination's fictions. He moves from a belief that "man is the intelligence of his soil, / The sovereign ghost" to "his soil is man's intelligence. / That's better" (22, 29). This concern to get closer to the real is a need to come to terms with the unending, changing flow of both the mind and the world and to distinguish the one from the other.

Crispin moves on to Carolina, in search of "the relentless contact he desired" with the reality of the earth. "America was always north to him" (27) and

> Perhaps the Arctic moonlight really gave
> The liaison, the blissful liaison,
> Between himself and his environment,
> Which was, and is, chief motive, first delight. . . .   (28)

Moonlight stands for the imagination, because it belongs to the night and dreams and because it is at a remove, reflected, shadowy. What Crispin and his poet are looking for is to feel connected to their surroundings, and this connection is provided by the imagination. This is the "chief motive" and the "first delight" of poetry – and another way of stating Stevens' true subject. "Liaison," which denotes a thickening for sauces, close connection, intimacy between a man and a woman, and cooperation between allied military forces, is a perfect word here, especially as it can denote a process.

Stevens no sooner states the possibility of this "blissful liaison" ("Perhaps" balances "really") than he takes it back: "It seemed / Illusive, faint, more mist than moon, perverse, / Wrong as a divagation to Peking" (28). The deepest need is never fulfilled. Connection, completion exist only as hypothetical, imagined states, supremely desired, supremely fictitious. Stevens continues to devalue the moonlight. Each statement is modified, negated, left hypothetical, or undecided. The moonlight "was an evasion, or, if not, / A minor meeting, facile, delicate" (28). Stevens resolves the contradiction by making it an alternation. As a result, Crispin conceives of "his voyaging to be / An up and down between two elements, / A fluctuating between sun and moon" (28). This is the antithesis of reality and the imagination that informs all of Stevens' later poetry. What is remarkable about "The Comedian as the Letter C" and so many of Stevens' poems is their optimism in the face of the unanswerable questions. Stevens is the poet of inconclusive, happy endings. His keen and vivid pleasure in the beauty of the earth – and language – overcomes, at least for a moment, his doubts. Crispin lives contentedly with his wife and daughters, delighted with his family and the world.

Harmonium was published in an edition of 1,500 copies at $2.00 a copy by Alfred Knopf on September 7, 1923, and was successful enough that

Knopf decided on a second edition of 1,500 copies at $2.50 a copy published on July 24, 1931. Stevens subtracted three poems and added fourteen, the best of which is the wonderful "Sea Surface Full of Clouds," where in five sections of modified terza rima Stevens gives five different versions of the appearance of the morning light on the Pacific, using a partial refrain from Baudelaire's "L'Invitation au voyage." *Harmonium* did not sell everywhere. During the 1924 Christmas season, two young poets, Richard Blackmur and Conrad Aiken, found that the first edition had been remaindered in the basement of Filene's, the Boston department store, at 11¢ cents a copy. They recognized the book's merit and bought all the copies to send as Christmas cards to their friends.[7] The poet took a more ironic view of the book's sales. Around July 1924, he wrote to Harriet Monroe: "My royalties for the first half of 1924 amounted to $6.70. I shall have to charter a boat and take my friends around the world" (*L* 243).

NOTES

1. William Carlos Williams, *Selected Essays of William Carlos Williams* (New York: New Directions, 1969), 12.
2. *Ibid.*
3. Jean Prévost, *La Création chez Stendhal* (Paris: Mercure de France, 1951), 207.
4. Williams, *Selected Essays*, 13.
5. Charles Darwin, *The Autobiography of Charles Darwin*, ed. Nora Barlow (London: Collins, 1958), 87.
6. William Wordsworth and S. T. Coleridge, *Lyrical Ballads 1798*, ed. W. J. B. Owen (Oxford: Oxford University Press, 1971), 115, 152.
7. Russell Frazer, *A Mingled Yarn: The Life of R. P. Blackmur* (New York: Harcourt Brace Jovanovich, 1981), 99.

3

ALAN FILREIS

Stevens in the 1930s

Play the present
– "Mozart, 1935"

I

Wallace Stevens ended his promising career as a poet once he published *Harmonium* in 1923. He had been a semi-active member of the New York avant-garde scene in the 1910s and early 1920s, and had helped Harriet Monroe's modernist venue *Poetry* get underway by publishing there several poems perfectly befitting the modernist mode. The poems in *Harmonium* are at turns luscious, sparely ironic, cubistic, rhetorically anti-rhetorical, post-Christian, and minimally meditative; several are brilliant verse exercises in modernist language philosophy. But it is said – no one really knows for certain – that his family and business lives finally held more interest for him than poetry. His was a brief career. Perhaps its implosion was predicted, even necessitated, by the irony and insularity of the poems.

The narrative above is wrong, of course, but it is not an unreasonable story one might have told about Wallace Stevens at the beginning of the 1930s. Here now is another version – more focused perhaps, more overtly political, but presenting something of the same outcome:

The poems of *Harmonium* demonstrated Stevens' modernism, a fetishism of words as words that seemed to stand satisfactorily for loss of depth and reality in actual life in the United States, an elaborate demonstration of social timidity. Here was further new evidence of American modernism's perhaps inherent conservatism. But *Harmonium* was a success, the poems individually striking – even, at times, astonishing – in their alternation of aversion and precision. To be sure, Stevens had been briefly part of the revivification of American poetry following a post-Victorian interregnum of such talented yet forgettable poets as William Vaughn Moody, who sensed that the Victorian mode had become blowsily hyper-rhetorical but could only evoke the dismal situation in formal, old-sounding verse. The overall message of Stevens' poems, if one could be construed, was that things had fallen apart (modernity) and might stand to be put back together in an utterly new cognitive way (modernism). The high hilarity of the "roaring" 1920s, as that decade advanced, did not offer venues conducive for this kind of writing, an era friendlier to the sensational, flapperish tales of poet and novelist Maxwell Bodenheim or the heartthrob modernism of best-selling verse by poets hailed as true free spirits, Elinor Wylie, Sara Teasdale, or Edna St. Vincent Millay. Then, at the onset of global economic depression, beginning in late 1929 and reaching a nadir in 1932–33, the Wallace Stevens of *Harmonium* became utterly untenable. He was a conservative modernist at a time requiring political radicalism and aesthetic realism.

The publication in 1931 of a new edition of *Harmonium* featuring several new poems, the appearance of new poems by Stevens in magazines in 1932 and 1933, and then a more or less continuous flow of them from 1934 through 1939, and a sequence of three books in just two years – *Ideas of Order* (1936), *Owl's Clover* (1936), and *The Man with the Blue Guitar & Other Poems* (1937) – forced promulgators of the first of these two narratives to abandon altogether their deciphering of Stevens' post-*Harmonium* silence. But, in a way, though it too wrongly predicted Stevens' poetic demise, the second narrative was *strengthened* by what happened to his work in the 1930s.

Let us consider how the next installment of that particular version of the story might go if its point of view were retained and extended to the end of the 1930s, a look back at that tumultuous decade. That tale would run as follows:

> Stevens on the modernist right was attacked by detractors on the communist left. He met radical critique head on and badly lost the confrontation. The left vilified him and it only made him more intransigent. What had been playfully ironic in *Harmonium* hardened into an adamant aestheticism in the mid-1930s, much more difficult for readers and fellow poets to swallow in a time of economic privation. Open-endedness now seemed obliviousness. Modernist irony now seemed mere social conservatism. Digression seemed but mere aversion. Clever titles ("The Curtains in the House of the Metaphysician") now seemed somehow intended to provoke or cajole ("The Revolutionists Stop for Orangeade"). It is no wonder that *Ideas of Order* received a stinging, negative review printed in the pages of the *New Masses*, the cultural magazine of the revolutionary Communist Party of the United States (CPUSA). The reviewer was the communist poet Stanley Burnshaw, a young and little-known political hack, a full-time *New Masses* editor and CPUSA favorite. Burnshaw dismissed Stevens' poems as evidence of incipient fascism. His review did communist dirty work in the war against modernism's willful obscurity and ignorance of political urgency. Stevens was so unnerved by the attack that he wrote a long poem, "Owl's Clover," in response. Blank verse was an unwise choice of mode for responding. The book-length rejoinder is politically incoherent and in all ways Stevens' worst performance. Judging from "The Man

with the Blue Guitar" and other post-"Owl's Clover" poems, we can see that Stevens learned little or nothing – beyond anti-political prejudice – from his one failed encounter with the American literary left, and went his own aesthetic way thereafter, beginning with *Parts of a World* in 1942.

Any contemporary assessment of Stevens' poems of the 1930s can productively begin with the story as told somewhat along these lines. There is plenty to be said for the idea that Stevens mistakenly swerved toward and then away from the left. But this view is at best a heuristic device, and it is founded on all manner of wrong assumptions. Actually, Stanley Burnshaw was a talented lyric poet and no Party hack; he admired Stevens' poetry and genuinely hoped his criticism of Stevens' new poems would engage Stevens in a conversation with the younger radical poets, who read him attentively and longed to learn from him. The brief *New Masses* review was not stingingly negative; nor was Burnshaw's position on modernism representative of American communism; nor was Stevens stunned by the review. Nor was he ignorant of communism before its publication; nor was "Owl's Clover," except partly, a response specifically to Burnshaw. The verse in *The Man with the Blue Guitar & Other Poems*, including the long, brilliant title piece, does suggest that Stevens learned a good deal from the inter-animations with and among young leftist poets of the time. The very notion that this was a mere "encounter" with the political left – an unfortunate affair, a bumping in the night, an inapt rendezvous – only contributes to a general sense that the 1930s was a bad time for Stevens and (thus) for modern American poetics.

II

In Stanley Burnshaw's personal copy of *Ideas of Order* – it was the same volume given him at the offices of the *New Masses* to read and prepare his review – he marked the following passage:

> Is the function of the poet here mere sound,
> Subtler than the ornatest prophecy,
> To stuff the ear? (116)[1]

Burnshaw's answer to the question was *no*, of course. But so was Stevens'. The poem "Mozart, 1935" answers this question as if it were raised as part of a grievance – answers it directly at first and then more discriminatingly in the poem's last lines. In the end, Stevens will have employed one principle of the literary left to counter another, the main claim against "pure poetry." The use of "Mozart" in the very title indicates that among the several levels of poetic subject-position – Stevens', the speaker's, and the pianist's – the speaker is most conscious of the inappropriateness of what he calls upon the pure poet to play.

The title of this poem permits Stevens to say for the speaker: *Surely you can find a version of Mozart for this time of crisis, the mid-1930s.* Thus, through the very title – "Mozart" and "1935" separated by a mere comma, suggesting one element inside the other or set in relation against the other – the speaker distinguishes himself from the addressed pure poet ("Poet, be seated at the piano. / Play the present" [107]), implying that if one should be criticized by the left for fingering a divertimento in the year 1935, the attack cannot be aimed at this modern ingénue, who is, after all, tutored by a more conscious poet-figure, the speaker who is the worthier antagonist of the two: he, in short, is the Stevensian figure of capable imagination, sheltering a beset pure-poetry trainee while half-wittingly exposing him to public dangers – imagining a certain outmoded art form as downright instigation, a calling card for political trouble.

The speaker of this poem is willing to admit his audacious sense of cause and effect: he imagines that "they" (unnamed antagonists outside the house in which the poet plays) will "throw stones upon the roof" – while at the same time, somehow, "they" (the very same antagonists?) "carry down the stairs / A body in rags" (107). Stevens here acknowledges extrinsic or extra-aesthetic forces at work on the lyric. One's arpeggios are perhaps disfigured, not in the way the poet-player plays but by the contemporary ("1935") hearing the lyric will receive. One can hardly imagine ignoring the stone-throwers, so the murderous, intrusive auditors are themselves making sound in return.

Later in "Mozart, 1935" the speaker urges the poet-pianist to be "the *voice*, / Not *you*" – to speak for others as well as to create identity for himself through his art. "Be thou, be thou / The voice of angry fear." If, in being merely oneself, the artist in mid-Depression must adapt the voice that shouts down one's art (be thou *that* intrusive voice, decrying thou and the self-reflexive "be thou" mode), then one must bespeak one's besieger. Finally the piano does smooth over the contradictions of "1935" on one hand and outmoded "Mozart" on the other; the voices raised up by one against the other are "absolved" and "placat[ed]" (107–8; emphasis added).

"Mozart, 1935" is not an encounter with the left, pro or con. It is a poem in which adaptation to extrinsic forces – the "outside agitators" so often vilified in speeches by anticommunists – is enacted and performed, and a poetics that must include politics or be out-sounded is formed before our eyes (or in our ears). Some conservative modernists, such as Harriet Monroe at *Poetry*, were convinced that young poets who had converted to communism were now abandoning lyric verse in favor of what was derisively called "poetry with a message," on the assumption that the communists' insistence on content had unequivocally repudiated the lyric. It had not, as a matter of fact, and the Stevens of "Mozart, 1935" shrewdly knows this. One definition of lyric poetry accepted at this time stipulated that it must be "the product of the pure poetic energy unassociated with other energies."[2] What "Mozart, 1935" achieves so interestingly is an integration of those "other energies" – a challenge to the development of the lyric poetic self, perhaps, but not inimical. It was the judgment of a poet-critic named Ben Belitt that Stevens' new "music is . . . of a more toughened sort, pruned of bravura and merging the logical with the lyric."[3]

III

The just-mentioned Ben Belitt was a regular reviewer and assistant literary editor at the *Nation*, a weekly magazine long associated with progressive politics. Belitt was probably the person responsible for Stevens' receiving the annual *Nation* Prize in 1936. He was given the award for a poem about the Spanish Civil War, titled "The Men That Are Falling." This poem is surely what one recent critic has called a "curiously ambivalent" elegy.[4] It certainly has its overt political rhetoric, an almost hysterical command: "Taste of the blood upon his martyred lips, / O pensioners, O demagogues and pay-men!" (174). The "pay-men" must be mercenaries. But whose "martyred lips"? Whose death does the elegy lament?

They are those of a man who has fallen – who has been killed in the strife. The head of the dead soldier appears on the speaker's pillow and causes a crisis of poetic identity and responsibility. In the view of one eminent critic, Helen Vendler, when the soldier's head intrudes on "the psychic problem of private misery," Stevens mistakenly "turn[s] his attention to those moral 'words' of heroic action 'that are life's voluble utterance,' insisting that right action is the arena for the resolution of inner pain."[5] Vendler feels, as many of Stevens' critics do, that Stevens' poems err and misstep when political responsibility limits aesthetic choices. Some readers of Stevens' 1930s poems have come to doubt that view, and "The Men That Are Falling" is arguably the poem with which to begin an exploration of these basic interpretive differences. Does Stevens' aesthetic sensibility permit the inclusion of "voluble utterance[s]" without compromise? It does well to think about this volubility in connection with the noisy outside agitators entering the house of "Mozart, 1935."

Because the Spanish Civil War (1936–39) has become a touchstone for the American cultural left – support of the Republic against fascist insurgents during this doomed struggle, the precursor to worldwide war against fascism, has been called "the good fight" – there is more than usual at stake among many of Stevens' readers and critics when they arrive at "The Men That Are Falling," one poem that seems certainly to set the poet's apparently characteristic isolation in the specific contemporary context of political martyrdom. Readers of this chapter are urged to consult the poem as an exercise of historical imagination. Contemplate why the editors of the *Nation* would have given it their annual prize. Was it an error, the result of a political misreading? Does the ending of the poem ("This man loved earth, not heaven, enough to die" [174]) merely bring Stevens' concerns about religion in "Sunday Morning" into the context of the secular, collectivist mid-1930s – but otherwise unchanged? Another view, consistent with our efforts to complicate the usual story about the fate of Stevens' poetics in an era demanding geopolitical responsibility, is that "The Men That Are Falling" formalizes an American aesthetic policy of isolation by doubting it – by finding in the course of such a meditation that isolation lacks moral legitimacy until private pain can be compared to that experience by a world of sufferers existing bodily beyond the room, as it were, of the poem.

Communists, in their way, understood this too. One hardliner thought it silly that a writer who held an "exaggerated idea of physical action" would feel "certainly . . . that unless he personally and physically fought he could cease to function fully as a writer." The sympathetic writer's responsibility was to observe and write, not necessarily to fight.[6] Once the point of view or perspective of a poem shifted to a place from which the speaker observes rather than engages, the verse might itself create an idea about the very problem of position, and the result might be, ironically, an end to isolation in both its political and bodily senses. The poet Horace Gregory, for instance, was prepared to find in the CPUSA "a hope for the future" and a "necess[ity] for living through these times of terror and destruction," but he knew enough, he said, to discern just when "it would be an impertinence for me to take sides," even while always generally endorsing radicalism. Indeed, Gregory's reputation among mainstream critics became that of "a poet giving expression to the inner intellectual and spiritual strains and dilemmas of the time," and the typical Gregory poem was deemed "a sensitive instrument on which *the pulls in various directions* are recorded."[7] In Stevens' poem about Spain, there is an incursion into the scene of private invention. The very act of "gain[ing] perspective" – the politics of observations decried by some Marxist critics as counterprogressive and celebrated by others as "sensitive" after Gregory's open admission ("I must remain in a position to observe,"[8] he said) – permitted an intensity of engagement that is not rare in Stevens' poetry but is too little heralded as a quality of his verse in this period.

IV

Whatever else it is, the long poem "Owl's Clover" embodies an elaborate – at times allegorical – exchange between various advocates of the public and private realms, and it certainly carries on the discussion in "The Men That Are Falling" of the fate of the isolated poet in a time of real political dangers. "Owl's Clover" asks: "Is each man thinking his separate thoughts or, *for once* / Are all men thinking together as one . . . ?" (583; emphasis added). The diction of the phrase "for once" implies that the speaker believes it is about time for such collectivity, yet we note that people here are not acting or doing but *thinking* together – a gesture, however unifying, that is still necessarily individualized.

This odd poem was first written and published in five titled sections. The second section, called "Mr. Burnshaw and the Statue," gave the project a referential definiteness that startled and delighted an emerging generation of communist poets (including Burnshaw himself) who were following every eminent modernist's response to challenges from the literary left, hoping for any sort of engagement, "regardless," as one communist writer put it, "of . . . even its hostility to communism."[9] Stevens had sent the first section of "Owl's Clover," "The Old Woman and the Statue," to be published in a magazine edited by an old modernist colleague – a man Stevens' own age – who Stevens knew had become a "red-hot"[10] revolutionary. The Burnshaw section of the poem seemed to be both a rejoinder and an accommodation to communist criticism.

The whole poem was published by a small press in 1936. The edition was tiny – just 105 copies were printed – and only a few readers saw this complete version. When the work next appeared, as one of the "other poems" in *The Man with the Blue Guitar & Other Poems* in 1937, published in a trade edition by Alfred A. Knopf, "Owl's Clover" had been cut drastically by 198½ lines. The titular reference to Stanley Burnshaw had been eradicated; in the Knopf edition, the second section was now titled "The Statue at the World's End."

Does this perturbed publication history hint at Stevens' deferred anxieties about political reference? Did he have almost immediate second thoughts? Which version should we prefer? Fortunately, the Library of America edition, *Wallace Stevens: Collected Poetry and Prose* (1997), offers both versions, and twenty-first-century readers coming across Stevens' poetry of the 1930s can confront the problem in a way that few people at the time or decades later could. The literary historian justifiably views this as a crucial point, for opinions about Stevens' political poetry, formed in the 1940s and early 1950s – before the full version of "Owl's Clover" was republished in

1957 in *Opus Posthumous* – were almost exclusively based on the cut version, with its impalpable and thus seemingly unsure references to political matters and figures.

Although no essay introducing Stevens' response to the political situation in the 1930s can properly avoid this poem, the obligation to discuss it itself raises an instructive question. If it was a bridge Stevens built between, on the one side, poems facing Depression-era social turmoil such as "Mozart, 1935" (or facing emergent fascism such as "The Men That Are Falling") and, on the other, the brilliant aesthetic dialectic of "The Man with the Blue Guitar," then should "Owl's Clover" be read today out of literary-historical interest, as a matter of instruction, a view to a transitional moment? Has the poem become a factoid, a piece of evidence trotted out for quick certification of a gone era to be characterized by the unlyric extremist challenging the great poet? A ham-handed Goliath fitted out by the desperate poet to face the David of the moment? Can "Owl's Clover" be said to fit along an aesthetic continuum (let us say, along an axis running from communism to modernism), or is it stylistically anomalous? And if it is an anomaly, is it then right to draw conclusions about the inefficacy not of antifascist views among modern poets but of antifascist poetry *as* poetry?

Such a fundamental question – it is a question of poetry and politics – cannot be answered for the whole of this long poem in so short a space, but engaged readers, especially those new to the maligned poem, might turn to its lines, to the poem itself, with some fresh sense of the reasons for the vilifications that have rendered it merely historical. The unsubtle figure appearing in the fourth poem, "the Bulgar," joins people in the park who are "Forgetting work, not caring for angels, hunting a lift," seeking "The triumph of the arcs of heaven's blue / For themselves" (582). Here these working-class people, sharing the poet's public park space, also share his post-Christian dreams of an "imperishable bliss" ("Sunday Morning") postdating traditional belief and now found, as a real alternative, in the lyricism of free space and free time, which the speaker attempts to offer right there in lovely lines describing them on a Sunday, their only free day (and his). However passingly the supposed conservatism of Stevens' characteristic speaker joins in sympathy with the apparent radicalism of the Bulgar's immigrant working-class comrades, Sunday in itself – the park, too, as a merged space – provides the chance for convergence. Such convergences – there are many in "Owl's Clover" – based on continuities from Stevens' pre-1930s modernism, are not well explained by a sudden appearance of political challenge inciting errant reaction.

V

That such a challenge was already inherent in Stevens' writing is made clear by his next major effort, "The Man with the Blue Guitar," which in an experimental, quasi-improvisational stanza form attempted to answer this dilemma: Can a million people play on one string? The conclusion, finally, is *no*, but along the way, in thirty-three stanza variations of offering an answer to this politico-aesthetic question, a great many people get their hands on his instrument. It is as if the radicals outside the house of the poet playing Mozart in 1935 had by 1937 broken all the way into the place, set their hands alongside his on the keyboard and produced a sound that delighted the art's begetter, induced strangely beautiful variations out of him, and taught him that the clashing, jangling, or wrangling of aesthetics could create a new modern sound that somehow accounted for the detractors of its previous impulse to isolate and exclude.

The poem's key phrase – "things as they are" (135) – becomes a kind of rhyming concept, a touchstone the reader's ear will grab to hear something familiar in a poem otherwise so disparate. It is the occasion for an actual rhyme ("'You have a blue guitar, / You do not play things as they are'" [135]), but the poem is largely made of unrhymed couplets; even rhythmic refrains, after the opening cantos, are few and far between. Nonetheless, "things as they are" is a phrase used twenty times in the poem's thirty-three cantos (and five more times in six cantos later discarded). The guitarist-poet's detractors employ the slogan against him: it refers to the reality they say he does not comprehend and cannot reproduce in his variable art. He concedes that he "cannot bring a world quite round" but counters that he can "patch it as I can" (135) – and so representations of reality are redefined to indicate what exactitudes can be managed. If a "serenade" that is "almost" truthfully human is what can be managed, then that is what is being "play[ed]" musically or phrasally in this poem.

Later, "things as they are" is repeated to reassure detractors who doubt the validity of realism's extended geography; sometimes it seems to be a deliberately empty political gesture, like a verbal half-salute or nod toward idiomatic piety. The dialogue between the imagined and real, thought to be temperamentally aligned with political right and left respectively – of "serene" voices in the clouds (aesthetic conservatives) versus the "grunted breath" of the detractors (aesthetic left) – plays "year by year" (145) a metapoetry, a poetry about poetry itself, in a style that is answerable to both parties at once, poetry that is about the contingent concept of things as they are. At that point the poem has itself become the sort of writing being imagined in this assertion.

Thus the detractors' idea of things as they are, introduced in the opening canto, is again refuted, even as it is borrowed from liberally. Still, a major point against them has been clinched, for even *their* version of the poem is finally a poem about poetry. The centrality of poetics has been re-claimed after initial defeats in the face of reality. This enables us to read subsequent Stevensian provocations – for instance, "He held the world upon his nose / And this-a-way he gave a fling" (146) – as responsive to realists rather than evasive or irresponsible. The guitarist-poet pushes variations of the real so playfully and so riskily far that, when he soon makes a natural, conventional definitional claim – "I am a native in this world" (147) – it strikes us as astonishingly fresh and full of strong sentiment.

Even readers who are new to the tendency in modern poetry to achieve through form what in novels and essays is typically explained through thematics will find in "The Man with the Blue Guitar" a means of discerning why poets feel they must answer questions about content through the way their words, phrases, and lines are organized – arranged on the page, given meter, endorsed, or undermined by choices of tone or rhetorical devices. What is perhaps so exciting about these stanzas strummed on an instrument by a poet-figure thirty-three ways is that form becomes his only means of addressing ethical complaints raised against his mode. "The Man with the Blue Guitar" is a poem that is organized, or styled, to account for charges to be made against the invariability of its ideas about art. It responds through sheer variability and an incessant shifting of positions. These positions are not just political ones, but are also the sitting, or setting, or arrangement that the guitarist-poet takes or assumes in relation to his guitar.

In the opening canto, for instance, the guitarist's instrument is something to be tried on, handled (not just held), adjusted, and maneuvered. In canto II the guitar seems to be an adhesive and an accessory at once. In canto III it is a sharp tool, knife, and hammer. In canto VI it seems to have become abstract although not metaphorical: an apparatus constructed out of place and space and able to resist change. In canto XXVI the guitar is a noisy swarming of thoughts. In canto XXIX it is a way of defiguring a figurative mask. By canto XXXI, two cantos from the end, it is a mode of unanticipated, painful posturing that paradoxically enables subtlety and even inspires rhapsody. In canto IX it is the one thing that embodies the power of invention. In canto XX it seems to have become improvisation itself. The guitarist's guitar is not quite analogous to the poet's poem; the poet's poem is a means but it is also of course the product of the writing, whereas the guitar is almost always not art itself but an instrumentalism, a way of making art happen. On the other hand, the people in the poem who dislike the art (those called "they" by the anxious speaker, who call themselves "we" in some of the poem's opening ten or so cantos) can be thought of as the same figures whether they assail poetry or the guitarist's improvisations. Although readers wonder at the many forms taken by the guitar – it is an agent, a means, a method, an envoy, a device, a vehicle, a contrivance or gizmo, and also (thanks to Pablo Picasso) a piece of the art itself – a second level of wonderment is required to contemplate how a poem, how *this* poem too, can also be all these things.

Wallace Stevens' poetics at this point will not be pinned down, but this is not a sign, contra the straw-man version of Burnshaw in the tales we sometimes tell about Stevens' 1930s, of the poet's inability to position himself with respect to those political artists who would seem to be his detractors. In "The Man with the Blue Guitar" he modernizes them by the very same strokes in which they politicize him, but he does so only because their concerns have become pressing matters of poetic form. The 1930s was a good decade for modern American poetry, in part because the discontinuities of the New Poetry of the 1910s and 1920s offered the only opportunity for continuity into a new era of concerns about the poet's role in the world of urgently competing ideologies. Surely Stevens sensed this continuity when he decided that the place to publish his first selection of "The Man with the Blue Guitar" cantos was *Poetry*, the venue most closely associated with pre-1930s modernism and, indeed, with the beginning of his own ongoing story as a poet.

NOTES

1. I consulted the copy of this book in Stanley Burnshaw's possession before his death in 2005.
2. John Drinkwater, *The Poet and Communication* (London: Watts & Co., 1923), 56.
3. Ben Belitt, "The Violent Mind," *Nation* 143 (December 12, 1936): 710.
4. Milton J. Bates, *Wallace Stevens: A Mythology of Self* (Berkeley: University of California Press, 1985), 184.
5. Helen Vendler, *Wallace Stevens: Words Chosen Out of Desire* (Knoxville: University of Tennessee Press, 1984), 20–21.
6. "A Conversation with Claud Cockburn," *The Review* 11/12 (1965): 51, 52.
7. Horace Gregory, "One Writer's Position," *New Masses* 14.7 (February 12, 1935): 20.
8. *Ibid.*
9. Alan Calmer, "Portrait of the Artist as a Proletarian," *Saturday Review of Literature* 16.14 (July 31, 1937): 14.
10. Alan Filreis and Harvey Teres, "An Interview with Stanley Burnshaw," *Wallace Stevens Journal* 13.2 (1989): 120.

4

MILTON J. BATES

Stevens and the supreme fiction

Is it possible to believe in something that you know to be a fiction? Though most people admit to beliefs that cannot be validated logically or experimentally, they would balk at believing in something that is "made up." Wallace Stevens thought it not only possible to believe in a fiction but also inevitable. As creatures that interpret experience mentally, we have no choice but to believe in the mind's made-up version of reality, whether the reality is material (tables and trees, for example) or spiritual (God, Goodness, Truth, Beauty). Some believers, perhaps the majority, distract themselves from the fictional nature of their belief-objects. Others acknowledge the epistemological quandary but are satisfied that their fictions are "true" in the sense that they correspond closely to a presumed reality. Belief, after all, entails a tolerance for mystery. Few people are prepared to take the final step with Stevens, to embrace what he called "the nicer knowledge of / Belief, that what it believes in is not true" (291).

To the ultimate object of this "nicer," more discriminating belief Stevens gave the name "supreme fiction." Though he wrote little about the supreme fiction until midway through his poetic career, he came to regard it as his central theme, the concept that unified his lesser themes. Consequently, in a retrospective note written for the *Collected Poems* in 1954, he said that his poetry explores "the possibility of a supreme fiction, recognized as a fiction, in which men could propose to themselves a fulfillment" (L 820). What kind of fiction deserves to be called supreme? What kind of fulfillment does it provide?

Stevens first used the phrase "supreme fiction" in "A High-Toned Old Christian Woman" (1922), an early poem that opens with the line, "Poetry is the supreme fiction, madame" (47). Inasmuch as the poem contrasts "fictive things" with the woman's religious creed, it implies that the two are antithetical. The poem nevertheless plays with the idea that conventional religion is as much a product of the imagination as the speaker's alternative fiction. Moreover, both may serve as the foundation for ethical behavior. Like the proper Christian woman addressed in the poem, we may respond by wincing at such an equation because it seems to demote a mythology that has proved conducive to virtue. Or, like the provocative speaker, we may welcome the change of perspective, not to mention the opportunity to unsettle a smug religionist.

"A High-Toned Old Christian Woman" dramatizes the central insight in George Santayana's *Interpretations of Poetry and Religion* (1900), published while Stevens was a student at Harvard and spent time in Santayana's company. According to Santayana, poetry and religion are both human fabrications, designed to express and at least partly to satisfy our longing for the ideal. They differ only in their relation to practical affairs. Religion is poetry in which we *believe*, usually without knowing it to be poetry; hence it affects our behavior. Santayana contends that the highest poetry is identical with religion. By allowing us a glimpse of the ideal, it likewise gives direction and meaning to our lives. Because many of the tenets of traditional religion – eternal damnation, for example – have become distasteful and no longer satisfy the imagination, Santayana maintains, poetry must step forward to provide us with a new mythology.

Thus did Santayana marry two of the contending schools of thought in Harvard's philosophy department – idealism and pragmatism. Idealism, as articulated by philosophers from Plato through Descartes, Kant, and (at Harvard) Josiah Royce, insists on mind and perception as the fundamental realities. Pragmatism, especially as propounded by Santayana's colleague William James, insists on empirical experience and behavior as the tests of an idea's validity: a good idea is one that *works* in the actual world. In a famous imaginary experiment James places a mountain climber before a chasm. He can either believe in his ability to leap the chasm successfully or doubt it. He is far more likely to succeed if he believes, though his belief is, in James's phrase, "voluntarily adopted"[1] – hence the title of the essay in which he describes the experiment, "The Will to Believe."

The strains of idealism and pragmatism converge in Stevens' most ambitious attempt at defining a supreme fiction, the long poem entitled "Notes Toward a Supreme Fiction" (1942). The first two words of the title reflect the tentativeness of the venture and its preliminary nature. They also acknowledge the possibility of notes beyond the three that he offers. "It Must Be Abstract," "It Must Change," and "It Must Give Pleasure" nevertheless provide all the scaffolding he needed for a poem of thirty cantos (ten cantos per note) plus invocation and epilogue. The idealist component of the supreme fiction is most evident in the cantos of "It Must Be Abstract." The pragmatist component emerges in "It Must Change," in "It Must Give Pleasure," and most explicitly in the epilogue.

Besides the philosophical challenges in "Notes Toward a Supreme Fiction," the reader encounters a couple of literary challenges. Though the poem's prosody remains consistent throughout – each canto is composed of twenty-one lines of blank verse, arranged in seven tercets – the tone and rhetorical form vary considerably. The cantos are by turns rhapsodic and satirical, musing and bemused, impassioned and detached. They take the form of addresses to an imaginary pupil, a lover, and a soldier. They tell stories, stage mini-dramas, and develop arguments. They ruminate on the past and speculate about the future.

We encounter variations in tone and rhetorical form as soon as we cross the threshold into the poem. The addressee in the first line of the invocation, "And for what, except for you, do I feel love?," seems not to be the same person addressed in the first canto, which opens with "Begin, ephebe, by perceiving the idea" (329). The invocation is a love poem, the first canto a pedagogical lesson. The tender feeling of the former, and the intimate rendezvous it reconstructs, suggests that the "you" is a particular person. Could it be Henry Church, whose name appears just above the invocation in most printings of the poem?

Stevens' friend Henry Church doubtless played an important role in the genesis of "Notes Toward a Supreme Fiction." It was he who sponsored a series of lectures at Princeton University that got Stevens thinking about a supreme fiction as he prepared his own contribution to the series, a piece entitled "The Noble Rider and the Sound of Words" (1940). The "you" of the invocation is not a human being, however, but rather a supreme fiction endowed with personal – indeed, with affective and vaguely sexual – qualities that seem at odds with its abstraction. This is, of course, the point: Stevens initially presents the supreme fiction not as an object of intellectual speculation, such as "the extremest book of the wisest man," but as a source of emotional fulfillment: "The vivid transparence that you bring is peace" (329).

Stevens returns to the affective atmosphere of the invocation in the final canto of "It Must Give Pleasure." The intervening cantos are tonally different from these, none more so than the "ephebe" cantos of "It Must Be Abstract." In these a master poet, someone very like Stevens himself, tutors a young disciple in the mysteries of their craft. This is not an entry-level course. Forgoing the usual content of Poetry Writing 101, the merely technical aspects of versifying, the master goes directly to the big questions: What is the ultimate aim of poetry? How does it help us to live our lives? The short answer, supplied in cantos VIII through X, is that poetry constructs a grand but credible image of humankind, a "major man," that lends significance to the lives of ordinary people.

Major man is a fiction conceived within an idealist theory of knowledge. Before the master poet can introduce major man, he must prepare the stage philosophically. This he does in cantos I–VII, all of which turn on the notion of a "first idea" (329). In the idealist scheme of things, we recall, the mind has no direct, unmediated access to realities outside itself. The closest it can come is already a mental construction, which Stevens calls the first idea. As canto IV suggests, Adam was the first idealist as well as the first human being. He is consequently the spiritual father of Descartes, who famously defined existence as thinking: *cogito, ergo sum* ("I think, therefore I am"). When the master urges the ephebe to become an "ignorant man" in canto I, he does not imply that anyone can dispense altogether with thought. The ignorant man, in his Adamic innocence, sees the world "in its idea" (329), before subsequent embellishments have begun to obscure it. In the case of the sun, for example, the myth of Apollo is a secondary or tertiary idea, a "name for something that never could be named" (329).

Our inability to experience the world "as it really is," prior to any mental image, has its *triste* aspect. According to canto IV, "we live in a place / That is not our own and, much more, not ourselves / And hard it is in spite of blazoned days" (332). Alienation is the human condition. Yet it is also our muse, for it is from our alienation, canto IV likewise tells us, that "the poem springs." Like Coleridge in the nineteenth century, Stevens develops a modern theory of creative imagination grounded in an idealist theory of perception. To see the world and to write poetry are essentially the same fiction-making activity, arising from the same desire to overcome our estrangement from reality.

Neither perception nor poetry can come any closer to reality than the first idea. Yet our efforts to possess and anthropomorphize a place that is "not our own" and "not ourselves" may succeed almost too well. As the first idea becomes encysted in second and third and fourth ideas, we lose our Adamic ignorance and innocence. When the first idea becomes a "hermit in a poet's metaphors" (330), we must turn paradoxically to metaphor to dislodge the hermit from his cave. Not just any metaphor will do. Only the most radical metaphor, such as the "Arabian" figure for the moon in canto III, can restore us to a primitive perception of the moon. The Arabian, too, will eventually join the repertoire of moon-clichés. The cycle of creative and perceptual desire mirrors the cycle of the seasons, proceeding from winter's "not having" to summer's "having what is not" and back again (330).

Some versions of idealism – Emersonian transcendentalism, for example – assume that the world is an idea in the mind of God, who allows us access to his thoughts. Though Stevens entertains the theological hypothesis in later poems (to be considered below), he explicitly waives it in "Notes," instructing the ephebe neither to "suppose an inventing mind as source / Of this idea" nor to imagine a godlike "voluminous master folded in his fire" (329). We can be perfectly content, he asserts, without "the giant, / A thinker of the first idea" (333), and to leave unresolved the question of who or what created the "myth before the myth began, / Venerable and articulate and complete" (331).

Unable or unwilling to assume a transcendent thinker of the first idea, the master poet projects instead a larger-than-life image of an ideal human being. If this seems an arbitrary maneuver, we might place ourselves in Stevens' position as he wrote "Notes Toward a Supreme Fiction." From letters written in 1940 we learn that he shared Santayana's view that the God of religion is a product of the poetic imagination. Because the will to believe persists after a particular object of belief loses its appeal, the imagination must invent a credible alternative. In theory, Stevens speculated, we might transfer belief from the object to the source and believe in the "idea of pure poetry" or "essential imagination." But he understood that most people find it easier to believe in something created by the imagination than in the imagination itself (L 369–70).

What form might that something take? "If we are to think of a supreme fiction," Stevens remarked in 1953, "instead of creating it, as the Greeks did, for example, in the form of a mythology, we might choose to create it in the image of a man: an agreed-on superman" (L 789). The historical circumstances of "Notes" further shaped the kind of superman that he created in 1940–42, when many nations in Europe, Asia, and Africa were engaged in cataclysmic warfare. As Stevens phrases it in "Asides on the Oboe" (1940), "the jasmine islands were bloody martyrdoms" (227). Though inspired by World War II, Stevens' idealized soldier lacks specific personal or national identity. He is an abstraction, indeed the "major abstraction," which allows him to appeal to a broader spectrum of humanity. He is "abler / In the abstract than in his singular, / More fecund as principle than particle" (336).

Stevens' major man has often been compared to Nietzsche's *Übermensch* ("overman" or "superman"), and there are similarities between the two. They differ markedly, however, in their relation to ordinary people. Whereas Nietzsche imagined the superman partly in revulsion against the "herd man," Stevens' master poet insists that the ephebe take common people into account when devising his hero. Canto X represents spiritual and civic leaders, the rabbi and the chieftain, lamenting the shabby human material with which they have to work. But neither they nor the poet can afford to ignore the man in an old coat and baggy pants who wanders aimlessly outside the town, fixated on the past rather than the future.

"It Must Be Abstract" leaves the ephebe with one final challenge: to confect from this clownish figure the "final elegance" (336) of major man.

Except for an apostrophe to the muse ("My dame") in canto IX, the cantos of "It Must Be Abstract" are addressed to the ephebe or could plausibly be spoken in his presence. The cantos of "It Must Change" and "It Must Give Pleasure" are more eclectic rhetorically. Rather than advance an argument point by point, as the cantos of "It Must Be Abstract" generally do, they are improvisations on a theme.

The first three cantos of "It Must Change" illustrate the difference in approach. Canto III presents a satirical description of a statue. General Du Puy, presumably a French war hero, is immortalized in bronze, while his contemporaries go directly from their funerals to the cemetery and oblivion. As a relic of the past, unfortunately, the general elicits contempt rather than admiration. This extreme example of changelessness follows subtler instances in cantos I and II. Like General Du Puy, the old seraph of canto I is a statue. He is situated, however, in an Italian garden, at the center of natural flux, rather than in a sterile public square. What could be more changeable than the generations of flowers, doves, bees, and girls that pass before the seraph's unblinking eyes? But, insofar as each generation merely duplicates the activity of the previous generation, its motion is repetition rather than change. The "obvious acid" of decay overpowers the "erotic perfume" (337) of regeneration. Genuine change begins with perception: were the seraph endowed with consciousness and able to change his mind (as General Du Puy cannot), he might be transformed from chaste seraph into lusty satyr.

Canto I thus identifies the chief sources of real change, namely, mind (in keeping with Stevens' idealist bias) and desire. Canto II, picking up the "booming" bees in the seraph's garden, reports the resurrection, by executive decree, of a dead bee. This, too, is a spurious form of change, a comic version of the gospel story in which Jesus raises Lazarus from the dead. Here, as in his early poem "Sunday Morning" (1915), Stevens affirms the need for death as a component of change. Death, not resurrection or immortality, is the mother of beauty, because death clears the way for new life. Without the winter of death there will be no spring "for lovers at last accomplishing / Their love" or the "booming of the new-come bee" (338).

Like cantos I–III, canto VI satirizes the failure to change. Following Eve's example in canto IV of "It Must Be Abstract," the birds in this canto try to make air the mirror of themselves. Their "Bethou me" is the granite text of the pathetic fallacy. Insofar as each succeeds, it becomes "a bird / Of stone" (341), incapable of change in response to some other. Thus the birds violate the principle laid down in canto IV, that change originates not in identity but in a dialogue between opposites: man and woman, day and night, the imaginary and the real, winter and spring, north and south, the captain and his crew, the sailor and the sea, the self and an alter-ego.

The cantos that illustrate this principle are all dialogic in nature, whether the dialogue is between a planter and his island (canto V), a pair of lovers (canto VII), Nanzia Nunzio and Ozymandias (canto VIII), or a man and a park lagoon (canto X). In all of these desire suffuses perception to produce change that is not merely repetitive motion or narcissism. Canto IX uses the dialogic model to suggest how ordinary speech (the "gibberish of the vulgate," the "lingua franca et jocundissima" [343]) relates to poetry (the poet's gibberish, the imagination's Latin). The poet's challenge is to wed the two. Except for its opening and closing propositions, canto IX consists of a series of questions. These befit the daring speculation that lies at its center, that there may be "a poem that never reaches words" (343) yet encompasses all of the word-poems ever written. Such a poem would qualify as "the idea of pure poetry" or "essential imagination" – or as a supreme fiction.

Turning from the second note to the third, we may wonder why the capacity to please should be a necessary predicate of a supreme fiction. The logic goes something like this: the abstraction of ideas and the fluidity of perception are conducive to change, which, if genuine, elicits pleasure. The spurious change of canto I in "It Must Change" produces "distaste" (337) rather than pleasure because it is mere repetition. Stevens implies, moreover, that pleasure is another name for the kind of fulfillment that we have experienced historically in religion and hope to experience again in surrender to a supreme fiction.

Canto III of "It Must Give Pleasure" recounts the history of Judeo-Christianity as a parable of pleasure. It opens with an oppressive image of Jehovah as a badly weathered stone face. The "sheep" (believers) "carouse" when their dead shepherd, Jesus, harrows hell and establishes the new dispensation. Did this really happen? Historical fact matters less, the canto implies, than the myth: "so they said" (346). But a myth that initially generates pleasure – children scattering flowers, in this case – loses its affective power as it is codified and ritualized. When Jerome translated the Bible into the language of the people, canto I suggests, he fathered the joy of choral song. As the song loses its spontaneity and degenerates into a "facile exercise" (344), the spiritual seeker sets out on another quest for the uncanny, for those unaccountable epiphanies to be experienced "when the sun comes rising, when the sea / Clears deeply, when the moon hangs on the wall / Of heaven-haven" (345).

The two poems just discussed compress whole libraries of religious history into brief anecdotes or fables. This is Stevens' procedure in most of the cantos of "It Must Give Pleasure" until he resumes the rhetoric of discursive argument toward the end. Like the cantos of "It Must Change," these focus on perception and desire. The story of the great captain and Bawda in canto IV, for example, echoes the numerous references to love and lovers in previous cantos. Their desire for one another is in turn grounded in their love of a cherished landscape. Catawba is a "marriage-place" (347) not only in the sense that the lovers are married there but also in the sense that it marries raw geography and their perception of it. It is, to modify a clause in line 3, a place dependent on themselves.

Besides the captain and Bawda, the anecdotes of "It Must Give Pleasure" present three heroes for emulation: the blue woman of canto II, Canon Aspirin's sister in canto V, and the canon himself in cantos V and VI. What distinguishes the blue woman is her tact. She came into being, Stevens remarked in a letter, as his impression of the weather – no doubt the sky, in particular – on a cool, clear morning in April (L 444). Hence her color does not signal, as it often does in Stevens, the impulse to transform reality. Taking our cue from the metaphors implicit in "feathery argentines" and "frothy clouds" (345), we might be tempted to view the flowers (probably silverweed cinquefoil) as cold silver and the clouds as foamy waves. The blue woman, in contrast, allows them to be themselves. Even when she dreams of August heat and the scent of pine trees, she takes pains to distinguish between memory and desire. To the blue woman's careful discriminations the canon's sister adds the dimension of feeling. Impelled by maternal love, she names, dresses, and "paint[s]" her daughters, who seem to be personifications of reality. As cherished fictions, they in turn enrich her life with the pleasure of "sensible ecstasy" (347).

It is Canon Aspirin who coins that phrase and whose nocturnal adventures are related in canto VI. His name, Stevens cryptically remarked, is meant to suggest the sort of person that he is (L 427). By day he lives a life "[a]ccording to canon" (993), like Crispin in Stevens' early poem "From the Journal of Crispin" (1921). In his canonical capacity, he praises his sister's rejection of dreams. At night he indulges the "aspiring" side of his personality suggested by his surname. His Miltonic dream-flight takes him first to an extreme sense of fact. Then, following a brief visit to his sister's sleeping children, it carries him to an extreme of imagination. Appropriating the language of "It Must Be Abstract," canto II, we might say that he proceeds from "not having" to "having what is not" (330). Must one choose between these kinds of nothingness? The canon demonstrates his sophistication by choosing both, along with all of the intermediate gradations of being.

It is natural to suppose that Canon Aspirin is the person who "imposes orders as he thinks of them" (348) in the following canto. However, the sensibility of this imposer of arbitrary orders seems antithetical to the canon's, and his behavior prompts the narrator's scornful "It is a brave affair" (348). We might think of this "he" as an ephebe who has become fixated on the lesson of the master poet in "It Must Be Abstract." He believes – in fact, clings desperately to the belief – that reality can be confronted in its first idea, the "fiction of an absolute" (349). Without the "crude compoundings" of metaphor, it will seem an alien and repellent creature, a "beast disgorged" (349).

The final tercet of canto VII abandons third-person narrative for an apostrophe to reality, addressed as angel rather than beast. This abrupt and unsettling rhetorical maneuver continues into canto VIII, where the speaker of the apostrophe ("I") displaces the ephebe-like "he" of canto VII. The effect is much the same as in metafiction, where an author shifts from the story to reflections on storytelling. In this case the shift from poetry to metapoetry allows Stevens to pose in its most direct and personal form the central question of "Notes Toward a Supreme Fiction": "What am I to believe?" (349).

What, indeed? Up to this point in "Notes," Stevens has considered several plausible objects of belief: major man ("It Must Be Abstract," VIII–X); the poem that never reaches words ("It Must Change," IX); and the fiction of an absolute reality. These are, after all, notes toward *a* supreme fiction, the indefinite article allowing for multiple possibilities. In canto VIII, Stevens allows the fiction of an absolute to unfold in all its majesty as "angel," whereupon he asks, "Am I that imagine this angel less-satisfied? / Are the wings his, the lapis-haunted air? / Is it he or is it I that experience this?" (349). It is obviously the poet who experiences the angel because he invented it. Consequently, he can be satisfied not only with his imaginary angel but also without it, for its majesty is really a projection of his own. Canto VIII thus enacts the self-reflexive process that Stevens called "decreation" in a 1951 lecture. "Modern reality," he asserted then, "is a reality of decreation, in which our revelations are not the revelations of belief, but the precious portents of our own powers. The greatest truth we could hope to discover, in whatever field we discovered it, is that man's truth is the final resolution of everything" (750–51).

Stevens implicitly equates man's truth with God's when, echoing Jehovah's "I am who I am" (Exodus 3:14), he proclaims, "I have not but I am and as I am, I am" (350). With these words the romantic fondness for comparing poetic and divine creation reaches its apex. In the post-romantic era, however, so bold and even blasphemous an assertion cannot stand unchallenged. The final tercet of canto VIII acknowledges that the poet, like Cinderella, is a child of the mirror-making Eve. Eve's narcissism, Cinderella's daydreams, and the poet's majestic angel are all "escapades of death" (350), brief if pleasurable diversions from the inevitable end. As the final canto of "It Must Change" puts it, "Time will write them down" (344).

Canto VIII is the climax of "Notes Toward a Supreme Fiction," the canto in which Stevens, risking all, simultaneously wins and loses everything. The remaining two cantos of "It Must Give Pleasure" are poems of accommodation to the discoveries in canto VIII. Though mindful of ultimate defeat, they dwell on the imagination's victories. Pursuing his metapoetic reflections in canto IX, the poet tells a couple of the "bethou" choristers from "It Must Change," canto VI, about his "angel" trope. He implies that, as a source of pleasure, his metaphor surpasses their "Mere repetitions" (350). But he goes on to concede that repetition, which he had previously contrasted to genuine change, may also be a source of enjoyment. He speculates further that major man, mentioned here for the first time since "It Must Be Abstract," canto X, may be simply the master of repetition. This is a far more modest role than he had originally imagined for the hero who was to take God's place as an object of belief.

With canto X, "Notes Toward a Supreme Fiction" comes full circle back to the invocation. The "Fat girl" is a personification of planet Earth, familiar from daily encounters but aberrant in the sense that she changes in the eye of the beholder. As a fiction of reality she lacks the majesty of an angel and the grotesqueness of a beast disgorged. Like the "you" addressed in the invocation, she has instead the qualities that elicit affection. She is an object of love and desire rather than study ("the extremest book of the wisest man") or logical exposition (the lectures at the Sorbonne). The "crystal" in which she revolves is part of her attraction, for, as Stevens remarked in a 1943 lecture, "It is the *mundo* of the imagination in which the imaginative man delights and not the gaunt world of the reason" (679).

"Notes Toward a Supreme Fiction" could well end with the "Fat girl" canto, and some readers think that it should. Historical circumstance rather than logical or narrative necessity may have inspired the epilogue, an apostrophe to a soldier in the same format as the preceding thirty cantos. Though American troops were already engaging Axis forces as Stevens wrote the epilogue, he addresses it to a French soldier. This cultivated European "Monsieur" may be based loosely on Eugène Emmanuel Lemercier, whose *Lettres d'un soldat* inspired Stevens' 1918 sequence of war poems bearing the same title.

Stevens is somewhat defensive in making his case for poetry as the moral equivalent of war. Though he claims that the poet and the soldier depend on one another, he dwells exclusively on the soldier's indebtedness to the poet. As the soldier reads his book in a barrack, he may – like the MacCullough in "It Must Be Abstract," canto VIII – experience the encroachment of a "leaner being" (335). Poetry is the bread that sustains him in life and gives him the courage to face death. Without real soldiers, of course, the poet would lack any empirical basis for his fictions. For this side of the exchange we need to recall the "major man" cantos of "It Must Be Abstract" and other Stevens poems of the early 1940s that derive the idea of the hero from the historical deeds of soldiers.

Is the epilogue an integral part of "Notes Toward a Supreme Fiction" or an afterthought, possibly a lame attempt at relevance? In its defense one might observe that, more than any other canto of "Notes," it explores the pragmatist dimension of a supreme fiction. In the behavior of real soldiers an ideal such as Virgil's Aeneas or Stevens' major man becomes flesh. By influencing ethical behavior, the fictive hero becomes the real.

Perhaps too real? In 1954 Stevens told a correspondent that he had long considered adding a fourth section to "Notes" under the heading "It Must Be Human," but decided to leave well enough alone (L 863–64). He may have realized that he could not make his supreme fiction more definite without contradicting the first note, "It Must Be Abstract." After "Notes," Stevens continued to write poems about the ideal hero, including "Montrachet-le-Jardin" (1942), "Examination of the Hero in a Time of War" (1942), "Gigantomachia" (1943), "Chocorua to Its Neighbor" (1943), "Paisant Chronicle" (1945), "The Pastor Caballero" (1946), and "Sketch of the Ultimate Politician" (1947).

These are among his most evasive poems, for he was trying to define an abstraction without being too definite. The evasiveness was not only inherent in the subject matter but also rhetorically purposeful. Speaking of "Paisant Chronicle" in 1945, he remarked, "[I]n dealing with fictive figures evasiveness at least supports the fiction. The long and short of it is that we have to fix abstract objectives and then to conceal the abstract figures in actual appearance. A hero won't do, but we like him much better when he doesn't look it and, of course, it is only when he doesn't look it that we can believe in him" (L 489).

The hero poems taper off quickly after World War II, as though to underscore one point of the epilogue to "Notes" – that the poet's war depends on the soldier's. Stevens' fascination with a supreme fiction persisted, however. Though never comfortable as a public speaker, he delivered a series of lectures in the postwar years – "Three Academic Pieces" (1947), "Effects of Analogy" (1948), "Imagination as Value" (1948), and "The Relations Between Poetry and Painting" (1951) – that explore the notion of a "central poem." He developed the idea poetically in "A Primitive Like an Orb" (1948), calling this poem of poems a "primitive," or archetype; an "orb," or planet; an "essential poem"; a "huge, high harmony";

a "miraculous multiplex of lesser poems"; a "vis"; a "principle"; a "nature"; a "patron of origins"; and a "skeleton of the ether" (377–80).

"A Primitive Like an Orb" is one of Stevens' less successful long poems. It veers between the trumped-up rhetoric of "whirroos / And scintillant sizzlings such as children like" (380) and mechanical echoes of successful earlier poems such as "Notes Toward a Supreme Fiction" and "Chocorua to Its Neighbor." In subsequent poems he took a different tack. Before writing "Notes," we have observed, he commented on the logic of transferring belief from the object of belief to the source, which he called "the idea of pure poetry" or "essential imagination." "Notes" reverses that process, proceeding from major man and a majestic angel to the person who imagines them. The decreative canto VIII of "It Must Give Pleasure" represents a poet who, discovering the "precious portents" of his own powers, declares that he can do "all that angels can" (350).

In several poems of the late 1940s and early 1950s, however, Stevens speculates that "essential imagination," the source of our fictions, may lie outside the consciousness of any individual. Canto VII of "The Auroras of Autumn" (1948), for example, represents a sublime and terrifying display of the aurora borealis in the northern sky. This natural phenomenon prompts a series of three questions: "Is there an imagination that sits enthroned . . . ? When the leaves are dead, / Does it take its place in the north . . . ? And do these heavens adorn / And proclaim it . . . ?" (360). The interrogative mood allows Stevens to advance a daring, quasi-religious proposition, namely, that a transcendent "crown and mystic cabala" is responsible for order and seasonal change in the universe.

In "Looking Across the Fields and Watching the Birds Fly" (1952), Stevens ascribes much the same view to Mr. Homburg, a Kantian idealist who is entirely at home in Emerson's Concord. He is one of those thinkers whom Santayana had in mind when he remarked that they "imagine that all reality might be a transcendental self and a romantic dreamer like themselves; nay, that it might be just their own transcendental self and their own romantic dreams extended indefinitely."[2] Mr. Homburg's belief in a "pensive nature" (439) is irritating rather than exhilarating because he expresses it incautiously. Hence Stevens at first maintains an ironic distance from it. Gradually, however, he warms to this notion of a "daily majesty of meditation, / That comes and goes in silences of its own" (440). The last three tercets of the poem introduce a "new scholar" who seems prepared to accept Mr. Homburg's transcendental idealism, amended so as to accommodate human agency and recognition of nature's "blunt laws" (440).

Among the last pieces in Stevens' *Collected Poems* is one of his more suggestive treatments of the supreme fiction. "Final Soliloquy of the Interior

Paramour" (1951) may serve as a fitting coda to a consideration of the nature of the supreme fiction and the kind of fulfillment that it afforded Stevens. "God and the imagination are one" is the soliloquy promised in the title, if words spoken by more than one person – presumably the speaker and his muse or "interior paramour" (444) – qualify as a soliloquy. The words that introduce the proposition, "We say," identify it as a "voluntarily adopted" faith, the product of a will to believe. This credo passes the pragmatist test, for its effects are immediate and profoundly satisfying. Like a candle, it illuminates the darkened chamber and transforms the meeting of poet and muse into a lovers' rendezvous.

It may seem ungrateful to probe too deeply into a proposition that seems, for Stevens, to have been so fulfilling. But what precisely does it mean to say that God and the imagination are one? Like the epigrammatic lines in several other Stevens poems, this statement was lifted from a notebook entitled "Adagia." Here is the complete notebook entry:

Proposita:

   1. God and the imagination are one.
   2. The thing imagined is the imaginer.

The second equals the thing imagined and the imaginer are one. Hence, I suppose, the imaginer is God. (914)

This is rather baffling. Does the unity of God and the imagination result from God assimilating the human imagination or from the imagination assimilating God? The notebook entry is ambiguous, perhaps deliberately so. In "Final Soliloquy of the Interior Paramour" the first proposition likewise allows for both interpretations, but the context seems to favor a God who encompasses the imagination. On the one hand, the speaker and his muse choose to "think / The world imagined is the ultimate good" (444). Changing "imagine" from the passive voice to the active and supplying a pronoun, we might construe this to mean that *they* imagine a world that is God or at least godlike. On the other hand, the lovers "feel the obscurity of an order, a whole, / A knowledge, that which arranged the rendezvous" (444). They become aware, in other words, of an imagination that seems to operate independently of human will and invention – though it does not, like Mr. Homburg's "pensive nature," preclude human agency. As "central mind," this version of the supreme fiction most resembles the heavenly "imagination that sits enthroned" of "The Auroras of Autumn," canto VII.

Stevens died of cancer four years after publishing "Final Soliloquy of the Interior Paramour." A Roman Catholic priest is one of several people who have testified that he accepted religious instruction and baptism in the

Catholic Church shortly before he died. Depending on how readers interpret the statement "God and the imagination are one," they will regard "Final Soliloquy" as a natural prelude to baptism or as circumstantial evidence that none was ever performed.

The kind of fulfillment to be found in the supreme fiction varies according to which option we choose. If "Final Soliloquy" merely reaffirms the mind's capacity to invent gods, it is a poem of decreation that invites us to revel in "the precious portents of our own powers." If it acknowledges the presence of a cosmic, superhuman mind, the nature of the fulfillment is harder to specify. It includes elements of the conventional religious emotions of awe and self-effacement before an all-powerful Other: "we forget each other and ourselves. / We feel the obscurity of an order, a whole" (444).

Yet the fulfillment is also unconventional, for it demotes the supreme fiction from an end to a means. Once the central mind has arranged the rendezvous, it has served its purpose. It participates in neither the affectionate intimacy of the poet and his paramour nor their quiet joy in creating and inhabiting a domestic space. It is as though the supreme fiction, having supplied Stevens with an encompassing vision of reality, gave him one last gift: the capacity to live without a supreme fiction. The final word of this final soliloquy nicely calibrates his satisfaction in simply "being there together" (444) with his muse. Insofar as we allow the poem's homely ambience to draw us in, we may find that for us, too, it is enough.

NOTES

1. William James, "The Will to Believe," *The Will to Believe and Other Essays in Popular Philosophy* (New York: Longmans, 1897), 2.
2. George Santayana, *Winds of Doctrine: Studies in Contemporary Opinion* (New York: Scribners, 1913), 195.

5

B. J. LEGGETT

Stevens' late poetry

When his last volume of new poems, *The Auroras of Autumn*, was published in 1950, Wallace Stevens was a month from his seventy-first birthday, and the publication of his *Collected Poems* was timed to coincide with his seventy-fifth. The final section of the *Collected Poems*, *The Rock*, comprised twenty-five previously uncollected poems, written when Stevens was in his seventies. These two collections affirm that age had diminished neither Stevens' energy nor his artistry – the title poem of *The Auroras of Autumn* is the work most often nominated as his greatest long poem, and many readers would agree with Harold Bloom that "Stevens' last phase (1950–55) was his best."[1] The poems written during this five-year period (the poems of *The Auroras of Autumn* were written between 1947 and 1949) also inaugurate a fresh pared-down style that makes them the most accessible of Stevens' poems.

Although difficult from the beginning, Stevens' poetry had become increasingly theoretical and abstract, and thus increasingly obscure, since *Parts of a World* in 1942, and *The Auroras of Autumn* represents the culmination of this tendency. Coming directly after this demanding poetry, the poems of *The Rock* are unexpectedly plain, stripped of the imaginative flourishes and epistemological quandaries of the preceding volumes. Stevens' late poems are thus not of a piece formally or stylistically, even if they address many of the same themes.

The publication of *The Auroras of Autumn* in 1950 coincided with the belated acknowledgment of Stevens as one of the great American poets of the twentieth century. The volume received the National Book Award, and earlier that year Stevens had been awarded Yale's Bollingen Prize (for 1949). In 1951 he was awarded the Gold Medal of the Poetry Society of America, and the *Collected Poems* received both the National Book Award and the Pulitzer Prize in 1955. Between 1951 and 1955 Stevens also received honorary degrees from Bard College, Harvard, Mount Holyoke, Columbia, and Yale. This new acclaim was also responsible in part for the decision of

Knopf, his publisher, to issue a collection of his critical papers on poetry, and these were published in 1951 as *The Necessary Angel: Essays on Reality and the Imagination*. It was not, however, that *The Auroras of Autumn* in itself initiated the succession of awards and honors. Although the reviews were generally favorable, the volume was not universally admired. Randall Jarrell, one of Stevens' early champions and one of the most influential reviewers of the time, thought it "not a good book," describing the poetry as "abstract" and "monotonous."[2] In his review Jarrell nevertheless labeled Stevens "one of the great poets of our century" (343), and for other readers as well *The Auroras of Autumn* no doubt represented the capstone of the career of a master poet whose relative inaccessibility had delayed recognition.

The long title poem (ten twenty-four-line cantos) is the key to the volume and one of the pivotal poems of the Stevens canon. Its reading depends to some degree on what preceded it in the earlier volumes, but it also foreshadows what is to follow in the last poems. Its relation to the earlier poetry may be seen, first of all, in the seasonal motif. "Credences of Summer" is the poem in the preceding volume that corresponds to "The Auroras of Autumn," and "Auroras" may best be read in the context of its earlier companion poem. (Stevens himself used "Credences" as a marker for the shift in orientation seen in the later poems.) Although he plays many variations on the imagination–reality binary, from *Harmonium* (1923) through "Notes Toward a Supreme Fiction" (1942), Stevens' poetry had tended to privilege the human imagination over external reality. The assumption behind these earlier poems is that the world is never accessible to us as it is in itself, but only as it is constructed by the imagination. "Credences of Summer," however, signals a change in its attempt to depict a reality beyond the mind. "From the imaginative period of the Notes I turned to the ideas of Credences of Summer," Stevens said, and he noted later, "At the time when that poem was written my feeling for the necessity of a final accord with reality was at its strongest," explaining that "reality was the summer of the title of the book [*Transport to Summer*] in which the poem appeared" (L 636, 719).

"Credences of Summer" depicts a moment of accord with a reality independent of the mind, beyond analysis, of which the speaker says, "Let's see the very thing and nothing else . . . / Without evasion by a single metaphor" (322). It attempts to describe a world in which the sound of a bird "is not part of the listener's own sense" (326), a world complete in itself that does not require the human imagination. Curiously, however, in a move that anticipates "The Auroras of Autumn," it requires an *inhuman* imagination. The final section of the poem depicts its summer reality as the fiction of an "inhuman author" (326), the meditation of a cosmic imagination. This fiction of a cosmic imagination is also central to "The Auroras of Autumn," where it assumes a greater significance.

"Credences of Summer" is a poem of stasis, the realization of a perfect moment "Beyond which there is nothing left of time" (322). "The Auroras of Autumn," and much of the volume in which it appears, is about flux, the breaking down of such moments. The accord with reality in the earlier poem is here threatened with another aspect of reality, its relentless change. The auroras of the title, as Stevens explained, refer to the aurora borealis, the northern lights, which could occasionally be seen from Hartford. "These lights," he wrote, "symbolize a tragic and desolate background" (L 852). From the opening canto's serpent as "form gulping after formlessness" (355) (the serpent shedding its skin), the poem depicts the breaking down of all forms, all attempts to order reality. Cantos II, III, and IV all begin "Farewell to an idea," which recalls Stevens' concept of the *idea* in *Ideas of Order* and "Notes Toward a Supreme Fiction" (the "first idea" [330]), the assumption that for the poet reality is always an idea, even if it is a "first" or fresh idea. But here all ideas, containers, points of order – the ancestral house of canto II, the mother and family of canto III, the father as creative principle of canto IV – are broken down by a universe in flux, symbolized by the auroras of autumn.

Canto V of what is the tightest and most carefully crafted of all Stevens' long poems pulls these threads together when the mother "invites humanity to her house / And table" and the father "fetches tellers of tales / And musicians" (358). These are means, the poem suggests – the earthly ties of family, the creative fictions of art – by which a formless reality is given form. But this attempt to impose order degenerates into a "loud, disordered mooch" (358), and by the end of canto VI all ideas of order have been destroyed. The source of these ideas, the human imagination, depicted in the poem as a single candle, is helpless in the face of a destructive universe aflame, depicted in the aurora borealis. The "scholar of one candle" looks up at "An Arctic effulgence flaring on the frame / Of everything he is. And he feels afraid" (359). It is at this point that the cosmic imagination of "Credences of Summer" makes its appearance. The auroras of autumn, curiously, represent not only a universal flux that destroys everything it brings into being but they also represent "an imagination that sits enthroned" in the northern skies "which in the midst of summer stops / To imagine winter" (360). It "meditates" (363) reality into and out of existence innocently, not maliciously, as Stevens takes great pains to emphasize in the poem's finale. This cosmic imagination simply wants to experience everything, all pleasures and all pains, and a poem that had begun with the aurora borealis as a symbol of tragedy and desolation ends with a justification of change and death as a part of "an innocent earth" (361). As in "Credences of Summer," Stevens is able to achieve this resolution through the introduction of the fiction of a godlike imagination. In his earlier poetry the unreal gods were the projections of the human imagination. In the fiction of many of the later poems the situation is reversed; we and our world, it seems, are a part of a larger imagination.

Many of the shorter poems of *The Auroras of Autumn* play variations on the themes introduced in the title poem. "Large Red Man Reading," one of Stevens' favorites from the volume, has been interpreted as a poem glorifying the poet, the large red man of the title. But Stevens' reader is larger than life, and red is Stevens' color for the sun, which in turn is his shorthand for reality. (An earlier red man in "Anecdote of the Prince of Peacocks" is "suncolored" [46], identified with the real, set against the unreal blue dreams of moonlight.) In "Large Red Man Reading" the reader is also associated with reality, set against unsatisfied "ghosts" who have returned to earth from the unreality of heaven and who "would have wept to step barefoot into reality" (365). In a figure akin to the cosmic imagination of "The Auroras of Autumn," reality is the poem of a mythic poet, "the poem of life" about the most ordinary objects – "the pans above the stove, the pots on the table" (365). The poet's words (from the imaginative "blue tabulae") become the physical objects themselves: "the literal characters, the vatic lines, / . . . Took on color, took on shape and the size of things as they are" (365).

"The Ultimate Poem Is Abstract" portrays this mythic figure as "The lecturer / On This Beautiful World Of Ours," who "hems the planet rose and haws it ripe, / And red, and right" (369). The *ultimate* poem of the title is then the material world, as in "Large Red Man Reading," and it is abstract because it is imagined, although not by the persona. (*Abstract* for Stevens is the opposite of real.) A day in which the speaker feels himself "Helplessly at the edge" is itself seen as mind: "It is an intellect / Of windings round and dodges to and fro" (369), although "Not an intellect in which we are fleet" (370), that is, nimble, adept. The day, the poem implies, is the composition of an external intellect, to which the human intellect, in this instance, finds it difficult to adjust, to be "at the middle" (370). "Puella Parvula" ("Young Girl") portrays this external intellect in a manner that also recalls "The Auroras of Autumn," where the change of season was attributed to a cosmic imagination that "in the midst of summer stops / To imagine winter." In "Puella Parvula" the coming of autumn is the triumph of a "mighty imagination" (390), and, as in the longer poem, autumn is associated with an apocalyptic ending of everything, which is at first frightening to the speaker ("Keep quiet in the heart, O wild bitch.

O mind / Gone wild" [390]). The effort of the poem, similarly, is to accept autumn's destruction as a part of the innocence of the earth, to change the "wild bitch" of the heart to the innocent young girl of the poem's title. And it is when the speaker accepts the change of seasons as the act of a godlike imagination, as the *"summarium in excelsis"* (390), that his fear subsides. This "mighty imagination" might well be the "large red man reading": "Hear what he says," the speaker concludes, "The dauntless master, as he starts the human tale" (390).

"A Primitive Like an Orb" toys with this theme, but in a somewhat different manner. In "Effects of Analogy," a Yale lecture that coincided with the composition of the poems of *The Auroras of Autumn*, Stevens advances speculatively a theory in which the poet comes to feel that his imagination "may be part of a much larger, much more potent imagination" (712). The conception of the poet as a component of a greater, perhaps supreme imagination, or the individual poem as a part of a greater poem, the *"summarium in excelsis,"* is offered as an aesthetic theory in "A Primitive Like an Orb." Its assumption is that there exists a "central poem" that cannot be known in itself, but is "seen and known in lesser poems" (378). This "essential poem" (377) is the perfect "mate" or "mirror" of the real world, and it is, in fact, "As if the central poem became the world" (379). Like the "ultimate poem" above, it is an "abstraction," and Stevens' poem attempts to give it a shape, settling finally on the figure of a "giant on the horizon," an ideal "virtuoso" encompassing all the arts, "the total / Of letters, prophecies, perceptions, clods / Of color" (380).

"A Primitive Like an Orb" imagines a prodigious abstraction, a "definition with an illustration" (380). "An Ordinary Evening in New Haven" appears at first to return us to the real. Stevens said of the poem that his interest was "to try to get as close to the ordinary . . . as it is possible for a poet to get. It is not a question of grim reality but of plain reality" (*L* 636). From this one might expect a bare, unadorned poem such as those that were to follow in *The Rock*, but it is the opposite of the later poems. He also said that the poem was a development of the ideas of "Credences of Summer" (*L* 637), but there is little resemblance. "An Ordinary Evening" was written in 1949, and two years earlier, in a Harvard lecture, "Three Academic Pieces," Stevens had noted, "What our eyes behold may well be the text of life but one's meditations on the text and the disclosures of these meditations are no less a part of the structure of reality" (689). "An Ordinary Evening" is not in fact about plain reality, what our eyes behold, but about the disclosures of Stevens' seemingly endless meditations (through thirty-one eighteen-line cantos) on what our eyes behold. Stevens also said that, "like most long poems," it was "merely a collection of short ones"

(*L* 640), and this accounts for the lack of any overall argument in the poem. It vacillates between the extreme positions of an acceptance of reality "as a thing seen by the mind," "as unreal as real can be" (399), on the one hand, and the search for "pure reality, untouched / By trope or deviation" (402), on the other, as well as any number of positions in between. In exhibiting a structure based on the many possible relations between mind and world, it resembles the much earlier "The Man with the Blue Guitar," which ran through similar variations on the relations between the imagination and reality.

"An Ordinary Evening in New Haven," at the end of the volume, and "The Auroras of Autumn," at the beginning, also illustrate its two extreme thematic tendencies – more or less abstract epistemological exercises and more personal confrontations with change and death. Many of the other poems of the volume may be aligned with one tendency or the other. "Page from a Tale," which follows "The Auroras of Autumn," is an almost literal working out of one of its figures. By the end of "Auroras" the speaker has come to see change and death as part of "An innocence of the earth" (361). His analogy is the world of childhood, which we accepted unquestioningly, perfectly at home: "We were as Danes in Denmark all day long" (361). "Page from a Tale" gives us the harsh, problematic world of "The Auroras of Autumn," the North Sea frozen solid, a steamer foundered in the ice. Tomorrow the crew will climb down the side of the ship and march single file to the foreign shore, "alert / For a tidal undulation underneath" (365). On shore, tending his drift-fire, very much at home in this desolate world, is Hans, the poem's Dane in Denmark. The men on the freighter are fearful; Hans is at peace in his harsh surroundings, and Stevens emphasizes this by a rare use of literary allusion, phrases Hans hears in the wind from Yeats's "The Lake Isle of Innisfree" and Heine's *Lyrisches Intermezzo*, both of which depict an innocent, unthreatening world antithetical to the world the crew of the freighter anticipate.

Following "Page from a Tale" and "Large Red Man Reading" is a group of five poems that ask, in effect, how one might respond to the problematic world of "The Auroras of Autumn." "This Solitude of Cataracts" shifts the symbol of change from the aurora borealis to a Heraclitus-inspired river of time: "He never felt twice the same about the flecked river" (366). The speaker's attitude toward the flux of existence here is similar to the initial response in "The Auroras of Autumn." He wishes to be "released from destruction," transformed into a kind of Yeatsian "bronze man," existing at the "center of time" (366). In the poem that follows, however, "In the Element of Antagonisms," the speaker finds this world of endless becoming, this "world without a genius," a god or center, "most happily contrived"

(366). "In a Bad Time" returns to the auroras and the man who "beheld the order of the northern sky" and "thereafter . . . belong[ed] to it" (367). He recognizes, that is, the tragic existence the northern lights signify, but, in another allusion to Yeats's "Lake Isle of Innisfree," his sense of tragedy and poverty becomes "his heart's strong core" (367). (How poverty and tragedy might become a source of strength is a seeming contradiction addressed in the poems of *The Rock*.) "The Beginning" also associates autumn with tragedy. In the progression of the seasons, the ending of summer is simultaneously the beginning of autumn, and the last birds of summer are also "the first tutoyers [those who speak familiarly] of tragedy" (368). "The Countryman," the last of the group, returns to the image of the river – in this case the Swatara, a stream in Stevens' native Pennsylvania. Here, however, it is the name "Swatara" that attracts the speaker. He associates it with "swarthy," dark; he is a "countryman" because he shares the river's "swarthy motion" (369) as it enters "the swarthy sea" (368). The speaker of "This Solitude of Cataracts" wants to be released from the destruction he associates with the river; the "countryman" identifies with it, takes it to heart.

Most of the remaining poems of *The Auroras of Autumn* have the same interest as "An Ordinary Evening in New Haven" in pursuing what Stevens calls in that poem "'The search / For reality'" (410). One of the ironies of such a search is that the poems that deal with perceiving the real are his most abstract, since they consider philosophically such issues as the relation of metaphor or sense or something named "presence" to the apprehension of reality. It is typical of Stevens that he takes no one position on the subject. In "Bouquet of Roses in Sunlight," for example, he argues that the roses are too real "to be changed by metaphor" (370), so their reality exceeds metaphor. Yet our sense of them is a consequence of the way we *feel*, so they are *not* real except in our sense of them. So pre-verbal sense ("meanings with no speech" [370]) is stronger than metaphor. "Saint John and the Back-Ache" makes a similar argument. In his dialogue with his backache, St. John argues that it is not the mind that creates reality but what he calls "presence" (as in a backache), which "fills the being before the mind can think" (375). Other poems in the volume disparage metaphor or rhetoric in the face of the real. In "The Bouquet," the bouquet is artifice; it "stands in a jar, as metaphor" (384), while the poet spends four stanzas speculating on the relation of the real and the unreal. In the last stanza a soldier enters the room, bumps the table, and knocks the poem's metaphor to the floor, implying that the intrusion of real events (with a world war fresh in mind) exceeds all metaphor.

The title of "Metaphor as Degeneration" would seem to make the same claim, but in fact the poem says the opposite. How, it asks, "is metaphor degeneration" (381) when the river Swatara may be used as a figure for the very nature of being? And in "Study of Images I," images awaken us to the object, help us to see it freshly; it may be that "images are all we have" (396). Perhaps, he speculates in "Study of Images II," there is a "center of images" (396) (like the central poem of "A Primitive Like an Orb") that contains the appropriate image for each object, awaiting its marriage to the real. Stevens' *practice* in the volume also gives the lie to his disparagement of metaphor. Poems such as "The Woman in Sunshine," "A Golden Woman in a Silver Mirror," and "Celle Qui Fût Héaulmiette" use feminine figures as metaphors for natural phenomena. "The Owl in the Sarcophagus," the most obscure poem of the volume, invents allegorical figures – "high sleep," "high peace," and "she that says / Good-by" (371) – in its attempt to replace a supernatural mythology of death with a "mythology of modern death" (374). In his musings on the real, Stevens, finally, has it both ways. The volume ends with a poem, "Angel Surrounded by Paysans," that directs us to the real, asks us to "see the earth again, / Cleared of its stiff and stubborn, man-locked set" (423), but the speaker of these lines and the agency of our seeing is an imaginary creation, an angel.

This emphasis on the real and the paradox it entails – the premise that the apprehension of the real requires a supreme act of the imagination, a supreme *fiction* – persists in the poems of *The Rock*. In 1954, Stevens was asked for a statement on the major ideas of his poetry, and he responded that the "central theme" was "the possibility of a supreme fiction, recognized as a fiction, in which men could propose to themselves a fulfilment" (L 820). Stevens' use of the term "supreme fiction" dates from *Harmonium*, where he had implied that the poet's supreme fiction, the poet's attempt to reconcile us to our existence in the world, would replace religion's supreme being, a fiction no longer credible. "Notes Toward a Supreme Fiction" was a tentative definition of the poetic fiction – it must be abstract, must change, must give pleasure – but in many of the poems of *The Rock* Stevens attempts to realize such a fiction, most often in his conception of a godlike imagination.

For years Stevens had resisted Knopf's requests for a collection of his published poems because, he said, "it puts an end to things" (L 832). When he finally relented in 1954, his inclusion of *The Rock*, twenty-five previously uncollected poems, made the volume something more than a retrospective. Here was something new and unexpected, personal poems from a poet known for impersonality, plain poems from a poet recognized for the density of his style, and, most gratifying of all, generally accessible poems from a poet whose previous volume had been his most obscure. The title poem does not entirely escape obscurity, and it is atypical in other ways, in its abstractness, for example. What it shares with many of the poems is its fiction of the cosmic imagination, first elaborated extensively in "The Auroras of Autumn." And "The Rock" looks back to the earlier poem in yet another way. The auroras had symbolized for Stevens "a tragic and desolate background." In the later poem the barren rock of the title is Stevens' symbol for the nothingness that underlies all existence, "That in which space itself is contained" (447), as the third of its three sections has it. Its subject is its speaker's sense of nothingness and his need to be cured of it.

The first section of "The Rock" is titled "Seventy Years Later," and to the seventy-year-old speaker the past seems unreal, an illusion. It is not simply that the events of the past *no longer* seem real; it is as if they *never* existed: "They never were" (445). Looking back, he can think of them only as the contents of a "fantastic consciousness," the inventions of an external imagination seeking to fill a universal nothingness. It is, he says, "As if nothingness contained a métier" (445), a vocation or genius by which the illusion of the speaker's world has been produced. The daring conceit of "Seventy Years Later" is that reality is an illusion created out of nothingness and that its purpose is to cover over nothingness. In the central figure of the poem, the bare rock of nothingness is covered with vegetation in what is called a "cure of the ground" (446). The second section, "The Poem as Icon," seeks "a cure of ourselves, that is equal to a cure / Of the ground" (446), and it draws a parallel between nothingness' métier and the poet's. If reality can be thought of as an attempt to escape nothingness by a "fantastic consciousness," then the parallel human attempt, the poem (which is an *icon* for the "cure of the ground" described in the first section), is equally an attempt to escape nothingness by creating meaning. The poem "makes meanings of the rock" so "That its barrenness becomes a thousand things / And so exists no more" (447). There are, then, two cures of nothingness in the poem, the "cure of the ground," reality itself, and the "cure of ourselves," the poem. "The Rock" is one of the strangest of the late poems and one of the least understood. That Stevens said it was a poem he particularly liked (*L* 833) and used it for the title of the whole collection is testimony of the appeal its central fiction held for him.

In "Looking Across the Fields and Watching the Birds Fly," this fiction is attributed to the Emerson-like Mr. Homburg of Concord, who makes the case for a "pensive nature," which thinks natural objects into existence and at night "think[s] away the grass, the trees, the clouds" (439). He argues that the afternoon is "Too much like thinking to be less than thought," and, further, that the human mind is merely an imitation, an "affectation" (440) of this larger intelligence. Similarly, in "The World as Meditation" Penelope, meditating on the return of Ulysses, perceives the coming of spring as "an inhuman meditation, larger than her own" (442). In "Final

Soliloquy of the Interior Paramour," the speaker, the interior paramour contained within a larger "order" or "knowledge," finds comfort in the thoughts that "The world imagined is the ultimate good" and "God and the imagination are one" (444). Although these lines have been read as glorifications of the human imagination, this was not the way Stevens read them. Here is his own gloss: "1. God and the imagination are one. 2. The thing imagined is the imaginer. The second equals the thing imagined and the imaginer are one. Hence, I suppose, the imaginer is God" (914). The "world imagined," by this logic, is not the world as *we* imagine it, but something closer to Penelope's "world as meditation," and the statement that "God and the imagination are one" is not an assertion of the godlike powers of the human imagination, but something like Penelope's "inhuman meditation, larger than her own" or the "enthroned" imagination of "The Auroras of Autumn," which "in the midst of summer stops / To imagine winter."

The association of this universal imagination with the change of seasons is the basis of two of the most successful poems of *The Rock*, "The Plain Sense of Things" and "Not Ideas About the Thing But the Thing Itself." Both depict states of nature – the coming of winter, the coming of spring – as states of mind, although the ambiguous constructions of both poems permit a more conventional reading. In the first, the loss of summer's foliage is characterized as a "return / To a plain sense of things," "an end of the imagination" (428). Whose plain sense and whose imagination? The poem is careful not to ascribe these to the speaker; we seem rather to have returned to Stevens' fiction of the enthroned imagination, which stops in the midst of summer to imagine winter, in this case apparently unsuccessfully. "A fantastic effort has failed," the speaker says, "a repetition / In a repetitiousness of men and flies" (428). This yearly repetition of flies is summer, which, in the poem, is conceived of as a fantastic effort of the imagination, which has now come to an end. (In "Long and Sluggish Lines" from the same collection, the appearance of the "first fly" [443] is associated with the coming of spring.) But the speaker's initial impression – that winter represents a failure of the imagination – is, he recognizes, wrong, since "the absence of the imagination had / Itself to be imagined" (428). This statement, too, is ambiguously phrased. It may be read to say that it takes an act of the imagination to depict the absence of the imagination. But if Stevens is faithful to his controlling fiction, then it also says that what appeared to be an absence of the imagination *had to be* imagined, since all natural phenomena are a part of this larger imagination.

A similar ambiguity of agency is present in "Not Ideas About the Thing But the Thing Itself," set at "the earliest ending of winter," when the speaker hears a "scrawny cry from outside" (451) that he first thinks of as a sound in his own mind. He comes to recognize, however, that it is the cry of a bird, like a newborn baby, that announces the coming of spring. "It was part of the colossal sun," he says, not part of his own mind. And yet it was a kind of knowledge, although not his own: "It was like / A new knowledge of reality" (452). Whose knowledge? The "it" refers to the bird's cry, associated with the coming of spring. If the winter can be figured as reality's plain sense of things, then spring is its new sense of things.

"Not Ideas About the Thing" is the final poem of *The Rock* and brings to a conclusion the seasonal motif that began with *Transport to Summer* in 1947. *The Rock* had begun "After the leaves have fallen" (428), and at its finish we are "At the earliest ending of winter" (451). The poem also exhibits another dominant feature of *The Rock*. Its epiphany occurs in a moment of weakness, in the midst of its speaker's drowsy and confused awakening from "sleep's faded papier-mâché" (452). Much of the poetry of *The Rock* associates its speaker's old age, weakness, and infirmity with his discovery of a reality that had eluded him through a lifetime. That link is made in "Long and Sluggish Lines," in "Final Soliloquy of the Interior Paramour," in "The Rock," in "An Old Man Asleep." "A Quiet Normal Life" associates the impoverishment of the speaker's world with his recognition that it is not the object of his own perception, not something constructed by him. It is "so frail, / So barely lit, so shadowed over and naught" that he concludes it "was not / In anything that he constructed" (443), as if its drabness were itself proof that it was not a product of his own imagination. A poem written in the same year with the awkward title "Lebensweisheitspielerei" also associates the speaker's indigence with his insight into the real. The title, which may be translated "playing with the wisdom of life," owes something to Schopenhauer's *Aphorismen zur Lebensweisheit*, a translation of which Stevens owned, and the poem's assumption that old age grants a true vision of things is also indebted to *Aphorismen zur Lebensweisheit*. Everything in the poem is diminished. The sunlight falls "Weaker and weaker" in "an indigence of the light." The speaker places himself among "the unaccomplished," those left after the "proud and the strong / Have departed" (429). It is in this "poverty" of autumn that "Each person completely touches us / With what he is and as he is" (430). The implication of the poem's imagery is that everything imaginative, fanciful, falsifying has been removed, and what is left is the "finally human" (429).

"Lebensweisheitspielerei" speaks of the "stale grandeur of annihilation" (430), and except for "stale" this might be a description also of one of the most admired of the poems of *The Rock*, "To an Old Philosopher in Rome."

The poem depicts "a kind of total grandeur at the end" (434) in imagining the final days of the philosopher George Santayana, dying in self-imposed poverty at a convent in Rome. Stevens had known Santayana briefly at Harvard, and the poem makes it clear that he sees something of himself in the philosopher and employs him as spokesman, asking the dying Santayana to speak of his misery and of the vision it has afforded him, "so that each of us / Beholds himself in you, and hears his voice / In yours" (433). Stevens had apparently read Edmund Wilson's account of a visit to Santayana in a *New Yorker* essay, which concludes with this image: "he reposes in his shabby chaise longue like a monad in the universal mind."[3] The vision Stevens grants Santayana is the realization of "living in two worlds" (433), one the immediate world of the convent, "a bed, a chair and moving nuns" (434), and the other a larger, more imaginative world that is not unlike the universal mind glimpsed by other speakers in *The Rock*. The poem also makes it clear that it is the poverty of old age that enables this vision. "It is poverty's speech" that Santayana speaks, and he seeks a final grandeur, "finding it / Only in misery." His final vision is "the afflatus of ruin, / Profound poetry of the poor and of the dead" (433). Santayana thus resembles other personae of the last poems, both in his imaginative vision and in the conditions under which it is realized. The poem concludes with Stevens' now-familiar image of an imagination transformed into reality: "As if the design of all his words takes form / And frame from thinking and is realized" (434).

"To an Old Philosopher in Rome," like *The Rock* as a whole, is a poetry of endings, and one of the final poems in the collection, "The Planet on the Table," allows Stevens to contemplate his own ending as a poet. The planet of the title is apparently his *Collected Poems* (perhaps, as Harold Bloom suggests, in manuscript [365]), the appearance of which he had dreaded because "it puts an end to things." He speaks of them as if that were indeed the case; Ariel, his persona, "was glad he had written his poems" (450), as if he were done. What he finds significant about them suggests one of the distinctions of the late poetry. The younger Stevens had set his imagination against reality; the aged Stevens alters that, recognizing that his poems exist simultaneously on two levels. As in "The Rock," he draws a parallel between the creations of the poet and creations of reality, the sun. "Other makings of the sun / Were waste and welter," but not these poems, which he describes as "makings of his self." Yet because he is himself a making of the sun, his poems "Were no less makings of the sun" (450). In subsuming the human imagination under a larger creative reality, the late poems dissolve the distinction between mind and world that had been maintained throughout most of Stevens' career. The planet on the table is both mind and world.

The poem is misleading, however, in implying that the poetry had ended. Milton Bates's revised *Opus Posthumous* contains twenty uncollected poems written in 1954 and 1955 (Stevens died in August 1955). As a group, these poems (added to the Library of America's *Collected Poetry and Prose*) are less accessible than the poems of *The Rock,* more abstract, less personal, although there are exceptions. "As You Leave the Room," "Of Mere Being," and "Reality Is an Activity of the Most August Imagination" would have been at home in *The Rock.* "The Sail of Ulysses" would not; it is as dense as anything Stevens ever wrote. The most ambitious of the very late poems, it was written for Columbia University's bicentennial, and Stevens was so unhappy with it that he said he would "never . . . allow anyone to see a copy of it" (*L* 834). He blamed its failure on the abstract subject – the uses of knowledge – furnished by the university (*L* 835), but its chief difficulty is that Ulysses' long soliloquy on knowledge, which makes up the bulk of the poem, is largely unintelligible. Stevens was able to salvage from it a twenty-four-line poem, "Presence of an External Master of Knowledge," and the title for "A Child Asleep in Its Own Life," both of which hint at the theme so pervasive in *The Rock,* that reality itself is a kind of knowledge or intelligence. "Reality Is an Activity of the Most August Imagination" does more than hint at the theme. It returns to the auroras as symbol of this imagination, observed as the speaker and his companion "drove home from Cornwall to Hartford, late" (471).

"Of Mere Being" is legendarily Stevens' last poem, and it sets itself the paradoxical task of describing a state of being that exists apart from human intelligence and feeling. His image for this state is a Yeats-like golden bird that sings in a palm "without human meaning, / Without human feeling" (476). Readers have found the image (and the poem) fascinating in part because it appears to be beyond explication, itself without human meaning, the coldest and most impersonal of the last poems. The most personal – arguably the most personal poem of the Stevens canon – is "As You Leave the Room," a late revision of an unpublished poem, "First Warmth." As Yeats does in "The Circus Animals' Desertion," Stevens here looks back on his poetic career at the end, referring to four earlier poems, including "Credences of Summer." Yeats, at the end, questions the powers of his imagination as an old man. Stevens, conversely, questions the basis of his *earlier* poetry – his privileging of the imagination, his skepticism concerning reality – on the basis of his late appreciation of reality. He asks if he has "lived a skeleton's life, / As a disbeliever in reality" (598). It is clearly his present sense of reality as something palpable, beyond the mind, that generates the question. In his leave-taking, the older Stevens re-states the pervasive theme of his last poems, the discovery and articulation of what he had called in a late essay "a solid reality which does not wholly dissolve itself into the conceptions of our own minds" (701). In "As You Leave the Room," it is, he says, "as if I left / With something I could touch, touch every way" (598).

NOTES

1. Harold Bloom, *Wallace Stevens: The Poems of Our Climate* (Ithaca: Cornell University Press, 1977), 338.
2. Randall Jarrell, "Reflections on Wallace Stevens," *Partisan Review* 18 (1951): 339, 344.
3. Edmund Wilson, "Santayana at the Convent of the Blue Nuns," *New Yorker* 22 (April 6, 1946): 62.

6

JAMES LONGENBACH

Stevens and his contemporaries

Back in the twentieth century, when such distinctions seemed to matter, readers often paired Wallace Stevens with other poets in order to highlight their differences. Hugh Kenner summed up Stevens' relationship with William Carlos Williams as "one of the most extraordinary misunderstandings in literary history."[1] Marjorie Perloff asked the question "Pound/ Stevens: Whose Era?" Many people delighted in repeating this anecdote about Stevens and Robert Frost: "The trouble with you is you write about things," Stevens said to Frost. "The trouble with you is you write about bric-a-brac," Frost retorted.[2]

Why the need to make Stevens stand apart? Stevens and Williams first met in New York in 1915, became close friends for the next decade and, despite the pressure of diverging careers, remained supportive of each other's work until the end of their lives. Stevens and Frost were not close friends, but both poets attended Harvard in the late years of the nineteenth century, absorbing there the pragmatist philosophy of William James. Marianne Moore, friend of both Williams and Ezra Pound, admired Stevens' poetry from its beginnings; by the time they finally met face to face in 1943, each poet had written crucial accounts of the other's career. Elizabeth Bishop, Randall Jarrell, James Merrill, John Ashbery – major figures from each subsequent generation of American poets – have been shaped by Stevens' seriously playful sensibility.

But what about Pound, who spawned a different poetic progeny, one that leads from Charles Olson to Robert Creeley to Susan Howe? And what about Pound's friend T. S. Eliot, who during his lifetime presided over the divided territory of American poetry absolutely? In part, poets such as Bishop and Merrill found Stevens' influence nurturing precisely because it allowed them to discover a way of escaping Eliot's indomitable presence. Stevens himself had little contact with Eliot, less with Pound, so by the middle of the twentieth century his friendships with Williams and Moore came to seem less important than they truly were.

Polemical distinctions began to arise. Williams could be placed with Pound along the imagist–objectivist line of modern poetry, in which language is meant to achieve the status of an object in itself. Stevens could be placed with W. B. Yeats along the symbolist line, in which language is meant to be suggestive, invoking associations beyond itself. "Le Paradis n'est pas artificiel," wrote Pound in an influential passage in the *Pisan Cantos*, turning on Baudelaire's *Les Paradis artificiels* and then on his good friend and early mentor Yeats.

> Le Paradis n'est pas artificiel
> and Uncle William dawdling around Notre Dame
> in search of whatever
>   paused to admire the symbol
> with Notre Dame standing inside it
> Whereas in St Etienne
>   or why not Dei Miracoli:
> mermaids, that carving. . . .[3]

Rather than the all-too-meaningful symbol of Notre Dame, Pound prefers the pristine beauty of Pietro Lombardo's tiny stone mermaids in the church of Santa Maria dei Miracoli in Venice; he wants the words of poetry to cleave to things, liberated from conventional associations. To readers who either lionized Poundian values or deplored them, Stevens could conveniently be described as doing something else: exploring the limitless exfoliation of a word's connotation. Even when we name the world "flatly," says Stevens at the end of "Notes Toward a Supreme Fiction," there remains "the irrational / Distortion, however fragrant, however dear" (351).

These distinctions hold up in theory better than in practice. Perloff demonstrated the fault line by insisting, in a reading of a poem by Frank O'Hara, that O'Hara's use of the word "Mayflower" does not "call to mind our Founding Fathers or the innocence of an Early America"[4] – which is a bit like asking someone not to think about an elephant. In addition, closer scrutiny of poets placed on either side of the divide inevitably breaks down the ideological barrier. Susan Howe, closely associated with Poundian traditions, reveres Stevens above all other twentieth-century poets. Louis Zukofsky, who first coined the word "objectivist," admitted late in his life that he felt closer to Stevens than to "any of my contemporaries in the last half century of life we shared together."[5]

What is more, Stevens himself attempted to complicate the division between objectivist and symbolist poetics, pointing out in "Nuances of a Theme by Williams" (1918) that the effort to stave off a word's aura of associations is in practice doomed to glorious failure. In a little imagist poem called "El Hombre" (1916), Williams had praised the morning star, Venus, for standing alone, for being nothing but itself; like Pound, he wanted to foster the impression that his words work in the same way, denoting only their objects and rejecting any extraneous associations.

> It's a strange courage
> you give me ancient star:
> Shine alone in the sunrise
> toward which you lend no part![6]

In "Nuances of a Theme by Williams," Stevens quotes "El Hombre" and adds to variations – variations that, as the title advertises, are implicit in the language of Williams' poem.

I

> Shine alone, shine nakedly, shine like bronze,
> that reflects neither my face nor any inner part
> of my being, shine like fire, that mirrors nothing.

II

> Lend no part to any humanity that suffuses
> you in its own light.
> Be not chimera of morning,
> Half-man, half-star.
> Be not an intelligence,
> Like a widow's bird
> Or an old horse.   (15)

Stevens' fancifulness may seem at odds with Williams' earnest plainness, but in fact Stevens is playing out the implications of Williams' poem, not turning against it. "Shine alone in the sunrise," says Williams to Venus, making the planet stand paradoxically for something other than itself: as it stands alone, it also becomes a figure for the poem's aesthetic. "Shine alone," repeats Stevens. "Shine nakedly," he continues, emphasizing the planet's singularity but also extending its figurative power: the morning star is not only like a poem but also like a human body. "Shine like bronze, / that reflects neither my face nor any inner part / of my being," he adds, continuing to describe the morning star's place in a chain of metaphorical associations. By the time we reach the final lines ("Be not an intelligence, / Like a widow's bird / Or an old horse"), the poem has pushed this paradox to the point of hilarity. We have forgotten utterly the object that the poem wanted to impress on our memories – we might as well be thinking of our Founding Fathers. But the playfulness of the poem feels serious: it suggests that we inevitably delight in the exfoliating connotations of words, however strenuous the urge to suppress them.

Stevens does honor that urge, however, and throughout his career we can see him alternating between an effort to name objects flatly and an effort to highlight the play of language. In the late poem "The Plain Sense of Things," he emphasizes that plainness is for him an achievement, the result of a never-ending struggle: "the absence of the imagination had / Itself to be imagined," he says, going on to offer a little parable.

> The great pond,
> The plain sense of it, without reflections, leaves,
> Mud, water like dirty glass, expressing silence
>
> Of a sort, silence of a rat come out to see,
> The great pond and its waste of the lilies, all this
> Had to be imagined as an inevitable knowledge,
> Required, as a necessity requires.   (428)

These final lines of the poem equate the recovery of the "plain sense of things" with the assumption of a rat's low perspective on the world. The rat sees muddy water for what it is; viewed from a higher point of view, the surface of the water would be clouded by reflections. Yet Stevens' construction of this earthbound point of view is itself a highly imaginative act: the poem both describes and enacts the paradoxical notion that the absence of the imagination must be imagined. It is impossible to be plain, Stevens suggests over and over again, without being fancy, and even if his poems tilt at times to either of these extremes, the poems always contain the specter of the opposite quality. Sometimes the poems emphasize the mind's ability to fabricate elaborate metaphors, reminding us that our values are not given naturally in the world but are imposed on the world by human consciousness. At other times the poems caution us to remember that those metaphors inevitably collapse in the face of events of which human consciousness can make no sense.

It would be too schematic to suggest that Stevens' oeuvre encompasses both objectivist and symbolist tendencies, reaching out to poetic positions we associate with Pound on the one hand and Yeats on the other. Instead, the full scope of his work reminds us that any poet is larger, more various, more complicated than the literary-historical terms we employ. This is true of both Pound and Stevens, just as it is true of Browning and Tennyson or Byron and Keats. Today, nearly a decade into the twenty-first century, we can see that, whatever their differences, whatever their declared affiliations or antipathies, Stevens, Pound, Eliot, Moore, H. D., and Williams were responding to the same cultural and aesthetic imperatives. We can hear that, however distinctive their poems, these poets were engaged in a shared effort to transform the sound of English-language poetry.

On the many occasions when Moore wrote about Stevens' poetry, she emphasized what he shared with his contemporaries. Reviewing *Parts of a World* (1942), she remarked, "Ezra Pound might, conceivably, address the 'Academy of Fine Ideas' as 'My beards'; and life on the battleship *Masculine* – 'the captain drafted rules of the world, Regulae mundi, as apprentice of Descartes' – puts the stamp of its approval on certain Pound cantos."[7] Reviewing *Owl's Clover* (1936), she noted a resemblance between Stevens and Eliot: "Better say each has influenced the other, with 'Sunday Morning' and the Prufrock-like lines in 'Le Monocle de Mon Oncle' in mind, . . . and the Peter Quince-like rhythmic contour of T. S. Eliot's 'La Figlia che Piange.'"[8] What interests Moore here is what interests primarily any poet: how the poetry sounds. She knows that Stevens has been listening to Pound and Eliot, just as she has been listening to Stevens.

In the early years of the twentieth century, when the practice of free verse was being established in English, these poets learned how to sound like themselves by listening to one another. Pound's characteristic free verse line, which is virtually always end-stopped –

> The silver mirrors catch the bright stones and flare,
> Dawn, to our waking, drifts in the green cool light;
> Dew-daze blurs, in the grass, pale ankles moving[9]

does not sound like Williams' line, which is often heavily enjambed:

> The sunlight in a
> yellow plaque upon the
> varnished floor
>
> is full of a song
> inflated to
> fifty pounds pressure. . . .[10]

Williams' enjambed line, which cuts against the turns of syntax, does not sound like H. D.'s more gently broken line, which parses the syntax, following its natural turns:

> The night has cut
> each from each
> and curled the petals
> back from the stalk
> and under it in crisp rows. . . .[11]

Stevens sometimes employs H. D.'s kind of line, as his "Nuances of a Theme by Williams" demonstrates. In his most powerful free verse poems, however, he employs all three of these kinds of lines in order to control the temporal unfolding of the poem. The opening lines of "The Snow Man" parse the poem's single sentence in the manner of H. D., confirming rather than interrupting its drive toward predication:

> One must have a mind of winter
> To regard the frost and the boughs
> Of the pine-trees crusted with snow. . . .   (8)

But in the second half of the poem, the lines become increasingly more radically enjambed, increasing the tension between syntax and line; we are no longer receiving placid observations, reinforced by the lineation, but are swept forward by the action of thought, which is interrupted by the lineation:

> Which is the sound of the land
> Full of the same wind
> That is blowing in the same bare place
>
> For the listener, who listens in the snow,
> And, nothing himself, beholds
> Nothing that is not there and the nothing that is.   (8)

By cutting against that syntax, these lines highlight the half-rhymes ("land" with "wind," "snow" with "behold"), forcing us to stress syllables that would otherwise remain unstressed. We feel the syntax rushing forward because we also feel the enjambments are holding it back. And when we reach the charismatic final line, the line sounds like the culmination of the poem because it is more syntactically complete, more rhetorically balanced, than the lines preceding it. We may not understand the line right away, but we trust it because of how it sounds: the poem has lured us into a soundscape of understanding.

By the time Stevens wrote "The Snow Man," the general practice of free verse had already entered its decadence; around 1917, Pound and Eliot had begun to write rhymed tetrameter quatrains in order to stem the tide of watered-down imagist poetry. Stevens himself had never abandoned metered verse; he continued to write masterful blank verse at the same time that he observed the imagist movement from a distance, absorbing and responding to its experiments with the free verse line. Unlike Williams, Stevens was not involved with the imagist movement even tangentially, but like every poet of his generation he nonetheless found himself confronted with a question Pound first posed publicly in 1915: "I am often asked whether there can be a long imagiste or vorticist poem."[12] The ambitious poetic achievements of the early 1920s – Stevens' *Harmonium* and Moore's *Observations* as much as Pound's "Hugh Selwyn Mauberley" or Eliot's "The Waste Land" – provide the answers to this question.

Consider for a moment Pound's early development. At the height of the imagist movement, around 1913, Pound was writing immensely influential poems that rarely strayed beyond a half-dozen lines; the most famous of them, "In a Station of the Metro," consists of just two lines, one of statement ("The apparition of these faces in the crowd"), one of pure image ("Petals on a wet, black bough"),[13] both of them distinguished by immense rhythmic delicacy. But, while Pound had become a lyric poet of extraordinary nuance, the world presented him with an unavoidable epic subject: the Great War, which broke out in 1914. Like every poet of his generation, Pound was deeply affected by the war, but he was also appalled by the epic challenge – and especially by other poets who rose to the challenge thoughtlessly. "O two-penny poets, be still! – / For you have nine years out of every ten / To go gunning for glory – with pop-guns," he wrote in "War Verse" (1914).[14] Pound was talking to himself, and he was asking another version of his question about the long poem: How does a maker of pristine lyric poems take on the most pressing issues and events of his time?

This question shaped Stevens' career as dramatically as it shaped Pound's. After "Carnet de Voyage" (a series of poems mostly written long before it was published in 1914), Stevens' first major publication was a sequence of war poems – "Phases," published in the 1914 war poem issue of *Poetry* magazine. Pound had objected strenuously to the notion of this issue; the idea of writing war poems to order seemed to him both aesthetically and politically corrupt. At the same time, he wanted to address the war in his own poems, but epic ambition seemed irreconcilable with lyric concision. In "Phases," Stevens responded to this dilemma by writing war poetry against war poetry, a lyric cry against the epic imperative.

> The crisp, sonorous epics
> Mongered after every scene.
> Sluggards must be quickened! Screen,
>
> No more, the shape of false Confusion.
> Bare his breast and draw the flood
> Of all his Babylonian blood.   (527)

Stevens never reprinted these lines, but several poems lifted from a later sequence of war poems called "Lettres d'un Soldat" (1917) were eventually reprinted in the second edition of *Harmonium*, where they do not seem out of place. Most pointedly, "Lunar Paraphrase" shows that many of the hallmarks of *Harmonium* became important to Stevens because of the war poet's predicament: the latent but ever-present threat of death; the inability of Christian belief to account for it; the reduction of the gods to beings "humanly near"; the need for human imagination to transform the "wearier end" (89) of bare reality.

All of the great postwar works of modern American poetry – "Hugh Selwyn Mauberley," "The Waste Land," *Spring and All*, *Harmonium*, *Observations* – were the product not so much of the war as such but of the war poet's predicament: a generation of lyric poets had been pushed despite themselves to make an epic statement. Those statements took different shapes. Despite his early antipathy for epic grandeur, Pound eventually succumbed to it; both "Mauberley" and the early cantos contain the kind of rhetoric Pound cautioned against in "War Verse." This is why Pound's long poem, like Eliot's, could seem to readers more obviously worldly, more engaged with historical necessity, than Stevens' *Harmonium* or Moore's *Observations*. This is also why Pound and Eliot could seem to other readers to have confused epic ambition with narcissism: "If it is the supreme cry of despair," said Stevens of "The Waste Land" when he read it in 1922, "it is Eliot's and not his generation's" (940).

Eventually, Eliot himself came to read "The Waste Land" much as Stevens did, urging readers to see the poem as a personal grouse against life rather than a considered statement about the fate of European culture. But Stevens' own position was closest to Moore's: she remained committed to a lyric poetry that addressed the epic challenge without succumbing to its potential for self-aggrandizement. In 1918, after the United States had entered the war, Moore published a poem called "Reinforcements" that began with these stanzas:

> The vestibule to experience is not to
>   Be exalted into epic grandeur. These men are going
> to their work with this idea, advancing like a school of fish through
>
> still water – waiting to change the course or dismiss
>   the idea of movement, till forced to. The words of the Greeks
> ring in our ears, but they are vain in comparison with a sight like this.[15]

Like Stevens, who insisted in "Phases" that the war "was not / Like Agamemnon's story" (526), Moore wants to remind us of the ways in which the language of poetry might itself become a "reinforcement" of war. The words of the Greeks ring in our ears; the sight of mobilized soldiers arouses the need for epic scope, for weighty poetic statement. But rather than succumbing to that urge, Moore wrote self-consciously little poems about big ideas, poems that interrogate a masculine arrogance by inviting us to mistake smallness for irrelevance. "The vulgarity of poetry is an insisting upon the subsidiary as major,"[16] said Moore in her review of Stevens' *The Auroras of Autumn*.

Stevens refused the prestige of major statement most craftily in "The Comedian as the Letter C," the longest poem of *Harmonium*. Though comparable in ambition to other great long poems of the early 1920s, "The Comedian" has none of the obvious grandeur of "The Waste Land"; nor does it bolster itself with the strategic rejection of grandeur that distinguishes Williams' *Spring and All*. "The Comedian" is a major poem about becoming minor, a big statement about the virtues of thinking small, a mock epic about the wisdom of giving up poetic statement altogether. Its protagonist, Crispin, begins his poetic career as a "lutanist of fleas," a connoisseur of insignificance, and he is consequently "washed away by magnitude" (22) when he undertakes a momentous voyage across the sea. In Yucatan, his first port of call, his ambition is aroused by the exotic landscape, but he finds that he lacks the epic poet's calling: he

> That wrote his couplet yearly to the spring,
> As dissertation of profound delight,
> Stopping, on voyage, in a land of snakes,
> Found his vicissitudes had much enlarged
> His apprehension, made him intricate
> In moody rucks, and difficult and strange
> In all desires, his destitution's mark.
> Qua interlude: Crispin, if he could,
> Would chant assuaging Virgil and recite
> In the oratory of his breast, the rhymes
> That drop down Ariosto's benison.   (25; 987)

The last four lines of this passage were deleted from the final version of "The Comedian as the Letter C," perhaps because they named Stevens' personal dilemma too precisely: Crispin refuses the epic challenge, admitting that he could not muster the grand music of Virgil and Ariosto even if he wanted to. "The Comedian" was the closest Stevens came to writing a poem with epic pretensions, but, as in "Phases," the poem's mock-epic irony is at war with his desire to make a major statement, and "The Comedian" tells a story of epic ambition renounced. By the end of his travels, Crispin gives up poetry altogether for a quiet domestic life – a salad bed, four daughters with curls.

"The Comedian as the Letter C" leaves us with this question: Has the poem described a failure of will or a rejection of poetic ambition that actually serves the true cause of poetry? If he wanted to, Crispin could "scrawl a tragedian's testament," attributing his fate to cultural rather than personal forces; he could "make / Of his own fate an instance of all fate" (33). Stevens was speaking presciently here, for just a few months after "The Comedian" was finished, he would sense that Eliot had done exactly that in "The Waste Land," transforming an intimate despair into a generation's.

Like Moore, Stevens preferred what she called a "feigned inconsequence / of manner" to "the fiercest frontal attack."[17] He understood that poetry is never served by an exaggeration of its power. So, rather than courting the signs of postwar cultural relevance, Stevens was willing to allow his own poems to appear inconsequential.

For many years, that appearance was accepted at face value. During the first half of the twentieth century, the most powerful stories told about modern poetry placed "The Waste Land" and "Hugh Selwyn Mauberley" at the center of the achievement: since poetic importance was bound up with the declaration of cultural relevance, Stevens and Moore seemed subsidiary – poets who were more purely decorative. In the second half of the century, when this sternly apocalyptic notion of modernism began to fall away, Stevens' stock rose sharply while Pound's and Eliot's fell; a poetry of linguistic play became more fashionable. Neither of these narratives will suffice, however, since neither of them allows us to see how Stevens' playfulness is bound up with his relevance, not opposed to it. Neither narrative allows us to see the full extent of the cultural predicament Stevens shared with Eliot as much as Moore, however differently each poet responded to it.

NOTES

1. Hugh Kenner, *A Homemade World: The American Modernist Writers* (New York: Knopf, 1975), 55.
2. Quoted in Peter Brazeau, *Parts of a World: Wallace Stevens Remembered; An Oral Biography* (New York: Random House, 1983), 160.
3. Ezra Pound, *The Cantos of Ezra Pound* (New York: New Directions, 1972), 528–29.
4. Marjorie Perloff, *Frank O'Hara: Poet among Painters* (Austin: University of Texas Press, 1979), 124.
5. Louis Zukofsky, *Prepositions: The Collected Critical Essays of Louis Zukofsky* (Berkeley: University of California Press, 1981), 27.
6. William Carlos Williams, *The Collected Poems of William Carlos Williams*, vol. I, *1909–1939*, ed. A. Walton Litz and Christopher MacGowan (New York: New Directions, 1986), 76.
7. Marianne Moore, *The Complete Prose of Marianne Moore*, ed. Patricia C. Willis (New York: Viking, 1986), 382.
8. *Ibid.*, 348.
9. Pound, *Cantos*, 13.
10. Williams, *Collected Poems*, 196.
11. H. D., *Collected Poems: 1912–1944*, ed. Louis L. Martz (New York: New Directions, 1983), 33.
12. Ezra Pound, *Gaudier-Brzeska: A Memoir* (New York: New Directions, 1970), 94.
13. Ezra Pound, *Personae: The Shorter Poems of Ezra Pound*, ed. Lea Baechler and A. Walton Litz (New York: New Directions, 1990), 111.

14. *Ibid.*, 253.
15. Marianne Moore, *The Poems of Marianne Moore*, ed. Grace Schulman (New York: Viking, 2003), 126.
16. Moore, *Complete Prose*, 430.
17. Moore, *Poems*, 108.

7

JOSEPH CARROLL

Stevens and romanticism

For Wallace Stevens, the romantic period extends from the late eighteenth century through the late nineteenth century, and it includes both English and American writers. The chief romantic influences on Stevens' poetry include Wordsworth, Shelley, Keats, Emerson, Whitman, and Tennyson. (There are lesser echoes of Blake and Coleridge; Byron seems to have had little impact.) Stevens was born in 1879, and both Whitman and Tennyson died in 1892. For Stevens, then, romanticism was not a remote historical episode. It overlapped with his own life, and it formed the immediate historical background to his life's work as a poet. Moreover, in Stevens' conception, romanticism is not just a single historical period. It is a recurrent mode of the poetic imagination, and for Stevens that mode constitutes the wellspring of all poetic vitality.

In a letter of 1940 – when he was sixty years old and writing the poems included in *Parts of a World* – Stevens succinctly sketched out a comprehensive theory of poetic history as a cycle. The cycle begins in romanticism, as a phase of imaginative vitality, moves in a degenerative direction leading to exhaustion, and then returns to romanticism. "I suppose that the way of all mind is from romanticism to realism, to fatalism and then to indifferentism, unless the cycle re-commences and the thing goes from indifferentism back to romanticism all over again" (L 350). The middle terms in this sequence take their inflection from the direction of the sequence. For Stevens, romanticism is the highest form of imaginative fulfillment. "Realism" might seem a neutral or even positive term, but "fatalism" has a sinister ring, and "indifferentism" is unmistakably negative in connotation. Indifferentism is a blank absence of interest and pleasure in the world. "Realism" and "fatalism" thus measure out stages in the descent from fulfillment to despair.

Stevens' theory of the romantic cycle generalizes from the immediate historical context of his own poetic career. As a comprehensive account of all poetic history, this theory no doubt merits a good deal of skepticism, but it nonetheless provides a central clue to Stevens' views on the nature of poetry and on his own mission as a poet. In this middle phase of his career, at the time he wrote this letter, he felt that his culture was coming to the end of the historical cycle, and he believed that his own mission was to create a new romanticism and thus to give new life to the imagination. "At the moment, the world in general is passing from the fatalism stage to an indifferent stage: a stage in which the primary sense is a sense of helplessness. But, as the world is a good deal more vigorous than most of the individuals in it, what the world looks forward to is a new romanticism, a new belief" (*L* 350). Stevens' use of the word "belief" as an appositive to the word "romanticism" suggests the broadest signification that he gives to the word "romanticism." The new "belief" is for Stevens a spiritual vision of the world.

Despite all the modernistic aspects of his poetic style, in his predominating concern to find a substitute for traditional religious belief, Stevens is among the last of the great Victorians. In the lives of many of the Victorians, the single most important imaginative event was the loss of religious faith. Many of the Victorians grew up in devout adherence to traditional forms of Christian worship, but as they entered intellectual maturity they found that they could no longer accept the literal truth of Christian doctrines – the divinity of Christ, the resurrection, salvation through belief in Christ, and the immortality of the soul. The loss of religious faith was profoundly disturbing and disorienting both for the Victorians and for Stevens. In his essay "Two or Three Ideas" (1951), Stevens evokes the subjective sensations produced by this loss. "To see the gods dispelled in mid-air and dissolve like clouds is one of the great human experiences. . . . It was their annihilation, not ours, and yet it left us feeling that in a measure we, too, had been annihilated. It left us feeling dispossessed and alone in a solitude, like children without parents, in a home that seemed deserted" (842). Stevens' phrasing in this late essay echoes that in his greatest early poem, "Sunday Morning." The occasion of "Sunday Morning" is a dialogue in which Stevens and a female companion are discussing the loss of Christian faith – a loss that leaves us in an "island solitude" (56). As Stevens puts it, simply and plainly, in another letter of 1940, "My trouble, and the trouble of a great many people, is the loss of belief in the sort of God in Whom we were all brought up to believe" (*L* 348).

Neither Stevens nor the great Victorians could rest content with a simple loss of faith. They sought substitutes that would give a sense of spiritual purpose to their lives. The Victorians identified two chief substitutes, one social and one literary. The social substitute was a belief in the progressive development of human society toward an ideal of harmonious individual

development and cooperative interaction. The idea of progressive development toward the realization of that goal provided a sense of purposeful
direction in human history and a framework for ethically meaningful action
in individual lives. (This ideal is still not dead, of course, but the great
historical cataclysms of the twentieth century, beginning with World War I,
subdued the facile confidence with which many of the Victorians had
embraced it.) The literary substitute for traditional religious faith was an
ideal of poetry that would satisfy all spiritual craving. The Victorians
identified this poetic ideal with the great visionary poems of the romantics
and especially with the poetry of Wordsworth.

The great romantic themes are consciousness, spirit, nature, individual
identity, personal growth, the imagination, and poetry itself. One current
Marxist school of thinking claims that the real and true themes of literature
can only be socioeconomic and political, and it thus identifies the typical
romantic themes as mere evasions of these real and true themes. Proponents
of this school present themselves as members of a "post-Romantic culture."[1] The romantics themselves would not of course agree that they were
evading the subject, nor would Stevens. The romantics sometimes speak of
social and political concerns, but they would argue that their other themes
are also real and true concerns and that these other concerns cannot legit-
imately be reduced to socioeconomic and political themes. The current
climate of theoretical opinion is generally favorable to Marxist theory, but
individual readers must still decide for themselves whether socioeconomic
and political themes exhaust the spectrum of real and true human concerns.
My own view is that they do not.

In some of his poems written during the Great Depression and World War
II, Stevens ruminates about the social role of the poet, but his genius was not
essentially social and ethical in character, and the poetry animated by these
concerns tends to be both ponderous and obscure. Stevens' genius was lyric,
mythic, and metaphysical. In exploring the spiritual role of poetry, he brings
the strongest forces of his imagination to bear, and it is in the poetry written
under this inspiration that he most completely succeeds in fulfilling his own
deepest purposes as a poet. Stevens believes "The major poetic idea in the
world is and always has been the idea of God" (*L* 378). When he speaks of
creating "a new romanticism, a new belief," he means creating "a poem
equivalent to the idea of God" (*L* 369–70). Creating that poem becomes his
own central mission as a poet, and in creating it he draws heavily and
directly on the great visionary poems of his romantic predecessors.

There is one crucial difference between the old romanticism and Stevens'
"new romanticism." In Stevens' view, the single most important change in
the epistemology of the modern world is the recognition that all "belief" is

"fictive"; that is, all beliefs are imaginative conceptions, products of the imagination. For the old romantics, the divine mind simply exists. The poet depicts it and by depicting it shares more fully in it. Thus Emerson affirms that "the heart which abandons itself to the Supreme Mind finds itself related to all its works";[2] and he declares that nature "always speaks of Spirit. It suggests the absolute. It is a perpetual effect. It is a great shadow pointing always to the sun behind us."[3] Wordsworth also describes a universal spiritual presence, and he evokes the awe, wonder, and meditative exaltation this presence creates in him:

> And I have felt
> A presence that disturbs me with the joy
> Of elevated thoughts; a sense sublime
> Of something far more deeply interfused,
> Whose dwelling is the light of setting suns,
> And the round ocean, and the living air,
> And the blue sky, and in the mind of man,
> A motion and a spirit, that impels
> All thinking things, all objects of all thought,
> And rolls through all things.[4]

In similar guise, Shelley invokes "The everlasting universe of things" that "Flows through the mind"; and he describes the sun god Apollo as "the eye with which the Universe / Beholds itself and knows it is divine."[5] These sources and others like them enter directly into Stevens' creation of a new romanticism. The one main thing that makes Stevens' romanticism "new" – the one thing that distinguishes it from the work of writers such as Emerson, Wordsworth, and Shelley – is the idea that the divine mind does not fully exist, or at least is not fully realized, until it is depicted in the images of poets.

In an early poem, "A High-Toned Old Christian Woman," Stevens declares that "Poetry is the supreme fiction" (47), and he contrasts poetry with traditional Christian religious belief. What he means in this context is that poetry is the supreme medium of imaginative activity. In Stevens' later thinking, the idea of poetry as the supreme medium becomes intermingled with the idea of God as the supreme image created by poetry. As he explains in a letter, "The idea of God is a thing of the imagination. We no longer think that God was, but was imagined. The idea of pure poetry, essential imagination, as the highest objective of the poet, appears to be, at least potentially, as great as the idea of God" (L 369). In Stevens' work, this "highest objective of the poet" has a number of synonyms: "essential imagination" – "essential unity" (195), "The essential poem at the center of things" (377); "pure poetry" – "the pure idea" (231), "pure principle" (361), "the first idea" (330), the "central heart and mind of minds" (229), "the whiteness that is the ultimate intellect" (372), the "imagination that sits enthroned" (360), and the "supreme fiction" (47, 329), among others.

For Stevens, "the idea of God is merely a poetic idea, even if the supreme poetic idea" (674). By declaring that the idea of God is "imagined" or that it is "merely a poetic idea," Stevens does not mean that this idea is simply false or illusory. In Stevens' poetic cosmology, the mind of God and the human mind are interdependent, and the supreme fiction consists in a circular process through which both minds achieve fulfillment. "The mind that in heaven created the earth and the mind that on earth created heaven were, as it happened, one" (913). The divine mind has a need for self-recognition, and that need makes itself felt, in the mind of the poet, as a need to create an image of the divine mind. God creates the poet, and the poet in turn creates an image of God. By creating images of the divine mind, poets are thus "fulfilling not only themselves" but also "the aims of their creator" (864). In Stevens' visionary poetry, the "creator" is not a person but only a generative source. As "The essential poem at the center of things," the creator produces all phenomenal appearances – of sea, land, and sky – but this essential poem is itself "something seen and known in lesser poems" (377–78). By "lesser poems" Stevens means all actual poems. Actual poems are "lesser" only in comparison with "The central poem" that "is the poem of the whole, / The poem of the composition of the whole" (379), that is, in comparison with the divine generative source. "A Primitive Like an Orb," from which these quotations are drawn, is one of Stevens' greatest poems; but it is itself nonetheless one of those "lesser poems"; it is a medium through which "essential imagination" comes to know itself.

More than most poets, Stevens conceived of all his poems as parts of a single, great poem. He came very close to titling his first volume not *Harmonium* but rather *The Grand Poem: Preliminary Minutiae* (L 237). As Stevens' poetry develops, it becomes ever more internally allusive. He frequently alludes to previous poems and develops and synthesizes the themes, images, and tonal inflections from those poems. The images thus become "motifs." Some of these motifs are "archetypal" or universal; some of them are directly inspired by figurations in the work of his chief romantic predecessors; and some are both universal and romantic. The chief motifs include the following: comedian, angels, the seasons, stars, sun, moon, day, night, sea, mountain, sky, earth, fire, wind, trees, mother, father, giant, shadow, house, diamonds, crown, scholar, candle, alphabet, book, mirror, waving farewell, breath, eye, whiteness, the color green, transparence, circle, orb, and center. To appreciate fully the meaning of such images in any given poem, it is often necessary to understand the way in which Stevens is responding to the work of his romantic predecessors, reflecting on his own previous moments of poetic experience, or both. Many of the later poems are so densely self-referential that they could hardly be understood except in the larger context of their allusive references to his earlier poems. It is thus important to read Stevens whole, taking in all the poems, and to follow the course of his writing chronologically, as a continuously evolving poetic meditation.

When Stevens says that "the way of all mind" is from romanticism through realism and fatalism to indifferentism, he is referring not only to whole historical periods but also to the range of imaginative experience available to individuals within any given historical phase, and he is himself included within this range. In describing the cycle, he is generalizing from the experience of one of his own poetic personae, Crispin, the protagonist of "The Comedian as the Letter C" (1922). Crispin is an "introspective voyager" (23). He sets out from the old world, in Bordeaux, rejecting romanticism as a mode grown stale and literary, and travels to the New World – to Yucatan and finally to Carolina. The purpose of his voyaging is to seek out raw, elemental experience and by assimilating that experience to revitalize his own poetic imagination. In the American homeland, he adopts the creed of the "realist" and projects a poetry that will be purely a poetry of local place. He intends to found a poetic colony but instead settles down, becomes a family man, and watches helplessly as his poetic aspirations dissipate within the absorbing hubbub of the mundane. "The Comedian as the Letter C" was written early in Stevens' poetic career, more than thirty years before the end of that career, but it comes close to being his own poetic epitaph. It is among the last poems Stevens wrote before entering into a lapse of poetic activity that lasted from about 1924 to about 1930.

The effort to create a new romanticism, as a distinct, conscious purpose, begins to take shape in Stevens' second volume of poetry, *Ideas of Order* (1936), and from that point on attaining this objective fundamentally shapes the course of Stevens' poetic development. In many of the poems of *Parts of a World* (1942) and *Transport to Summer* (1947), Stevens is making "notes toward a supreme fiction," and his development as a poet thus assumes the character of a quest. The protagonist of that quest is variously depicted as a "figure of capable imagination" (226), as "major man" (336), and as the "father" (358), among other personae. Most often, the protagonist is identified simply by the third-person masculine personal pronoun – "he." Stevens' quest culminates in a series of major visionary poems in 1947 and 1948, and especially in three great longer poems, "The Owl in the Sarcophagus," "The Auroras of Autumn," and "A Primitive Like an Orb." In the poems that follow this visionary culmination, Stevens looks back wistfully on this achievement, evaluates its significance and its limitations, and tries to adjust to the sad feeling of belatedness, the painful decline of his powers, and the frightening prospect of death.

From the period of *Ideas of Order*, Stevens' poetic career has the unity of a dramatic progression, with a goal, conflicts, a rising action, a climax, and a denouement. Most of the conflicts in this drama arise not from Stevens' interaction with other people but from his arguments with himself. Stevens' poetry is introverted – that is, solitary and meditative. It contains mythic human figures such as those of the "father" and "mother," but these figures are usually symbolic elements within Stevens' own poetic universe, and often they are aspects of his own psyche. For instance, the centrally important mythic female image – "Sister and mother and diviner love" (70) – figures frequently as an embodiment of the poetic imagination and, in her larger significations, she represents life, experience, and consciousness itself. She is an agent or personification of sentient change, and she is thus a medium both for the exhilaration of "discovery" (374) and an elegiac sense of loss and grief. As an affective influence, in both her erotic and maternal aspects, she provides an element of human warmth and tenderness to Stevens' figurations of "essential imagination."

In its largest movements, both within and between poems, Stevens' poetry progresses dialectically through thematic and tonal oppositions. The largest opposition is that between a poetry of mystical vision and a poetry that celebrates the enjoyments of common life. In an address of 1955, Stevens declares that poetry can move in either of two directions. "In one direction it moves toward the ultimate things of pure poetry; in the other it speaks to great numbers of people of themselves, making extraordinary texts and memorable music out of what they feel and know" (834). Pure poetry is the mode through which Stevens seeks to create a new romanticism, and it is this mode that dominates his poetic ambitions and gives direction to his development as a poet. The poetry of common life forms the chief dialectical tension for the poetry of mystical vision. In the letter in which he describes the cycle from romanticism to indifferentism, Stevens also describes one phase of his own career in terms of pure and common poetry. "About the time when I, personally, began to feel round for a new romanticism, I might naturally have been expected to start on a new cycle. Instead of doing so, I began to feel that I was on the edge: that I wanted to get to the center: that I was isolated, and that I wanted to share the common life" (*L* 352). Throughout his poetic life, Stevens continues to alternate between the modes of pure and common poetry. From the perspective of common poetry, he is disposed to think of "the romantic" in a disparaging way. In one of his adages, for instance, he remarks, "The ideal is the actual become anaemic. The romantic is often pretty much the same thing" (904). From the opposite side of his modal dialectic, Stevens affirms, "The whole effort of the imagination is toward the production of the romantic" (849), and even more simply, "The imagination is the romantic" (903).

Pure poetry or the poetry of mystical vision is most often associated with night, sleep, and solitary meditation. The poetry of common life is associated with day, summer, and festivals. As Stevens' poetry develops, both modes assimilate images and tonal inflections from the other, but each also achieves culminating moments of realization as a distinct mode. Some signal instances from the poetry of common life include "On the Road Home," "The Latest Freed Man," and, above all, "Credences of Summer." Poems that contribute most directly to the development of pure poetry include "Montrachet-le-Jardin," "Chocorua to Its Neighbor," and "Description Without Place." Some of the major long poems – including both "Esthétique du Mal" and "Notes Toward a Supreme Fiction" – are not so much whole poems as, rather, collections of shorter poems, and these shorter poems include instances of both pure and common poetry. In a number of single poems, Stevens sets the modes of pure and common poetry into direct dialectical tension with one another. "Crude Foyer" provides a striking instance. There are two personae in the poem: one a protagonist of pure poetry, and one of common poetry. The protagonist of pure poetry sits within "paradise"; that is, within "A foyer of the spirit in a landscape / Of the mind" (270). The protagonist of common poetry is a "comedian" (like Crispin); he stands outside this foyer and writes a "critique of paradise." The protagonist of pure poetry reads this critique and rejects it, but the poem ends ambiguously, with no clear resolution.

Common and pure poetry reflect phases of a temperament that ranges from robust celebrations of common life, on the one side, to sublime figurations of spiritual vision on the other. These modal differences are partly differences of mood, but each type of poetry is grounded in a complex of distinct and conflicting metaphysical ideas. The poetry of common life is dualistic and pluralistic. It is dualistic in the sense that it presupposes a metaphysical dichotomy between "reality" and "the imagination." Reality is the physical world, and the imagination is the mind of the individual person. This metaphysical scheme is "pluralistic" in the sense that reality or the external world consists of "parts" or "particles" that are never united in a single, ultimate reality. The culminating moments of fulfillment within common poetry consist in vivid sensual apprehensions of the particulars of reality within a physical world. Pure poetry, in contrast, is transcendental and monistic. Within this mode, both the physical world and the individual human mind are contained within a "pure principle" of sentient relation. The pure principle is itself the ultimate reality, and it is essentially mental or spiritual in character. It is a "mind of minds" that contains both the individual human mind and external reality.

When Stevens was a student at Harvard, his mother gave him a complete set of the works of Emerson, and this gift was perhaps the most important he ever received. Emerson exercises a deeper conceptual influence on Stevens' poetic cosmology than any other writer, and Emerson provides the most incisive formulations of the ideas that govern this cosmology. In "The Transcendentalist," Emerson outlines the metaphysical and epistemological dichotomy that shapes the modes of pure and common poetry. "What is popularly called Transcendentalism among us, is Idealism; Idealism as it appears in 1842. As thinkers, mankind have ever divided into two sects, Materialists and Idealists; the first class founding on experience, the second on consciousness; the first class beginning to think from the data of the senses, the second class perceive that the senses are not final."[6] These alternative positions are those that Crispin envisions in "The Comedian as the Letter C." Before setting out on his poetic voyage, Crispin accepts the idealist credo: "man is the intelligence of his soil" (22). Once he has encountered raw reality, he reverses this formula and affirms the credo of the materialist: "his soil is man's intelligence" (29). Throughout the poems of *Ideas of Order, Parts of a World*, and *Transport to Summer*, Stevens works variations on this basic theme, sometimes adopting one perspective and sometimes the other. The dominant perspective, for both Emerson and Stevens, is ultimately that of the idealist or transcendentalist. As Emerson explains, "These two modes of thinking are both natural, but the Idealist contends that his way of thinking is in higher nature."[7] The transcendental perspective is "higher" for two reasons. It resolves oppositions within an ultimate unity, and it identifies that unity as a "mind" or "spirit." In Emerson's formulation, the "central Unity" of nature "betrays its source in Universal Spirit."[8]

To give a more particular sense of the way in which Stevens assimilates the themes and images of his romantic heritage, it should be helpful to look at some specific instances. One of Stevens' greatest visionary poems, "The Owl in the Sarcophagus" (1947), will serve for this purpose. This poem was written in the state of mind that followed the death of Stevens' closest friend, Henry Church. The poem is both elegiac and celebratory. It expresses grief at the passing of the dead, and it envisions life and death as part of a universal process reaching resolution in the "central Unity" invoked by Emerson. There are three mythic figures in the poem – High Sleep, High Peace (also identified as "peace after death" [373]), and a more complex and elusive feminine figure identified as "The earthly mother and the mother of / The dead" (371). The poem consists of six main sections,

each of several tercets (three-line stanzas). The first section introduces the
three figures. The second section describes the poetic protagonist who
"walked living among the forms of thought / To see their lustre truly as it
is" (372). The "forms of thought" are the three mythic figures, and the next
three sections each give an elaborated description of one of the three
figures – first Sleep, then Death, then the earthly mother and the mother
of the dead. The final section is a coda in which Stevens identifies the nature
of the poem – "This is the mythology of modern death" (374) – and creates
a mood of meditative serenity and fulfilled poetic need.

Sleep and Death are quasi-allegorical figures rendered in mythic form for
the occasion of this particular poem. The third figure, the earthly mother, is
the single most important motif in all of Stevens' poetry. She emerges in the
earliest poetry and becomes the main image through which Stevens synthesizes the many themes, tonal inflections, and motifs that ultimately constitute the supreme fiction. In his essay "The Noble Rider and the Sound of
Words," Stevens refers to life itself – "the never-ceasing source" – as the
"ancient mother" (660), and that is the designation I shall use for this
mythic feminine figure in "The Owl in the Sarcophagus." (As a mythic
figure within pure poetry, the ancient mother should be distinguished from
female personifications of common poetry such as the "Fat girl, terrestrial"
[351] in "Notes Toward a Supreme Fiction.") In discussing the romantic
antecedents of Stevens' mythic figurations, I shall first consider the ancient
mother, then examine some of the images that enter into the figuration of
"sleep realized" (372) and "peace after death."

The three figures in the poem are said to "move among the dead." In this
region, the three figures hold complex and ambiguous kinship relations with
one another and with "us" – humans both living and dead:

> There sleep the brother is the father, too,
> And peace is cousin by a hundred names
> And she that in the syllable between life
>
> And death cries quickly, in a flash of voice,
> Keep you, keep you, I am gone, oh keep you as
> My memory, is the mother of us all,
>
> The earthly mother and the mother of
> The dead.   (371)

The grouping of these figures – two brothers and an earthly mother – seems
to have been inspired most directly by Tennyson's "Demeter and
Persephone." Demeter is the Greek goddess of grain and fertility. Her
daughter Persephone was abducted by the god of the underworld, but in

Tennyson's poem Demeter has found Persephone. Demeter explains that she was able to find Persephone because Persephone's image or shadow had come to Demeter to tell her what had happened to her:

> thy shadow past
> Before me, crying, "The Bright one in the highest
> Is brother of the Dark one in the lowest,
> And Bright and Dark have sworn that I, the child
> Of thee, the great Earth-Mother, thee, the Power
> That lifts her buried life from gloom to bloom,
> Should be for ever and for evermore
> The Bride of Darkness."[9]

In Stevens' rendering, the "Bright one in the highest" is "Sleep realized," an image of "the whiteness that is the ultimate intellect" and also of central unity. The "Dark one in the lowest" is "peace after death, the brother of sleep, / The inhuman brother so much like, so near, / Yet vested in a foreign absolute" (373). For the third figure, the earthly mother and mother of the dead, Stevens blends the image of "the great Earth-Mother" with the image of her daughter. Persephone is herself calling out to her mother from the land of the dead. Stevens' figure, in contrast, calls out to those who are passing into death.

The elegiac pathos of the mother's cry in Stevens' poem draws on his long experience in the romantic tradition of the elegiac sublime. His earliest major achievement in this mode is "Waving Adieu, Adieu, Adieu," from *Ideas of Order*:

> That would be waving and that would be crying,
> Crying and shouting and meaning farewell,
> Farewell in the eyes and farewell at the centre,
> Just to stand still without moving a hand.   (104)

This exercise in pure elegiac lyricism seems to have drawn inspiration directly from both Keats and Tennyson. In "Ode to Melancholy," Keats depicts Melancholy as a mythic female figure who "dwells with Beauty – Beauty that must die; / And Joy, whose hand is ever at his lips / Bidding adieu."[10] The image of "Bidding adieu" would naturally associate itself in Stevens' mind with similar phrasing in section 57 of Tennyson's *In Memoriam*, and the sweeping movement of Stevens' verse, gaining momentum through repetition, probably owes a good deal to Tennyson's verse:

> I hear it now, and o'er and o'er,
> Eternal greetings to the dead;
> And "Ave, Ave, Ave," said,
> "Adieu, adieu" for evermore.[11]

The ancient mother is a personification of elegiac passion, and her character as a mythic figure – a figure invested with divinity – suggests another association from Tennyson. In "The Ancient Sage," Tennyson's persona describes the elegiac sensations that have always possessed him: "A height, a broken grange, a grove, a flower / Had murmurs, 'Lost and gone and lost and gone!' / A breath, a whisper – some divine farewell."[12] The ancient mother in Stevens' poem cries out, "I am gone." She gives eternal greetings to the dead, and these greetings consist in "inventions of farewell" (371).

Stevens' linking of death with figurations of the ancient mother first appears in "Sunday Morning." Having rejected the idea of an insipid traditional "paradise," Stevens declares, "Death is the mother of beauty, mystical, / Within whose burning bosom we devise / Our earthly mothers waiting, sleeplessly" (55). The "earthly mothers" in this context are actual human mothers. By "devising" these mothers in death, Stevens invests death itself with a maternal character. In "The Owl in the Sarcophagus," the human mother has metamorphosed into a divine mythic figure. As we have already seen, this metamorphosis draws inspiration from Tennyson's depiction of Demeter and Persephone and from Keats's depiction of Melancholy, and it probably also draws inspirations from Keats's depiction of the Greek goddess Moneta in "The Fall of Hyperion: A Dream":

> But for her eyes I should have fled away.
> They held me back, with a benignant light,
> Soft mitigated by divinest lids
> Half closed, and visionless entire they seem'd
> Of all external things – they saw me not,
> But in blank splendor beam'd like the mild moon. . . .[13]

In this second Hyperion poem, Moneta replaces the Mnemosyne of the first Hyperion poem; she is the mother of the muses, and Keats addresses her as "'Shade of Memory.'"[14] The ancient mother in Stevens' poem calls out "oh keep you as / My memory" (371). Moneta's eyes beam "in blank splendor," and the ancient mother in Stevens' poem moves "With a sad splendor, beyond artifice, / Impassioned by the knowledge that she had, / There on the edges of oblivion" (374).

The ancient mother mediates between life and death, and it is in this region that Stevens seeks to penetrate into the secrets of the divine mind. "High sleep" is one of the personages of this poem because for Stevens sleep is the medium of mystic vision. Both in making visionary use of sleep and in rendering it as a mythic personage, Stevens has an antecedent in Keats. In "Sleep and Poetry," Keats apostrophizes Sleep and asks, "But what is higher beyond thought than thee? / . . . More strange, more beautiful, more smooth, more regal . . . ?"[15] In section three of "The Owl in the Sarcophagus," Stevens "saw well the foldings in the height / Of sleep" (372). These "foldings" in the height of sleep are vague and vast motions that are ultimately absorbed within central unity. They are "moving masses" that are "moving through day / And night, colored from distances, central / Where luminous agitations come to rest, / In an ever-changing, calmest unity" (372).

Stevens' evocation of sleep realized as a form of central unity seems to synthesize images from Emerson, Wordsworth, Whitman, and Tennyson. Emerson speaks of "central Unity," and in Wordsworth's *The Excursion*, a solitary sage declares that the universe imparts "'Authentic tidings of invisible things; / Of ebb and flow, and ever-during power; / And central peace, subsisting at the heart / Of endless agitation.'"[16] Whitman too declares that within the "central heart" of the earth "nestles the seed perfection."[17] Stevens designates the central unity as "The unique composure, harshest streakings joined / In a vanishing-vanished violet" (372). In Tennyson's "The Ancient Sage," the sage describes the divine presence as an infinite regress in material reality, as "in the million-millionth of a grain / Which cleft and cleft again for evermore, / And ever vanishing, never vanishes."[18]

In the course of this section, "high sleep" as the medium of mystic vision modulates into "Sleep realized" – the object of mystic vision. "Sleep realized / Was the whiteness that is the ultimate intellect, / A diamond jubilance beyond the fire" (372). The "fire" is the fire of death, an association suggested forcibly by a passage in Whitman's "Chanting the Square Deific," from "Whispers of Heavenly Death." "Santa Spirita, breather, life, / Beyond the light, lighter than light, / Beyond the flames of hell, joyous, leaping easily above hell."[19] Brilliant fire, light, and the connotative kinship of the words "joyous" and "jubilant" link Stevens' poem with Whitman's, and, like Whitman, Stevens associates these images with an image of breathing that taps into the root sense of "spirit" as "breath." "Then he breathed deeply the deep atmosphere / Of sleep, the accomplished, the fulfilling air" (373). Stevens often uses the image of diamonds as a symbol of poetic realization. In "Notes Toward a Supreme Fiction," he identifies the diamond crown as "the spirit's diamond coronal" (342). (The dialogue in which this phrase appears features Ozymandias, a name presumably suggested by Shelley's poem about this ancient king.) This spiritual crown has a close affinity with that evoked in "Crude Foyer": "there lies at the end of thought / A foyer of the spirit in a landscape / Of the mind, in which we sit / And wear humanity's bleak crown" (270). The diamond jubilance beyond the fire assumes its full meaning only within the larger context of all these associations.

Despite Stevens' claim to see "beyond the fire," death remains the most inaccessible and forbidding figure in his poetic mythology. Peace after death is "An immaculate personage in nothingness" (373). Stevens can gain imaginative access not to death itself but only to the poetic tradition about death. Death has "the whole spirit sparkling in its cloth, / Generations of the imagination piled / In the manner of its stitchings" (373). These "stitchings" are for Stevens primarily those of the romantic tradition, and for his figuration Stevens seeks out those associations that emphasize "peace" and that tend toward a softening and humanizing of this "inhuman brother." In "Ode to a Nightingale," Keats says he has often "been half in love with easeful Death,"[20] and Stevens says that the image of death "by its brilliance calmed" and that "Its brightness burned the way good solace seethes" (373). The robe of death in Stevens' depiction contains "an alphabet / By which to spell out holy doom and end, / A bee for the remembering of happiness" (373). The bee in this context seems to evoke an association with Shelley's "To Night": "Thy brother Death came, and cried, / Wouldst thou me? / Thy sweet child Sleep, the filmy-eyed, / Murmured like a noontide bee, / Shall I nestle near thy side?"[21] Sleep and death are kin, and evoking sleep as a sweet child mutes the harsher connotations of this kinship.

The final image Stevens contrives for death is that of "a king as candle by our beds / In a robe that is our glory as he guards" (374). In "The Auroras of Autumn," Stevens presents himself as "The scholar of one candle" (359), and this self-designation gives us a clue about the provenance and connotative aura of the candle in "The Owl in the Sarcophagus." In "Society and Solitude," Emerson declares, "A scholar is a candle which the love and desire of all men will light,"[22] and in "The Man with the Blue Guitar" Stevens had said, "A candle is enough to light the world" (141). The candle is a metaphor of the human imagination. The "robe" of death is the work of "Generations of the imagination" (373). By invoking these generations with allusive imagery, Stevens deflects the sense of solitude and nothingness in death. He tacitly places himself in the company of his romantic ancestors, and his communion with these figures provides spiritual solace. The character of that solace makes itself felt in one of the finest poems of his last period, "Final Soliloquy of the Interior Paramour":

> We say God and the imagination are one . . .
> How high that highest candle lights the dark.
>
> Out of this same light, out of the central mind,
> We make a dwelling in the evening air,
> In which being there together is enough.   (444)

The "central mind" is the mind of God, but it is also a single candle, the light of the human imagination. In "Of Modern Poetry," Stevens had described the purpose and character of modern poetry – his own poetry – as "The poem of the mind in the act of finding / What will suffice" (218). In the quiet figuration of divinity in "Final Soliloquy of the Interior Paramour," Stevens finds what will suffice. Simply being there, together with those who share "this same light," is "enough."

Stevens' work can of course be set within a wide range of illuminating contexts, historical and theoretical, but romanticism has a special claim on the attention of his readers. It is the context that Stevens himself identifies as his own central tradition. For him, romantic visionary poetry constitutes the highest form of imaginative achievement, and it is the norm against which he measures all other forms of imaginative experience. He could not, of course, simply repeat the achievements of his romantic predecessors. That would have been a case of the "ideal" becoming "anaemic." His own style and manner draw heavily on the style and manner of the great romantics, but it also has behind it the historical experience of realism, aestheticism, symbolism, and modernism. Stevens' new romanticism incorporates this experience, and it incorporates also the modern belief that all metaphysical ideas are merely constructs of the imagination. Unlike his romantic predecessors, Stevens could not simply depict and affirm an ultimate spiritual reality. He had himself to fashion the figurative structures through which "the essential poem" becomes a living presence. The supreme fiction consists only in the imaginative realizations of poetry, and its only purpose is to fulfill a need of the imagination. In an autobiographical note written the year before he died, Stevens explains that his work "suggests the possibility of a supreme fiction, recognized as a fiction, in which men could propose to themselves a fulfilment" (*L* 820). Stevens achieved the fulfillment he sought, and because he achieved that fulfillment, romanticism remains, in his work, a living tradition.

NOTES

1. Jerome J. McGann, *The Romantic Ideology: A Critical Investigation* (Chicago: University of Chicago Press, 1983), ix.
2. Ralph Waldo Emerson, *The Complete Works of Ralph Waldo Emerson*, 12 vols. (Boston: Houghton, Mifflin, 1903), vol. II, 276.
3. *Ibid.*, vol. I, 61.
4. William Wordsworth, *Lyrical Ballads, and Other Poems, 1797–1800*, ed. James Butler and Karen Green (Ithaca: Cornell University Press, 1992), 118–19.
5. Percy Bysshe Shelley, *The Complete Works of Percy Bysshe Shelley*, 10 vols., ed. Roger Ingpen and Walter E. Peck (New York: Gordian Press, 1965), vol. I, 229; vol. IV, 42.

6. Emerson, *Works*, vol. I, 329.

7. *Ibid.*, 330.

8. *Ibid.*, 44.

9. Tennyson, Alfred, *The Poems of Tennyson*, 3 vols., ed. Christopher Ricks (Berkeley: University of California Press, 1987), vol. III, 167.

10. John Keats, *The Poems of John Keats*, ed. Jack Stillinger (Cambridge: Harvard University Press, 1978), 375.

11. Tennyson, *Poems*, vol. II, 375.

12. *Ibid.*, 145.

13. Keats, *Poems*, 484–85.

14. *Ibid.*, 485.

15. *Ibid.*, 69.

16. William Wordsworth, *The Poetical Works of William Wordsworth*, 5 vols., ed. E[rnest] de Selincourt and Helen Darbishire (Oxford: Clarendon Press, 1940–49), vol. V, 145.

17. Walt Whitman, *Leaves of Grass*, ed. Harold W. Blodgett and Sculley Bradley (New York: New York University Press, 1965), 226.

18. Tennyson, *Poems*, vol. III, 140.

19. Whitman, *Leaves of Grass*, 445.

20. Keats, *Poems*, 371.

21. Shelley, *Works*, vol. IV, 84.

22. Emerson, *Works*, vol. VII, 11.

8

BART EECKHOUT

Stevens and philosophy

I

Among the great modernist poets in English, it is T. S. Eliot who, on the face of it, can lay most claim to being a philosophical poet. After all, Eliot is the only poet of his generation to have enjoyed an extensive academic training in philosophy. He even wrote a doctoral dissertation in the field. Yet, in spite of this professional training and its patent influence on especially his late masterwork, *Four Quartets*, it is not Eliot who has gone down in history as the most philosophical of modernist poets in English. That honor has been bestowed on another Harvard student from around the turn of the twentieth century: Wallace Stevens.

This may seem strange to anyone who still associates the name of Stevens with that of a reclusive lawyer working in the insurance industry and a playful, dandy-like poet indulging in the most sophisticated verbal jugglery. The claim to fame becomes even stranger if one takes a quick look at this poet's collection of aphorisms, "Adagia," only to come across antagonizing proclamations of the following sort: "The poet must not adapt his experience to that of the philosopher" (909). Or, more provocatively still: "Perhaps it is of more value to infuriate philosophers than to go along with them" (906). In a letter of 1951 to the young scholar Bernard Heringman, Stevens can be seen to mount the same warhorse when he goes on to claim, "I have never studied systematic philosophy and should be bored to death at the mere thought of doing so" (*L* 636). So how could this man be considered the most philosophical among modernist poets in English?

The animosity that speaks from the previous quotations is, unsurprisingly, not the whole story. For one thing, Stevens was not quite consistent in his attacks on philosophy and its practitioners. For another, the urge he felt to set off his own writings from those of philosophers already betrays a number of shared concerns and interests. Most poets, after all, are not much inclined to dwell on the topic of how their poetry relates to philosophy; they simply take this to be a non-issue. Yet here is another story about Stevens and philosophers, this time in the recollection of one of the most gifted poets to succeed him, Richard Wilbur. After Stevens gave a public reading at his alma mater in May 1952, he was being fêted at a small party, which included the young Wilbur. As Wilbur recollected the occasion many years later:

> Stevens became very comfortable, sitting in a corner chair as he talked at great length about the Harvard of his days, about Royce and Santayana. We were all so interested that we just asked him questions that made him talk a little more. I cannot remember anything save that it was all about his teachers in philosophy. Those were the people he talked about, and we went out feeling *that's* what happened. Not the publication of a few poems in the *Advocate*, but his philosophy courses.[1]

The revelatory value of this little anecdote is enhanced further when we look up the courses the young Stevens actually took during his three years at Harvard (1897–1900): they were all courses in English, French, and German, with some history and economics thrown in on the side. Not a single one was in philosophy. Yet, more than half a century after the fact, when he was back at Harvard and surrounded by people celebrating him as one of the greatest living poets, Stevens' mind did not go back to any of his literary classes nor to his first attempts at writing and publishing poems. What had left the most indelible impression on him, apparently, were the philosophers who had been around when he was an undergraduate.

II

"Philosophy" can mean a lot of different things depending on the cultural and historical context in which the word is used. It is this semantic instability, arguably, that accounts for much of the ambiguity surrounding Stevens' relation to it. The word's several connotations allowed him to be defensive and flippant on one occasion, inspired and deeply committed the next. The etymology of the word does not help us much to restore clarity: the Greek composite noun *philo-sophia* simply points to a love of wisdom. However, the very vagueness of the term "wisdom," and the fact that what is wise often depends on circumstances and contexts, already communicates something of vital importance. It suggests that the word "philosophy" for more than two and a half millennia has managed to survive in Western languages by dint of its offering a sufficiently open arena – both a battleground and a playground – for ideas. To be a philosopher is not to enter a beautifully closed-off terrain of intellectual operations, let alone an institutional discipline certified with a degree, but to display a fundamentally questioning spirit. The first question of philosophy, it has even been argued, is simply: What is the question?

There can be no doubt that Stevens was a lifelong questioner who was given to meditating intensely upon the world and that he was both an original, independent thinker and someone who liked to develop his ideas in confrontation with established philosophers. Two illustrations should be enough to flesh this out. Here is the older poet giving some avuncular advice about the value of independent thinking to a young admirer of his:

> True, the desire to read is an insatiable desire and you must read. Nevertheless, you must also think. Intellectual isolation loses value in an existence of books. I think I sent you some time ago a quotation from Henry James about living in a world of creation. A world of creation is one of the areas, and only one, of the world of thought and there is no passion like the passion of thinking which grows stronger as one grows older, even though one never thinks anything of any particular interest to anyone else. Spend an hour or two a day even if in the beginning you are staggered by the confusion and aimlessness of your thoughts. (L 513)

The same "passion of thinking," untroubled by any need for systematicity, recurs in my second illustration. When the aging Stevens heard that his old mentor from his Harvard days, George Santayana, was living out his life in a convent in Rome, he felt prompted to compose a moving tribute, "To an Old Philosopher in Rome," in which he made abundantly clear how strongly he identified with Santayana's philosophical attachment to intensified aesthetic experiences. Yet, when in 1952 he was informed of Santayana's death, he also made sure to characterize him as not only a philosopher but also a poet and to dramatize the tension between both sides of Santayana's personality. "Fifty years ago," he reminisced to a friend, "I knew him well, in Cambridge, where he often asked me to come to see him. This was before he had definitely decided not to be a poet. He had probably written as much poetry as prose at that time. It is difficult for a man whose whole life is thought to continue as a poet. The reason (like the law, which is only a form of the reason) is a jealous mistress" (L 761).

Stevens' occasional animosity against philosophy must be regarded in its context, then, as tapping into specific connotations of the word. When he lashed out at "systematic philosophy" and wanted to "infuriate" philosophers, he was not just guarding his poetic inspiration against the jealous mistress of reason, nor simply pitting his own attachment to beautiful things against an attachment to truth; he was also associating philosophy with a particular institutionalized discipline with which he felt fundamentally out of step. Already in his own day, and even more so since then, what has come to dominate in Anglo-American philosophy departments are various strands of so-called analytic philosophy. Yet this kind of philosophy, with its insistence on formal logic, would-be scientific objectivity, and highly theoretical, disembodied, almost scholastic case studies, happens to constitute the one tradition that is most antithetical to Stevens' own interests and poetic manner of thinking. To understand Stevens' relation with philosophy more fully, we need to distinguish between different cultural, national, and institutional traditions.

A small, recent anecdote will clarify this. When at the end of 2004 the French philosopher Jacques Derrida died, a massive effort on the part of mainstream journalists and academic philosophers in the English-speaking world was mounted to persuade the general public that Derrida had not really been a philosopher at all, or else no more than a kind of intellectual fraud who was considered third-rate at best by his professional colleagues. Yet, by leading scholars in the humanities and social sciences *outside* Anglo-American philosophy departments, Derrida is commonly regarded as one of the twentieth century's three or four most important thinkers. Typically, in Stevens criticism, too, a Derridean-inspired approach became widespread for a while (in analyses from the late 1970s through much of the 1980s), when readings inspired by the French thinker helped articulate a number of insights that until then were formulated only inadequately. This was an understandable development also, given that Derrida himself was fascinated by the relation between philosophy and literature all his life and provided much food for thought in this respect. Often engaging directly with the work of difficult writers, he explored issues such as the paradox of defining literature, the never-ending way in which texts produce meaning, the impossibility of deciding upon one interpretation at the expense of others, or the constant struggle between singularity and generality within any literary text. There has been no comparable enthusiasm for engaging with the work of poets or novelists among analytic philosophers, who feel they have simply nothing to say on the topic.

Although the antagonism between analytic philosophy and the so-called deconstruction practiced by Derrida and his admirers postdates Stevens' life, a similar kind of antithesis was already in place during the poet's own days, and it drew complaints from him that "most modern philosophers are purely academic" (L 476). Indeed, when we try to situate Stevens' poetry within the most important philosophical traditions in Western history, we cannot but be struck by how relevant almost all of them are to his kind of thinking and writing – with one major exception: that of analytic philosophy. Let me try to demonstrate this with regard to two major European traditions (Greek and German philosophy) and one more native tradition that did *not* become hegemonic in American philosophy departments (pragmatism). This will already take us so far that I will be forced to remain silent on the many connections that can be equally established with French philosophers (especially Henri Bergson, Maurice Merleau-Ponty, and Maurice Blanchot) or Italian ones (such as Benedetto Croce).

<h1 style="text-align:center">III</h1>

The Greek founding fathers of what we now call philosophy are not often mentioned in Stevens criticism, yet they make up an important part of the poet's intellectual background. As a student at the end of the nineteenth century, Stevens was more deeply versed in the classics than the generations of critics and readers coming after him. Thus, he is the kind of writer who would have been quite aware of the affinity between much of his own worldview and the ideas of somebody such as Heraclitus (who held that the world is in constant flux) or who was likely to ponder his conflicting personal affinities with philosophical movements from antiquity such as Skepticism, Stoicism, and Epicureanism. The hypothetical formulation of this claim is of some importance, though, for connections of this sort do not simply jump at us when we look at the poems on the page. Stevens' poetry does not parade philosophers' names, nor does it include direct quotations from them. Unlike his contemporaries Ezra Pound and Eliot, Stevens is not the kind of writer who will tell us where he got his ideas or will start dropping names. Of all the Greek philosophers with whose work he was familiar, the only names that get an actual mention in his poetry are Plato, Aristotle, and Socrates, and these only three times, twice, and once, respectively (out of a total of some 120,000 words).

The connections between Stevens' poetry and the ideas of certain philosophers, in other words, are principally those of association – which is why critics continue to have a field day exploring ever-new ones. It suffices for anyone to be struck by some parallel between Stevens' poetic ruminations and certain ideas that in the history of philosophy are identified with particular philosophers to start wondering about similarities and dissimilarities. Among Greek philosophers, Plato is probably the best case in point: Stevens' endless playing off of sense impressions against abstractions, and his shifting allegiances in this respect, constantly invites comparison with Plato's classic theory about the relation between fickle sense objects and their underlying forms/ideas (which in Plato's view are eternal and immutable and can be arrived at through reason). Take, as an example, Stevens' notion of "the first idea," which is sometimes attributed a pivotal place in his theory of poetry. The phrase was first introduced in the early parts of his most famous long poem, "Notes Toward a Supreme Fiction," which opens with the following two stanzas:

> Begin, ephebe, by perceiving the idea
> Of this invention, this invented world,
> The inconceivable idea of the sun.
>
> You must become an ignorant man again
> And see the sun again with an ignorant eye
> And see it clearly in the idea of it. (329)

What strikes us immediately in this overture is the insistence on the "idea" of the sun. This is not the kind of language we expect from poetry, where we normally assume we will be treated to a wealth of particular descriptions and arresting metaphors, not to a philosophical-sounding search for ideas. Nor is the occurrence of the word "idea" in these lines exceptional for Stevens: in its singular or plural form, the word appears seventy-eight times in his poetry. Several of these occurrences, moreover, take up prominent positions: one of the poet's volumes is entitled *Ideas of Order* and there are poems with titles such as "Extracts from Addresses to the Academy of Fine Ideas" and "The Role of the Idea in Poetry" – titles that are almost too soaked in philosophical parlance.

But Stevens' use of the word "idea" in the above lines is treacherous. To understand it better, we need to remind ourselves of the etymological history of the word. Stevens is a poet who was constantly digging into dictionaries for extra layers of meaning. In this case, he clearly sought to catch the reader's attention by what some theorists of modernism have called a defamiliarization technique. What he gives us is not the familiar modern meaning of "idea" but a reactivation of the word's original meaning in ancient Greek, from before the days of Plato. Originally, *idea* referred to the realm of the visible; deriving from the verb *idein* (to see), it meant as much as "look, semblance." If we bear this past layer of the word in mind, we begin to understand how Stevens can invite his addressee (who is himself called, with a reference to Greek antiquity, an "ephebe") to "perceiv[e]" the "idea of the sun" by becoming ignorant again of earlier conceptions and seeing the sun just as it looks and appears to us. Simultaneously, however, Stevens' use of the word "idea" is tainted and impure – and inevitably so. To a modern readership, the word cannot but retain some of the everyday meaning of abstract concept it has acquired since Plato. The proposed idea of the sun may be "inconceivable" all right (which is to say that, literally, no concepts may be derived from it), yet the poet also calls what is thus being seen an "invented world" (with another ambiguous play, this time on the

Latin etymology of the word "invention"), and he has put an even more confusing subtitle over these opening stanzas: "It Must Be Abstract." Seeing and thinking, perceiving and conceiving, concrete materiality and abstraction are thus getting entangled in the text to form an almost indivisible Gordian knot. It takes a reader with a philosophical bent to want to unravel such a knot.

This does not mean, fortunately, that the first-time reader of "Notes Toward a Supreme Fiction" is forced to brush up on his knowledge of Greek philosophy and the etymology of words before he can even go on to read beyond the opening stanzas. What my brief example demonstrates, rather, is that Stevens loved to make surprising, frequently counterintuitive proclamations of a more abstract, theoretical nature that invite us to ponder a variety of questions with a long philosophical pedigree. For readers with some expertise in philosophy, moreover, there appears to be a wide range of opportunities for deepening the interpretation of poems along age-old philosophical lines – so much so, even, that the main risk for novice readers is not so much one of underestimating philosophical implications as of overestimating them. Whatever it is, for instance, that Stevens was getting at in the opening lines of "Notes Toward a Supreme Fiction," it would be wrong to treat these lines as foundational building blocks for a coherent theory. As the title of the poem does well to remind us, Stevens was merely trying out a number of poetic "notes toward," not developing a systematic theory. Or, in the words of Frank Kermode, echoing the poet's own at the start of this chapter: "Critics who systematize Stevens, work out what, under all his vatic obscurities, his tranced and sometimes impassioned mimesis of thinking, he was really getting at, have occasionally come quite close to making him a bore."[2]

IV

In the history of philosophy, the relation between sense impressions and abstract thinking is at the heart of what is called epistemology, and much of Stevens' work is epistemological in inspiration. Its central question, in philosophical terms, is that of the knowledge relation between subject and object: How can we know (and, no less important for a poet, describe and represent) the external world around us? This is a question that in the intellectual history of the West reached a stage of intense crisis during the era in which Stevens was writing – roughly the early half of the twentieth century. We find it informing the work of a great many other modernist writers and artists as well. Stevens stands out among these only because of the consistency, the near-obsessiveness, and the endless originality with which he pursued it in poem after poem.

Given the importance of epistemological questions in his work, we cannot be surprised that his thinking has been situated frequently in the context of German philosophy since Kant. The late eighteenth-century writings of Immanuel Kant are widely held to constitute a watershed in the history of Western philosophy, in particular when it comes to understanding the importance of human subjectivity and perspectivity in our knowledge relation with the external world. Kant was the first major thinker to argue that we cannot know the thing itself (the *Ding an sich*) but that we perceive the world always from a specific human perspective, which is conditioned, among other things, by our concepts of space and time. Stevens did not necessarily read much of Kant (who is frequently arid and tough-going) but he grew up at a time when neo-Kantians were everywhere, and Stevens' worldview and concerns unmistakably stand in a Kantian tradition. Kenneth Burke, a contemporary thinker, even mocked Stevens in this respect. "Is it not a bit ironical," Burke wondered in a letter of 1944 to the poet Allen Tate, "to see a supposedly fairly relatively new poet like Stevens trying to explain his supposedly fairly relatively new esthetic by discovering the Kantian line-up somewhat more than 150 years late?"[3] For much of his life, Stevens was visibly intrigued by questions of how to grasp and evoke "the thing itself." Almost too conspicuously, the very phrase makes a few appearances in his work. It is even introduced pontifically in its German form when Crispin, the protagonist of his first long poem, "The Comedian as the Letter C," sheds his old self and marvels, "Here was the veritable ding an sich, at last" (23). Thirty years later, in "The Course of a Particular," Stevens was still writing of "the thing / Itself" (460), and he chose to conclude his *Collected Poems* in 1954 with a poem entitled "Not Ideas About the Thing But the Thing Itself."

Whether or not he drew a lot of immediate inspiration from Kant in composing such poems is moot and ultimately of little importance. What Kant initiated is, in the words of M. H. Abrams, a "Copernican revolution in epistemology."[4] Abrams coined this image in his famous study of romanticism, *The Mirror and the Lamp*, which in turn helps to show the main genealogical line that connects Stevens to Kant. The most important advocate and translator of Kant's ideas in the English-speaking world was the romantic poet Samuel Taylor Coleridge, the first writer in the history of English literature to make a name also as a critic and theorist reflecting on the activity of writing. It is from Coleridge, above all, and from the other great romantic poets and thinkers who followed in his footsteps, that Stevens drew inspiration – sometimes extending ideas in a direct line, at other times disputing and resisting them, but always in a virtual dialogue.

His lifelong habit of opposing "reality" and the "imagination," among other things, clearly derived from Coleridge.

The opportunities for pursuing links between Stevens' poetic ideas and the work of various idealist and romantic philosophers in the tradition of Kant have been many. Some critics have explored affinities with, or the possible influence of, thinkers such as Arthur Schopenhauer and Friedrich von Schlegel. Still others (such as the famous gender and queer theorist, Judith Butler) have teased out interesting connections with G. W. F. Hegel.[5] But, for a better understanding of Stevens' worldview, the most important philosopher in the nineteenth-century tradition of Kant remains Friedrich Nietzsche. We need only return to the opening canto from "Notes Toward a Supreme Fiction" to see how Stevens follows up the already-quoted stanzas in a seemingly Nietzschean manner:

> Never suppose an inventing mind as source
> Of this idea nor for that mind compose
> A voluminous master folded in his fire.
>
> How clean the sun when seen in its idea,
> Washed in the remotest cleanliness of a heaven
> That has expelled us and our images . . .
>
> The death of one god is the death of all.   (329)

The speaker's denunciation of a divine mind as possible origin of (the idea of) the sun and his insistence on staring into a heaven that has been emptied by the death of God are formulated in terms that would seem to derive at least some inspiration from Nietzsche's epochal and polemical work. Stevens' own complex attitude toward religion and belief and his vaguely Nietzschean concept of a supreme fiction are discussed in greater detail elsewhere in this volume. For present purposes, it should suffice to point out that much of his poetry from especially the early and middle periods shares a number of concerns with the radical work of Nietzsche – concerns about the social need for heroes (from Nietzsche's *Übermensch* to Stevens' major man); about the existential value of fictions, illusions, and metamorphosis; about the liberating quality and life-affirming vitality of art as the supreme human vocation; about the unsuspected powers of rhetoric. The precise extent to which Stevens was influenced by Nietzsche is again a point of contention; he himself preferred to downplay the connection on several occasions. However this may be, the critic B. J. Leggett has found enough material to write a substantial book on the subject and his explanation of the connection between both writers is worth quoting because the same qualifications apply to nearly all the philosophers with whose work Stevens has been cross-fertilized. "According to the perspective we adopt," writes Leggett, we may say that Stevens is a Nietzschean poet because he exemplifies qualities we associate with Nietzsche, because he has been a frequent subject of critics who are themselves influenced by Nietzsche's theories of language, because his poetry may be glossed usefully with passages from Nietzsche, because his concepts, ideas, and tropes parallel Nietzsche's in striking ways, because certain of his assumptions, values, themes, images have their source in Nietzsche, because his concepts and figures are generally identified with Nietzsche even if Stevens acquired them elsewhere – there are presumably a number of other possible combinations and nuances.[6]

A similar tentativeness is apt when we extend the Kantian–Nietzschean tradition in German philosophy still further to the twentieth-century phenomenologists Edmund Husserl and Martin Heidegger. Again, both of these figures – approximate contemporaries of Stevens himself this time – have been presented repeatedly as either sources of inspiration or thinkers with remarkably analogous worldviews. Especially in the early days of academic Stevens criticism, during the 1960s and 1970s, parallels with phenomenology were frequently drawn. One of the most sophisticated longtime champions of Stevens' poetry, J. Hillis Miller, started out in this way. Under the influence of Heidegger, who famously asked the question "Why are there beings at all, and why not rather nothing?," Miller would make claims about how in the later poetry of Stevens "nothingness is source and end of everything, and underlies everything as its present reality."[7] But also Husserl's founding principles of phenomenology have helped critics reformulate Stevens' poetic worldview in more prosaic philosophical terms. As a French Husserlian, Pierre Thévenaz, explains these principles,

> phenomenology is neither a science of objects nor a science of subject; it is a science of *experience*. It does not concentrate exclusively on either the objects of experience or on the subject of experience, but on the point of contact where being and consciousness meet. It is, therefore, a study of consciousness *as intentional*, as directed towards objects, as living in an intentionally constituted world.[8]

This may not be the kind of language or discourse that lovers of poetry invariably welcome, nor does Thévenaz's general point contribute much to the specific enjoyment or appreciation of Stevens' wonderfully inventive, unpredictable poems, yet the drift of such philosophical definitions does help us whenever we wish to recast this poet's idiosyncratic inventions in a more sober theoretical language and seek to moor his poetical thinking in its own day and age.

V

As we have already seen with Coleridge's appropriation and popularization of Kant, or with a figure such as Nietzsche, the thinkers who most influenced Stevens are often hard to label as either literary or philosophical in any strict sense. Such is the case again when we finally turn to the ostensible influence of American pragmatism on the poet. The first major figure in this tradition is Ralph Waldo Emerson, the central voice in American romanticism – or what is more often called American transcendentalism. The two different terms already betray how Emerson sits astride two genres: while "romanticism" is more readily associated with literature and the arts, "transcendentalism" points to a more philosophical interest in metaphysical questions. Emerson was too much of a poet, a rhetorician, and an aphorist to be simply embraced by academic philosophers today as one of their own. Yet, among those who do see themselves as continuing the tradition of American pragmatism, he stands as a towering figure. And at least since the critical work of Harold Bloom, there has been no doubt that Stevens' writings are steeped in Emerson's ideas and language. Indeed, if Stevens' own poetry and prose so patently distrust any philosophy based on rigorous logic and sterile rationality, he is naturally much happier in the company of a thinker such as Emerson, who loved to proclaim that "A foolish consistency is the hobgoblin of little minds."[9]

One of the reasons why by the middle of the twentieth century Stevens felt impelled to turn up his nose at the "purely academic" quality of contemporary philosophy is exactly that the reputation of American pragmatism was at an all-time low.[10] With its humanistic inspiration, antiessentialism, and antisystematicity, American pragmatism is probably the tradition within which Stevens' ideas are most easily inscribed. It is a tradition of thinking that prefers vagueness and ambiguity, if that is what it takes to get closer to the bone of lived experience and stimulate individual creativity. The most important foundational figure after Emerson, the thinker also to have launched the label "pragmatism," happened to be one of those teachers who was around at Harvard when Stevens was a student: William James, the older brother of the novelist Henry James. The kind of philosophy James stood for, and the example he set for Stevens, was a multidirectional, freely exploratory one. As Russell Goodman explains, James's major opus, *Pragmatism* (1907), gives us "at least six accounts of what pragmatism is or contains: a theory of truth, a theory of meaning, a philosophical temperament, an epistemology/metaphysics stressing human interest and action, a method for dissolving philosophical disputes, and a skeptical anti-essentialism."[11] In the same book, James, for example, writes:

The philosophy which is so important in each of us is not a technical matter; it is our more or less dumb sense of what life honestly and deeply means. It is only partly got from books; it is our individual way of just seeing and feeling

BART EECKHOUT

the total push and pressure of the cosmos. . . . The history of philosophy is to a great extent that of a certain clash of human temperaments.[12]

An idiosyncratic, eager, and self-reliant thinker such as Stevens would have willingly concurred with words such as these. In fact, the inspiration for his early poem "Thirteen Ways of Looking at a Blackbird" may well have derived at least in part from a classic paper published by Arthur Lovejoy in response to James's *Pragmatism*, for that paper carried as a title "The Thirteen Pragmatisms." Thirteen has long been the favorite number for anyone wishing to represent uncontainability and irreducible plurality.

Predictably, then, critics have sought to enlist Stevens' poetry also in an antiteleological, pragmatist project that especially values concepts such as contingency, provisionality, and transitionality. Richard Poirier is the clearest case in point. In two explicitly Emersonian and pragmatist books from the late 1980s and early 1990s, Poirier set out to argue that to read literature is to learn to live in transition, to remain inside the process of thinking, to resist the desire for secure meanings, and to dissolve the self. "We do not go to literature to become better citizens or even wiser persons," according to Poirier, "but to discover how to move, to act, to work in ways that are still and forever mysteriously creative."[13] Such a stance, in his opinion, is at the core of the pragmatist tradition that began with Emerson, ran through William James, and found its best twentieth-century representatives in the poetry of Robert Frost and Wallace Stevens. The work of such writers "depends on certain key, repeated terms. But to a wholly unusual degree it never allows any one of these terms to arrive at a precise or static definition. Their use is conducive less to clarification than to vagueness."[14] Along analogous lines, Thomas Grey has offered a refreshing analysis of Stevens' poetics from the point of view of a pragmatist law professor. For Grey, too, the conclusion should be that "Stevens can speak to the lawyer or legal theorist as a kind of therapist for the habitual and institutional rigidities of binary thought."[15]

VI

If Stevens' poetry may be read as a kind of antidote to rigid thinking, we must nevertheless be careful not to overemphasize such utilitarian arguments or overlook the more intrinsic pleasures of reading poetry. To remind ourselves of this, let me return, by way of conclusion, to the title of this chapter and give it a slight twist. What happens when we reverse the word order in "Stevens and Philosophy" and instead choose to address the question of "Philosophy and Stevens"? At first sight, nothing much would appear to be altered. Logically speaking, the two formulations amount to

114

the same thing: $A + B = B + A$. But in the world of Stevens one quickly becomes wary of logic.

Upon closer inspection, trying to explain Stevens and philosophy, as I have been doing for most of this chapter, is different from inquiring into philosophy and Stevens. In the first instance, we posit an interest in the poet as our central topic of investigation and then go on to ask ourselves what this poet may have derived from his reading in, and interaction with, philosophy. This is what literary critics or literary historians are most inclined to do. In the second instance, however, we are interested primarily in philosophical questions and want to know what insights we may derive in turn from Stevens. This is a question more often raised by readers who are themselves philosophers. The slight difference in perspective can have serious consequences, for it is able to stir up the age-old animosity between poetry and philosophy and rekindle debates about which of the two activities is of most value. In the case of a recent book on Stevens by the British philosopher Simon Critchley, this animosity can be seen to flare up in the guise of an implicit hierarchy between the two kinds of writing, which slips into his text only to be suppressed promptly and ostensibly retracted. According to Critchley, it is important that we understand his own approach to Stevens' poetry to be as follows:

> I am not mining Stevens's verse for philosophical puzzles and *aperçus* in pleasing poetic garb. Nothing would be more fatuous. On the contrary, I am trying to show two things: first, that Stevens's poetry – and by implication much other poetry – contains deep, consequent and instructive philosophical insight, and second that this insight is best expressed poetically. It is not, therefore, a question of paraphrasing obscure poetic rumination in clear philosophical prose, but rather of trying to point towards an experience of mind, language and things that is best articulated in poetic form.[16]

Critchley is clearly writing about "Philosophy and Stevens" here. To him (and to most of his implied audience), the notion of providing a "pleasing" aesthetic "garb" to philosophical ideas is anathema and any attempt at treating philosophy as subservient to the aesthetics of art-making is quickly dismissed as "fatuous." (Compare this to Stevens' own observation that "I like my philosophy smothered in beauty and not the opposite."[17]) From Critchley's point of view as a professional philosopher, Stevens' poetry can be validated only if it can be raised to the level of "deep, consequent and instructive philosophical insight." Since Stevens' poetry, *as* poetry, is in the final analysis more aesthetic in impulse than philosophical, this means that an argument must be developed in which the poet is seen to outdo the philosopher at his own game. Such an argument is what Critchley goes on to provide in his own book, which proposes that "Stevens's poetry allows us to recast what is arguably the fundamental concern of philosophy, namely the relation between thought and things or mind and world, the concern that becomes, in the early modern period, the basic problem of epistemology. It will be my general claim that Stevens recasts this concern in a way that lets us cast it away."[18]

As a philosopher, in other words, Critchley appears to be at once condescending and deferential. He is condescending toward those who would rather address questions of aesthetics (he pays little or no attention to how Stevens gave actual shape to his poems), while he shows himself humbly deferential to a poet who manages to be a full philosopher in his own right precisely insofar as he leaves one aspect of philosophy behind. A residual antagonism between poetry and philosophy, then, is noticeable in even the most elegant and admiring attempts at bringing the two together. As the quotations at the outset of this chapter already demonstrated, Stevens himself was given to expressing this antagonism on occasion. In spite of all his own attraction to philosophy, and his well-attested appeal to philosophically oriented readers, we should not be made to forget too soon that he remained a poet first and foremost, someone who could protest that "it must be an odd civilization in which poetry is not the equal of philosophy" (L 378).

NOTES

1. Quoted in Peter Brazeau, *Parts of a World: Wallace Stevens Remembered; An Oral Biography* (New York: Random House, 1983), 169.
2. Frank Kermode, Preface to 1989 edition, *Wallace Stevens* (1960) (London: Faber and Faber, 1989), xvii.
3. Quoted in Alan Filreis, *Wallace Stevens and the Actual World* (Princeton: Princeton University Press, 1991), 97.
4. M. H. Abrams, *The Mirror and the Lamp: Romantic Theory and the Critical Tradition* (1953) (Oxford: Oxford University Press, 1971), 58.
5. See Richard P. Adams, "Wallace Stevens and Schopenhauer's *The World as Will and Idea*," *Tulane Studies in English* 20 (1972): 135–68; Anthony Whiting, *The Never-Resting Mind: Wallace Stevens' Romantic Irony* (Ann Arbor: University of Michigan Press, 1996); Judith Butler, "The Nothing That Is: Wallace Stevens' Hegelian Affinities," *Theorizing American Literature: Hegel, the Sign, and History*, ed. Bainard Cowan and Joseph G. Kronick (Baton Rouge: Louisiana State University Press, 1991), 269–87.
6. B. J. Leggett, *Early Stevens: The Nietzschean Intertext* (Durham: Duke University Press, 1992), 18–19.
7. J. Hillis Miller, "Wallace Stevens," *Poets of Reality: Six Twentieth-Century Writers* (Cambridge: Harvard University Press, 1965), 277.
8. Quoted in Gyorgyi Voros, *Notations of the Wild: Ecology in the Poetry of Wallace Stevens* (Iowa City: University of Iowa Press, 1997), 12.

9. Ralph Waldo Emerson, "Self-Reliance," *Ralph Waldo Emerson: Essays and Lectures*, ed. Joel Porte (New York: Library of America, 1983), 265.
10. See Russell B. Goodman, Introduction, *Pragmatism: A Contemporary Reader*, ed. Russell B. Goodman (New York: Routledge, 1995), 1.
11. *Ibid.*, 3.
12. Quoted in Goodman, *Pragmatism*, 10.
13. Richard Poirier, *The Renewal of Literature: Emersonian Reflections* (New Haven: Yale University Press, 1988), 44.
14. Richard Poirier, *Poetry and Pragmatism* (London: Faber & Faber, 1992), 129.
15. Thomas C. Grey, *The Wallace Stevens Case: Law and the Practice of Poetry* (Cambridge: Harvard University Press, 1991), 6–7.
16. Simon Critchley, *Things Merely Are: Philosophy in the Poetry of Wallace Stevens* (London: Routledge, 2005), 4.
17. Quoted in Milton J. Bates, "Stevens' Books at the Huntington: An Annotated Checklist," *Wallace Stevens Journal* 2.3/4 (1978): 49, 50.
18. Critchley, *Things Merely Are*, 4.

9

GEORGE S. LENSING

Stevens' seasonal cycles

Familiar perhaps with only a handful of anthology pieces, readers of Wallace Stevens will be aware of the reappearance of the four seasons throughout his poems. Two of his volumes are called *Transport to Summer* and *The Auroras of Autumn*, and many other poems such as "Autumn Refrain," "The Snow Man," "The Paltry Nude Starts on a Spring Voyage," and "Credences of Summer" make the repetition of the trope unignorable. Queried once about whether he was doing a formal "seasonal sequence," Stevens denied it. However, he acknowledged that the writing of "An Ordinary Evening in New Haven," then in progress, was a "development" of the ideas of "Credences of Summer," adding, "That sort of thing might ultimately lead to another phase of what you call a seasonal sequence but certainly it would have nothing to do with the weather: it would have to do with the drift of one's ideas" (*L* 637).

How, one might ask, did the "drift" of Stevens' ideas lend itself to his reiterative adaptations of the seasons in so many poems throughout each of his volumes? Examining the scores of these poems, one quickly discovers that seasons are more than pastoral backdrop or lyrical evocation: they evolve from setting into trope and from trope into a larger mythos that lends a unity to what Stevens eventually came to call his cumulative "grand poem" (*L* 237). Additionally, the seasons of nature also evolve into a highly personal psychodrama, even a mode of survival, for a poet who found himself for the most part estranged from the supporting ties of family (parents, wife, siblings, daughter), friendships, and religious faith. "[O]ne might say that my father lived alone" (*SP* 4), said his daughter. As if in reply, the poet declares, "I have no life except in poetry" (913) and "There is no life except in the word of it" (257).

When Stevens draws the seasons into his descriptions of human interactions with the world, it is done in terms of various degrees of disengagement and engagement. In the poems of autumn and winter, the complex self willfully withdraws from its own makings and markings upon the world.

Such severings are often harsh, like foliage stripped from branches. Seeking a unity with nature itself in its denuded and snowy landscapes, the self hungers for an unmediated or nearly unmediated possession of essential reality. The poems of winter conceive of a self like a snowman, innocently but perfectly assimilated with all that it regards and beholds.

For Stevens, however, the issue is not mere epistemology. For a variety of reasons, he gradually became estranged from the bonds and rewards of human love in his own immediate world and, having undergone a "decreation" (750) in his relation with God, he found himself thrown back upon the world itself – which in one essay he calls his "inescapable and ever-present difficulty and inamorata" (838). If human love also disappoints and disappears, the "other" that consists of the world never does. One must first possess it as it is as fully as one can by suppressing one's powers of distortion, even the distortions of perception itself. The rigors of autumn and winter install the poet upon that hard but rewarding path.

Such abnegations of the self are discarded with the coming of spring and summer. As nature adorns itself in new growth and color, the self awakens from its earlier suppressions, eagerly indulging now its own intrusive perceptions and inventions. The "mortal no," says Stevens in "Esthétique du Mal," has its "emptiness and tragic expirations." But in "the imagination's new beginning," there comes the irrepressible "yes": "under every no / Lay a passion for yes that had never been broken" (282). The poet can now love the world as a man and a woman love each other, a joyous and placating coupling with the real. The poems of spring often mark an incipient journey out upon the world, or an awakening from sleep, or a child growing into maturity. Summer is culmination and consummation, the end for which the previous seasons have been prelude. Self and world attain a perfect harmony and accord. "It comes to this and the imagination's life" (322), the poet exclaims in "Credences of Summer." However, such makings of the self soon grow stale or excessively distorted or too distant from the real. The cycle of the seasons recommences. The rude disengagements of autumn must be undertaken anew.

The poems of the seasons remind us that Stevens' romance with the world was born of a boyhood love of the fields and hills around the home of his birth and youth in Reading, Pennsylvania; that same love was later transferred to other locations he inhabited, especially the Hudson River valley above New York and the large Elizabeth Park in Hartford, Connecticut. As a young attorney living in New York in 1909, he wrote to his fiancée back in Reading: "The truth is, it gets to be a terror here. Failure means such horror – and so many fail. If only they knew of the orchards and arbors and abounding fields, and the ease, and the comfort, and the quiet. One might preach the country as a kind of Earthly Paradise."[1] In one sense, that earthly paradise never failed him, even if human love did. If he could not *possess* another, he could passionately *pursue* the other as sun, field, star, and sea. But in another sense, the world itself remained always at a remove, divided by the Cartesian chasm, "not an external world but an image of it and hence an internal world" (857). Even so, Stevens never tired of pursuing the external world, longing to possess it in its essential verity. If not always close, that world was at least constant and requiting. As a result, he was willing to subject himself to the chastisements of autumn and winter in order to arrive at the dispensations of spring and summer. It follows that the poems of the seasons indulge in a wide range of emotional responses – between abstemious denial and sensuous indulgence, sadness and delight, isolation and communion-with-the-world, fiction-denying and fiction-creating. These are not the poems of a detached and disinterested observer – as Stevens is sometimes taken to be – but of a passionate man of intense longing.

Autumn

The poems of autumn are always poems of departure, dislocation, and an enveloping destitution. A part of the self is abjured in the interest of drawing the pure and unfalsifying eye (and the other senses of perception, as well) into conjunction with nature as "pure principle" (361), "first idea" (330), "veritable ding an sich" (23). This self-effacement is a kind of asceticism (far from the hedonism by which Stevens is often identified): "To project the naked man in a state of fact, / As acutest virtue and ascetic trove" (237).

Stevens' own life underwent a similar process of reduction. In the years immediately preceding the writing of perhaps his best-known poem, "Sunday Morning," he gradually surrendered the doctrinal faith of his Presbyterian youth in favor of an agnosticism that often left him feeling disinherited. The surrender was reluctant and regretful. In his essay "Two or Three Ideas," he reveals in unusually personal terms the wrenching sense of loss that follows the "annihilation" of the "gods": "It left us feeling dispossessed and alone in a solitude, like children without parents, in a home that seemed deserted, in which the amical rooms and halls had taken on a look of hardness and emptiness" (842). In the face of that same hardness and emptiness, Stevens sought the compensation of the beautiful earth in his poem "Sunday Morning." In "The Death of a Soldier," another early poem, the "season of autumn" enfolds the fallen soldier who can look up to no resurrected deity, no "three-days personage," as the clouds above him move at their own pace and "In their direction" (81). In the absence of God there remained the earth, what in a letter to his fiancée in 1907 Stevens regarded as if it were "my dearest friend," one he wished to share "with nobody, not even with you" (*L* 99).

In his daily business habits at the Hartford Accident and Indemnity Company, where he eventually became a vice president, Stevens reviewed claims against surety bonds on behalf of the company, becoming "for many years before his death, the dean of surety-claims men in the whole country."[2] To the adjustors who worked under his supervision, he was remembered as one who "would just relate the facts,"[3] and by another as one who "was very precise,"[4] and from the widow of another, "Jim learned a lot [from Stevens] about succinctness, not this gobbledygook they put into briefs nowadays."[5] Precision in quest of facts shaped both the businessman and the poet of autumn. But the "no-nonsense guy when it was business"[6] appeared to many of his associates as aloof, possessing a caustic tongue, and condescending.[7]

The man who wrote the poems of autumn and others as well was not a caustic poet, but he was a lonely one, alone by temperament, by habit, and by choice. In 1952, he wrote to Sr. Bernetta Quinn in an autumnal mode of despondency: "For a long time now there has been so much to do at the office that I have not felt like doing anything elsewhere. This morning I walked around in the park [Elizabeth Park was near the Stevens home in Hartford] here for almost an hour before coming to the office and felt as blank as one of the ponds which in the weather at this time of year [October] are motionless" (*L* 762). The park, the pond, and the blankness ("this blank cold" [428]) he made into his poem "The Plain Sense of Things."

The title of the poem defines the purpose of Stevens' autumnal meditation: "After the leaves have fallen, we return / To a plain sense of things" (428). It is, he declares directly, "as if / We had come to an end of the imagination" (428), as if we had arrived at a state of mental blankness ("inert savoir"). The poet denies himself everything but reduction and inertia. House, greenhouse, and chimney all seem near collapse. No exotic turban relieves the squalor. The failure of the "fantastic effort" (428) is the failure of fantasy itself, and the poet allows none of fantasy's impositions. The plain sense of things, forbidding as it is, cannot, however, absent itself entirely from the poet's knowledge as a perceiver – even if it is knowledge of muddy waste that is hospitable only to flies and a rat. The speaker is a man made minimum, but he is not moribund. Rejecting fantasy, he remains a seeing agent of perception; he has *not* arrived at the end of the imagination, nor is his *savoir* or knowing completely dead. "Inevitable knowledge" replaces "inert savoir": the "absence of the imagination had / Itself to be imagined" (428).

What Stevens has gained in "The Plain Sense of Things" is a return to what, in describing another poem, he called the urge "to try to get as close to the ordinary, the commonplace and the ugly as it is possible for a poet to get" (L 636) because the ordinary, the commonplace, and even the ugly are occasional qualities of the real. He must get "as close to" them as his separate and perceiving mind will allow, even though in this and the other poems of autumn such a regimen is rigorously straitening to the beholder. In the poems of autumn, loss is gain, purgation leads to purification, and the bright contours of the real are made newly accessible.

Winter

The poems of winter are like those of autumn, except pushed further and, in some cases, to an extreme. They set up an intriguing hypothesis and question: What would it be like to be one with the earth in an absolute sense, to erase altogether the Cartesian rupture? Stevens hints at such a longing in an explanation of one of the cantos in "The Man with the Blue Guitar": "I want, as poet, to be that in nature, which constitutes nature's very self. I want to be nature in the form of a man, with all the resources of nature" (L 790). Under such an arrangement, any doubt of the other would be dissolved in certitude; the essence of things, outside time and freed from mortality and human inconstancy, would yield its eternal efficacy and bliss. Such a condition, however, is only hypothetical because perceiver and perceived stubbornly remain in time – each intractably divided from the other.

For Stevens the hypotheses of winter are worth entertaining because they draw one as close as humanly possible to the beloved world from which the lover's imagination may later commence to act. Because the imagination "loses vitality" as it "ceases to adhere to what is real" (645), and because "The real is only the base. But it is the base" (917), one must make the real a constant quarry. The prospect of drawing near it, if not uniting perfectly with it, is both possible and profoundly satisfying. The lights of the aurora borealis in "The Auroras of Autumn" are a pure "innocence of the earth" and "no false sign." Their revelation portends a great requital: "we partake thereof, / Lie down like children in this holiness" (361).

In poems of winter, Stevens introduces the notion of a "nothing" to describe the idealized but perfectly unified state with the other. But, one might protest, "nothing" as no-thing suggests absence from, rather than unity with, the object. Yet, nothingness-as-something remains the only way the poet can accurately codify the pure and undistorted state of being: a condition of reality utterly independent of a perceiver who, by his very action, distorts the object in the act of beholding. If the falsifying eye is removed and the perceiver set aside, reality is then a something per se, though a nothing to any looker-on.

At the end of Stevens' celebrated lyric "The Snow Man," the "One" with whom the poem begins (its first word) has evolved into the snowy "listener" who as "nothing himself, beholds / Nothing that is not there and the nothing that is" (8). Only the snowman can claim perfect absorption into the wintry milieu of pine trees, spruces, and "junipers shagged with ice" (8). Stevens described the poem in a letter as "an example of the necessity of identifying oneself with reality in order to understand it and enjoy it" (L 464). But such an identity of enjoyment comes to rest in a "nothing that is," and it has been gained at a terrible price, the final forfeiture of the human presence otherwise remade into a snowman. A poem written four decades after "The Snow Man," "The Course of a Particular," again sets forth the nothingness of winter. Here the sound of leaves in winter is marked by the "absence of fantasia" and "the cry of leaves that do not transcend themselves" (460). That thin cry of leaves becomes the "final finding of the ear" until the ear itself dissolves and "until, at last, the cry concerns no one at all" (460). The ear as "no one" is kinsman to the eponymous snowman, the "nothing himself" into which the "One" was transformed in that poem.

Stevens' poems of absolute winter possess a mysterious, almost ghostlike presence lingering in the wake of human effacement. A snowman, a dissolving ear, or, in "Vacancy in the Park," a man who walks into the margins of the poem – all are remnant presences who are unselved into the nothingness of winter until, as "Man Carrying Thing" observes, "The bright obvious stands motionless in cold" (306). Inevitably, these are poems of "as if," hypotheses of nothingness. The final irony of these poems is a great one: an arrival at pure being that allows for no consciousness of its cleanest efficacy.

Other poems of winter are less extreme in their demands upon the perceiver, though their wintry setting is no less severe. Written in 1943, "No Possum, No Sop, No Taters," with its images of human dismemberment, owes something to the reports of casualties from the battlefields of World War II. In the opening couplets, stalks from a harvested cornfield are counterparts to human decreation: stalks that are "broken," arms that are "without hands," trunks "Without legs or, for that, without heads" (261). So pared down and dismembered, however, human presence is not eliminated in the manner of the snowman. A final syllable remains to intone "its single emptiness" (262). And to the syllable is added the presence of a mysterious "One" who joins the rusty crow at the end of the poem: "One joins him there for company, / But at a distance, in another tree" (262). Stevens may be suggesting that the "One" is not merely another crow, but the person who possesses the final syllable, a human presence now conjoined to the scene of winter but at the necessary "distance" of "another tree."

In all the poems of winter Stevens stands alone among the surroundings of what "No Possum, No Sop, No Taters" calls "deep January" (261). His pleasure is unwarmed by human company, and his own ascetic denials are unrelieved. But his distress leads to a company with the real that is as true and unembellished as he can conceptualize it: "It is here, in this bad, that we reach / The last purity of the knowledge of good" (262). In another poem set "At the end of winter," "The Poems of Our Climate," he describes the same reward as he views pink and white carnations in a "bowl of white, / Cold, a cold porcelain": "Note that, in this bitterness, delight" (179). His preference for such chilling assuagements was outlined by Stevens in his commonplace book, a preference for the impersonal over the personal: "For myself, the indefinite, the impersonal, atmospheres and oceans and, above all, the principle of order are precisely what I love; and I dont see why, for a philosopher, they should not be the ultimate inamorata" (*SPBS* 33). In one of his "Adagia," he professes that same love for the essence of things over their existence: "To live in the world but outside of existing conceptions of it" (904). But living in the world outside existing conceptions is too onerous a burden even for Stevens, and, with his abnegations of autumn and winter faithfully endured, he turns eagerly to the happier dispensations of spring and summer.

Spring

The harsh abrasions endured in the quest for winter's lucidity yielded, as we have seen, a good in bad, a delight in bitterness. Now the ensuing season offers a different delight. It signals the beginning of subjectivity reemerging, a tentative and childlike reaching out to the world while remaining amenable to the minimum. The harsh suppressions of the self in the decreations of the poems of autumn and winter are now relaxed. It is possible to discover "a *meaning* in nothingness" (376; emphasis added) instead of a pure "nothing that is." The movement away from unmediated nothingness by means of a subjectivity no longer suppressed is to advance toward a new and different something.

The poems of spring share certain qualities: a waking at daybreak, for example, or the beginning of a symbolic journey, or initiating a symbolic sexual coupling with the world. One of Stevens' great poems written toward the end of his life, "The World as Meditation," situates Penelope at daybreak, yearning for the long-delayed return of her husband Ulysses and imagining his approach in the rising of the sun. Stevens' Penelope possesses the "barbarous strength" (442) of her own meditative imagination. She reaches out to husband/sun and both finds him and does not: "It was Ulysses and it was not. Yet they had met, / Friend and dear friend and a planet's encouragement" (442). It is the real Ulysses whom she ultimately awaits ("His arms would be her necklace / And her belt" [442]), but his "coming constantly so near" (442) through the agency of her imagination sustains and ennobles her.

The wife in this poem seeking the separated husband had become for Stevens in many ways a counterpart to his own role as husband who, for many complicated reasons and over many years, found himself distanced from his wife. Penelope's loneliness is Stevens' loneliness, just as her compensation through meditating upon the world is likewise his.

The chilled relation between poet and wife is important especially to the background of many poems of spring where Stevens (or the speaker in the poem) is the isolated lover finding in the trope of spring's greening revival a kind of surrogate lover identified with the fecundity and lushness of the budding earth. What, one might ask, had made such a transferal so necessary for Stevens? During the courtship itself, before their marriage in 1909, his letters indicate over and over that Elsie is his "Muse" (L 115), or "*une vrai princess lointaine*" (a true faraway princess) (SP 146), or "Elsie, Ilsa, Ilsolda-Isolda. Sylvia – Yseult – to embrace so many famous histories in your name alone."[8] For his fiancée's birthday in 1908 and 1909, Stevens composed a series of undistinguished lyrics in some of which he celebrated her as muse, princess, Columbine to his Pierrot. A few years later, following their marriage, Stevens would write in the pedestrian "Dolls," "The thought of Eve, within me, is a doll / That does what I desire, as, to perplex, / With apple-buds, the husband in her sire" (517). Not surprisingly, Elsie shrank from such passively designated roles. Differences in age (he was more than seven years her senior), education (Elsie failed to complete one year of high school), her predilection for the country over the city – all led to later strains between husband and wife. By the time of their daughter's birth in 1924, Stevens was writing a poem such as "Red Loves Kit," a thinly disguised account of his troubled marriage: "Her words accuse you of adulteries / That sack the sun, though metaphysical" (556).

Stevens eventually responded to his marital disappointments by removing Elsie from his poems and reconfiguring her into the beautiful earth itself, a lover more constant, more controllable, and more requiting. In "Yellow Afternoon," for example, the speaker finds in "earth only" the thing "that I could love, / As one loves visible and responsive peace" (216); in "Arrival at the Waldorf," "the wild poem is a substitute / For the woman one loves or ought to love, / One wild rhapsody a fake for another" (219).

Most of these poems, however, make little comment on the circumstances of Stevens' private life, though such circumstances linger in the background. In "The Paltry Nude Starts on a Spring Voyage," the nude is Venus as she appears in the painting by Botticelli. She is the mind beginning to embark upon a new knowledge of the world as she "scuds the glitters" of the waves aiming toward the "high interiors of the sea" (4). Her actions now are minimal: she remains "discontent" (4); her play is "meagre" (5); she is "paltry." But the paltry nude will become the "goldener nude / Of a later day" (5). Ten years before writing the poem, Stevens had described his fiancée as a "mermaid, with seaweed and shells."[9] In this poem, however, Elsie is nowhere to be detected.

Unlike poems of the other seasons, many of the poems of spring depict obstacles, false starts, and misdirections. Having sustained the long suppressions of autumn and winter, the mind is sometimes slow in its awakening or even initially resistant to its new life. On the first day of spring when he was twenty-seven, Stevens tried to outline for his fiancée similar feelings of impatience and dismay. People themselves he found "grimy and puffy and it makes me misanthropic." He then goes on:

> "Spring fills me so full of dreams that try one's patience in coming time. One has a desire for the air full of spice and odors, and for days like junk of changing colors, and for warmth and ease, and all the other things that you know so well. But they come so slowly. – Earth and the body and the spirit seem to change together, and so *I* feel muddy and bare and rusty." (*SP* 174)

One might speculate that there must have been a natural hesitancy on Stevens' part to woo the world itself because it was only the world itself and because he would have to know it only as a fiction. But to such hesitancy Stevens never long succumbed.

Describing himself in the lines above as feeling "muddy," Stevens anticipates the later poem "Mud Master." Like the "muddy rivers of spring" that are "snarling," so, too, "The mind is muddy," and "The mind snarls" (119). Spring's revelations remain concealed: "As yet, for the mind, new banks / Of bulging green / Are not" (119). The speaker of "The Sun This March" is aware of his "dark nature" (109) at the end of winter; the "exceeding brightness of this early sun" (108) is like "an hallucination come to daze / The corner of the eye" (109). "Something of the trouble of the mind / Remains in the sight, and in sayings of the sight, / Of the spring of the year" (460) in "How Now, O, Brightener . . ." That speaker possesses a "restlessly unhappy happiness" (461).

The awakening mind in spring may be full of muddy snarlings or dump heaps ("The Man on the Dump") or a shadowy "dark nature." But having begun her "irretrievable way" (5) out upon the world, the paltry nude need not encounter only resistance and reluctance. Even in its incipiency, the freshness of spring can powerfully placate its beholder. To the "Infant" of "The Red Fern" Stevens admonishes: "But wait / Until sight wakens the sleepy eye / And pierces the physical fix of things" (317).

Stevens chose "Not Ideas About the Thing But the Thing Itself" as the final poem of his *Collected Poems*, even though it is a transitional one between the extremes of winter and summer. Like Penelope at daybreak in "The World as Meditation," another figure awakens from sleep and hears the "scrawny cry" of a bird "At the earliest ending of winter, / In March" (451). The first two stanzas describe the bird's cry; the next two present the sun "rising at six" (452) (the latter again like the object of Penelope's meditation). Cry and sun are synthesized into a unity by the poet's "choral rings" (452) in the final stanza. Three times the word "outside" reminds us that this sound and this sight are exterior to "sleep's faded papier-mâché" (452). Yet, the perceptions, though of the "thing itself," are also of the perceiver's own intuitions and syntheses: "He *knew* that he heard it [the scrawny cry]" (451; emphasis added). Inevitably, the poem is also not the thing itself but ideas about it. The "scrawny cry" of "Not Ideas About the Thing But the Thing Itself" is a new manifestation of a restless and energetic mind released upon the world. Like a lover seeking his beloved, Stevens pursues his world in a solitary journey. His seasonal vigil concludes in the poems of summer.

Summer

The imagination's happiest and most requiting pairings with the world find celebration in the fullness of summer, though devised from and depending upon the preceding seasons: "Winter devising summer in its breast, / Summer assaulted, thundering, illumed" (172). The eight cantos that make up "Credences of Summer" sustain a high pitch of excitation and wonder, a telling and retelling of a revelatory moment "Now in midsummer" (322) among hay fields, mountains, and pastoral ripeness. It is as if, in some moment of mystical transport, the poet attains perfect harmony between himself and all that lies beyond: "Now the mind lays by its trouble and considers." On this "last day of a certain year," one arrives at "this and the imagination's life" (322). All the autumnal and wintry austerities and even the tentative and minimal awakenings of spring were undertaken in order to arrive at the pleasures of this supreme moment. It is as if, Stevens insists, time itself were arrested ("Beyond which there is nothing left of time") and space also stops ("Things stop in that direction and since they stop / The direction stops and we accept what is / As good" [324]). In the end, time and space cannot be transcended; Stevens' mystical revelations are secular – though the poem draws heavily upon certain traditional conventions of religious mysticism in creating its antiphonal credences: "The rock cannot be broken. It is the truth. . . . / Things certain sustaining us in certainty" (324).

In canto VII, Stevens announces how the "concentred self" (325) fixes upon the objects around him, all associated with the memories of his youthful idylls around the Oley valley near Reading. He grips the object in "savage scrutiny":

> Once to make captive, once to subjugate
> Or yield to subjugation, once to proclaim
> The meaning of the capture, this hard prize,
> Fully made, fully apparent, fully found. (325)

Such revelatory moments are partly constructed ("Fully made") by the perceiving mind and partly revealed ("fully apparent"), as if they were a gratuitous gift bestowed. In "Lines Composed a Few Miles above Tintern Abbey," Wordsworth, in another pastoral setting, describes himself as a "lover" of the "green earth" revealed by eye and ear and "what they half-create, / And what perceive."[10]

One would expect that the poems of Stevens would consistently require a making and creating, and such is the case in the poems of autumn, winter, spring, and many of the poems of summer. Even in "Credences of Summer," the beholder is instructed to undergo a decreation – first to see the sun in "essential barrenness" (323) and "Without evasion by a single metaphor" (322). Then, he continues, "Fix it in an eternal foliage" (323). One then achieves "the barrenness / Of the fertile thing that can attain no more" (323). Such programmatic directives (makings) are everywhere in Stevens' poetry.

In a poem such as "Sea Surface Full of Clouds," a deliberate making is expressed. As the poet describes the wind and various reflections of clouds upon the surface of the sea creating a congeries of brilliant colors and metaphorical associations, "that November" becomes transformed into a "summer" that "hued the deck" (82) and, again, a "summer-seeming" (83). But the poet is no mere passive onlooker. Each of the five parts of the poem contains a summary sentence in French, placing the source of these phenomena in the poet's own creations: "C'était mon enfant . . . ; C'était mon frère . . . ; C'était mon extase . . . ; C'était ma foi . . . ; C'était mon esprit bâtard . . ." (83–85). It is the possessive pronoun (*ma/mon*) that unites all these responses leading to "fresh transfigurings of freshest blue" (85).

Other poems of summer, however, seem to be unmerited intimations of a kind of authenticity and perfection. In fact, Stevens refers in "Notes Toward a Supreme Fiction" to "a kind of Swiss perfection" made up of "balances": "not balances / That we achieve but balances that happen, / As a man and woman meet and love forthwith" (334). "Meditation Celestial & Terrestrial" remembers the role of "bluest reason" (101) and "will" (102) when we earlier "hardened ourselves . . . / In a world of wind and frost" (101). In summer's plenitude, however, such faculties can be discarded: "But what are radiant reason and radiant will / To warblings early in the hilarious trees / Of summer, the drunken mother?" (102).

Stevens' own presence as speaker in the poems of summer continues to be a solitary one. Although "erudite in happiness" (225), he finds his company in a world so pleasing to his total person that the sublimation is hardly noticed. In "The Woman in Sunshine," the warmth and movement of summer "are like / The warmth and movement of a woman" (381). The surrogate woman's "abundance of being" is for him "the only love" (382). As in "Variations on a Summer Day," a voyage by boat occurs in "Sailing After Lunch." The poem first mocks the "romantic" as something that "must never again return" (99). But then the imagination's own projection of the romantic is what the poet finally wants to stake everything upon, even though, in this case, it includes the elimination of all other persons: "To expunge all people and be a pupil / Of the gorgeous wheel and so to give / That slight transcendence to the dirty sail" (99–100).

In a few poems of summer Stevens suggests that expunging all people – a program as radical as any poet ever offered – had tested his own powers to efface an unquenchable guilt and regret. "World Without Peculiarity" surrounds the poet with "the spices of red summer" (388). But it is not enough. A father figure is introduced and remembered as "strong." But he "lies now / In the poverty of dirt" (388). Stevens' own father, Garrett, Sr., died two years following Stevens' marriage to Elsie in 1909. Communication between them was severed. One of Stevens' business associates recalls the estrangement that occurred during the courtship: "He'd rush over to the girl's place, and the family would never see him until it was time for him to leave. . . . After that had gone on for some time, his father said, 'If you're going to consider our home just a hotel, just a place to bring your laundry, you might as well not come at all.' They had words, and this was the last he saw of his father. He regretted this very much, because the father died without ever having spoken to him. He brooded over that over the years."[11] Thirty years after his father's death, Stevens recalled the man for the benefit of a niece: "I think that he loved to be at the house with us, but he was incapable of lifting a hand to attract any of us. . . . The result was that he lived alone" (L 454). The pronouncement might well be a self-portrait.

Stevens' mother, Margaretha Catharine Zeller, died a year after her husband's death. The poet visited her in Reading as she was dying; he was unable afterwards to conceal the guilt he felt in the breakdown of his relationship with her: "I have not been able to see her often for ten years or more" (*SP* 253). Stevens quotes his mother's words on her deathbed: "She said that she had had her 'boys' and asked, 'Do you remember how you used to troop through the house?'" (*SP* 255). In the case of her second son, she had had him *only* as a boy.

In the same poem, the mother as well as the father is evoked: "But what his mother was returns and cries on his breast," but as a "hating woman" (388). "She is the fateful mother, whom he does not know" (388). Stevens had recorded as an isolated entry into his early notebook of titles and phrases, "The mother, the one unknown."[12] In the lines of "World Without Peculiarity" the poet struggles, not very convincingly, to draw solace from the pain of parental alienation in the one thing that remains for him: "It is the earth itself that is humanity" (388). He abases himself as the "inhuman son" (388). Somewhat desperately, the poem seeks to resurrect the mother in day, walk of the moon, and breathless spices. After the death of his parents, one should add, Stevens' break with his two brothers and two sisters also became complete, though he would survive them all and later attempt to establish friendships with nephews and nieces in the last years of his life.

The other major figure in Stevens' family life is his daughter and only child, Holly. One can speculate that the strains between her parents must have made her childhood and adolescence difficult. She later tersely summarized the relationship: "[W]e held off from each other – one might say that my father lived alone" (*SP* 4). Holly was herself a high-spirited and independent-minded person. One of her companions during her adolescence remembers her unflatteringly: "Holly was boisterous, crass, playful, witty, sentimental, boorish, rebellious, loyal, iconoclastic, easily distracted, daring, selfish, self-centered, usually undisciplined and always terribly stubborn. Occasionally, she could be dishonest with even her oldest and best friends."[13] Shortly after Holly's reluctant enrollment at Vassar College, World War II broke out and Holly, against her father's vehement protests, withdrew, returned to a boardinghouse in Hartford, and took a job. Two years later she married a serviceman for office equipment, again against the outspoken wishes of her father. As one of Stevens' co-workers recalled: "[Before her marriage to John Hanchak in 1944, the couple went to Stevens' office to tell him of their plans.] . . . He was really upset. He let everybody know that he was mad about it. I didn't know what was going on. I heard him with this very high voice raising hell. The only time I saw him mad."[14] When Holly was still in her teens, Stevens wrote to some friends mentioning why he and Elsie had never had a second child: "There is nothing that I should have liked more, but I was afraid of it" (L 321). In the last years of his life Stevens and his daughter were reconciled, and some harmony was restored to the relationship.

It was during his estrangement from his daughter that Stevens wrote "The House Was Quiet and the World Was Calm," though Holly is nowhere alluded to in the poem. The speaker of the poem indulges the serenity of the summer night as if a respite from a world otherwise overbearing: "The house was quiet because it had to be. / The quiet was part of the meaning, part of the mind: / The access of perfection to the page" (312). Here again Stevens draws his sustenance from the "perfection [of] the page" over the perfection of the life.

The season itself perhaps afforded Stevens his greatest personal delight over the years, in spite of the great demands he placed upon it. "Summer has always made me happy" (L 760), and "I cannot get the idea of summer out of my head" (SP 155). From his earliest years those warm months beckoned Stevens to the outdoor world. But, like the other seasons, this one too comes to an end: "It is one of the peculiarities of the imagination that it is always at the end of an era" (656). Even in "Credences of Summer," the poem concludes as "A complex of emotions falls apart" (326), and the mind becomes "aware of division" (325). "[Y]ou detect / Another complex of other emotions, not / So soft, so civil" (326).

In one of his "Adagia," Stevens acknowledges that "The imagination consumes & exhausts some element of reality" (911). That reality must be reclaimed by once again undergoing the decreations of autumn and winter. In "Banal Sojourn," "Summer is like a fat beast, sleepy in mildew" and the garden is a "slum of bloom" (49). The poem concludes: "One has a malady, here, a malady. One feels a malady" (49).

In one letter Stevens spoke of the transition away from summer by comparing it to "a mosaic of a man": "Yesterday it was summer: today it is autumn. The change pervades everything and I suppose, therefore, that a mosaic of a man is something like a mosaic of the weather" (L 612). No season is final or fixed; as a result, no single poem co-opts other poems belonging to other seasons and addressing other needs. And so it is with his poetics, though this is not always appreciated by his readers. Stevens is a tentative poet who has "no wish to arrive at a conclusion" (L 710). Like the seasons, Stevens' poetics is itself incremental, cyclical, and variously composite.

It is no wonder that Stevens made the weathers of the seasons into the weathers of his poetry, but the same weathers also became his personal society with the world. Stevens' daughter remembers, for example, "My father's bedroom and private bath were at the top of the front stairs facing the garden. He rearranged his furniture with the seasons, so that he could lie in bed and look out at the pleasantest angle."[15] A neighbor in Hartford recalls, "Every Sunday he used to walk over to the park. Rain, or sometimes it'd be sleeting, he'd walk over. He'd spend an hour; all kinds of weather."[16] Although the poems of the seasons make Stevens into one of the great pastoral poets of modernism, they also trace over four decades the subtle and only partially hidden attempts on his part to justify his own place in the world as an isolated social being. His "grand poem," in which he found both frustration and placation, was also his personal refuge and self-appointed cure.

NOTES

1. Wallace Stevens, *The Contemplated Spouse: The Letters of Wallace Stevens to Elsie*, ed. J. Donald Blount (Columbia: University of South Carolina Press, 2006), 199–200.
2. Peter Brazeau, *Parts of a World: Wallace Stevens Remembered; An Oral Biography* (New York: Random House, 1983), 67.
3. *Ibid.*, 44.
4. *Ibid.*, 41.
5. *Ibid.*, 89.
6. *Ibid.*, 20.
7. *Ibid.*, 14, 22, 24, 27, 29, 31, 64.
8. Stevens, *Contemplated Spouse*, 52.
9. *Ibid.*, 202.
10. William Wordsworth, *"Lyrical Ballads," and Other Poems*, ed. James Butler and Karen Green (Ithaca: Cornell University Press, 1992), 119.
11. Brazeau, *Parts of a World*, 256.
12. George S. Lensing, *Wallace Stevens: A Poet's Growth* (Baton Rouge: Louisiana State University Press, 1986), 159.
13. John Crockett, "Of Holly and Wallace Stevens in a Hartford Light," *Wallace Stevens Journal* 21.1 (1997): 5.
14. Brazeau, *Parts of a World*, 251.
15. Holly Stevens, "Bits of Remembered Time," *Southern Review* 7 n.s. 3 (1971): 654.
16. Brazeau, *Parts of a World*, 239.

10

HELEN VENDLER

Stevens and the lyric speaker

Because the lyric poem so often speaks in a first-person voice, we uncon-
sciously expect to hear in its lines someone saying, "No, I am that I am"
(Shakespeare) or "I wandered lonely as a cloud" (Wordsworth), or "I too
dislike it" (Marianne Moore) or "Black like me" (Langston Hughes).
Wallace Stevens sometimes writes poems of this openly personal sort:

> The exceeding brightness of this early sun
> Makes me conceive how dark I have become. . . .   (108)

But Stevens' use of the naked first-person voice is relatively rare. The most
frequent substitute in lyric for the first-person singular is the first-person
plural: "Like as the waves make toward the pebbled shore, / So do our
minutes hasten to their end" (Shakespeare); "Oh joy, that in our embers / Is
something that doth live" (Wordsworth); "We outgrow love, like other
things" (Emily Dickinson). Stevens is much attached to this first-person
plural voicing, which serves him, as it has many poets, as a philosophic
resource in asserting something true of all human beings:

> We live in an old chaos of the sun,
> Or old dependency of day and night. . . .   (56)

But the capacious pronoun "we" can equally serve Stevens as the sign of
collective American reference – "Deer walk upon our mountains" (56) – or
as the sign of intimacy between two people – "Only we two are one" (118) –
or as an indirect way of speaking of himself: "If sex were all, then every
trembling hand / Could make us squeak, like dolls, the wished-for words" (14).
  Besides referring to themselves as "I" or as part of a collective "we,"
poets sometimes talk to themselves by means of the second-person pronoun
"you," either in imperative or declarative terms: "No, no, go not to Lethe"
(Keats). Stevens uses this roundabout way to say "I" as well, addressing
himself from a distance: "You like it under the trees in autumn, / Because
everything is half dead" (257). Finally, even when speaking of themselves,

poets sometimes resort to impersonal pronouns; for Stevens the indirectness of the impersonal "one" often enables the disclosure of suffering: "One has a malady, here, a malady" (49).

But of all the fashions of saying "I" in lyric, Stevens prefers "he." To refer to oneself persistently in the third person has not been common in lyric; Stevens is the first poet who has made this practice a characteristic of his work. Why would this poet choose to write of himself as "he" rather than "I"? The chief reason is that in doing so he must make an effort to see himself from the outside, as if he were a character in a story. He adopts the novelist's or dramatist's view: what is this character doing, or thinking, or describing now? In separating the described self from the describing voice, Stevens wishes to combine expressive accuracy with the truthfulness of detached observation.

In "The Man with the Blue Guitar," Stevens (who in his youth had played a guitar) refers to himself both as "he" *and* as "I," beginning the poem with an objective view – "The man bent over his guitar" (135) – then shifting, in the second canto, to the subjective statement of the guitarist – "I cannot bring a world quite round" (135). Later, in canto XXXII, he addresses himself in the second person – "You as you are? You are yourself. / The blue guitar surprises you" (150) – then ends the poem in the "we" of universality: "The bread / Will be our bread" (151). This fluidity of self-reference has influenced the work of later poets, notably John Ashbery, who shares with Stevens a sense of the multiplicity of ways in which the self can regard the self, from the indivisible unity of the subjective "I" to the dyadic intimacy of "you" to the collectivity of "we" to the apparent objectivity of "one" and "he."

Because readers of poetry begin by thinking of utterances in "I" or "we" as sincere declarations from the heart, and utterances in "he" or "one" as detached and impersonal, they have sometimes found Stevens' voice "cold" or "inhuman." Perhaps they have not perceived how very personal and deeply felt, even if impersonally phrased, his lyrics are. Not only did the use of "he" and "one" help Stevens to work toward an objective view of his emotions and convictions, it also shielded his griefs from too devastating a self-exposure. Stevens was a reticent man, and admired reticence. As early as 1907, noting in his journal the death of the French philosophical poet René Sully-Prudhomme, he added, "There is something *piquant* about a poet who leaves the feeling of reticence" (SP 185). Later, the idea that the reader's interest is piqued by encountering a veil of reticence will become an axiom in Stevens' poetics: "The poem must resist the intelligence / Almost successfully" (306).

Why did Stevens wish his poem to resist the reader's intelligence "almost" – but not entirely – successfully? He alerts us, by that qualifying adverb, that the package the poem offers is not unintelligible. Eventually our intelligence will unwrap it, he promises (it is a promise he always keeps), but we may at first find ourselves in a state of some bafflement, and may have to struggle with the poem almost to the end of our encounter with it. Stevens leads us to replicate, as we read, the struggles he undergoes in analyzing into composition his own feelings and motives. "A poem," Robert Lowell once said in a course I took from him, "is an event, not the record of an event." If we, as readers, are to "live[] along the line"[1] with the poet, then our bewilderment must mirror his. In "Man Carrying Thing" – Stevens' allegory of this difficulty – the eye perceives, in the obscurity of winter dusk, a figure that it can only inexactly define as that of a man carrying something. Then a snowfall begins, gradually intensifying throughout the night. In the morning, with the evening darkness gone and the night-long snowstorm over, we suddenly see what we had not been able to see before – "A horror of thoughts that suddenly are real":

> We must endure our thoughts all night, until
> The bright obvious stands motionless in cold. (306)

Our apparently incorrigible difficulty in seeing our passions and thoughts free of the surrounding storm of uncertainties is enacted in Stevens' poem; there, we struggle through those uncertainties until we see what they have been concealing from us: a horror of truth that, once admitted, is seen to be the inescapable "bright obvious."

Stevens takes a great risk in replicating in his poems, often by means of an impersonal voice, his own turn from tormenting perplexity toward clarity. Yet, if the reader persists, the reward is a dramatic sense of unfolding, even of astonishing insight, as the poem achieves its brilliant finality. Stevens never lost his sense that "Description is revelation" (301); his first duty was to enable that revelation by describing the ever-changing life of human emotional response. In 1906, he had written, "[M]y opinions generally change even while I am in the act of expressing them. So it seems to me and so, perhaps, everyone thinks of himself. The words for an idea too often dissolve it and leave a strange one" (SP 165). The rapidity of the evolution of his opinions and ideas seemed to him at first an impediment to his search for "the" truth, a systematic truth that could replace the Christianity of his churchgoing childhood. When he addressed this theme in "Sunday Morning," Stevens resorted to the stratagem of writing of himself in the third person, not as "he" but as "she," adopting a female persona for reflections that might at the time have seemed too "unmanly" to be voiced with a masculine pronoun: "Divinity must live within herself" (53), declares the woman who has decided to celebrate Sunday at home with "Coffee and oranges" instead of going to church. But her attempted hedonism cannot by itself blot out the old Christian "Dominion of the blood and sepulchre" (53), and so she must think through her attitude toward past and future religion. Rejecting the totally celestial Jove and the half-human, half-divine Jesus, she hopes for a fully human god in the future.

Soon, however, Stevens realized that the complexity of the self could not be satisfied with a single truth: "Where was it," he asks, that "one first heard of the truth? The the" (186). We must hear the closing words of this line as "*the* truth? The *the*" – the article emphasized to specify singleness, a unique truth proclaimed as the sole and all-sufficient one. In the poem immediately following, "On the Road Home," Stevens adds, "It was when I said, / 'There is no such thing as the truth,' / That the grapes seemed fatter. / The fox ran out of his hole" (186). As Stevens came to acknowledge multiple points of view and to elaborate the multiple scenes that served him as symbolic landscapes, he began a sustained celebration of partial truths, theorized in "Landscape with Boat":

> [I]f nothing
> Was divine then all things were, the world itself,
> And that if nothing was the truth, then all
> Things were the truth, the world itself was the truth. (221)

Acceptance of a proliferation of truths (matched by a consequent abundance of symbolic images) led Stevens to imagine a multitude of personae for himself – no longer merely the "one" or "he" of detached self-observation, but fleeting allegorical embodiments of points of view. The most striking (and funniest) voice among his early personae comes from the bantam rooster in pine woods who confronts a huge cock with "henna hackles," who is adorned by his tan feathers and "blazing tail" as Aztec chieftains were adorned by their sumptuous feather-capes. The little bantam hails and halts the giant rooster:

> Chieftain Iffucan of Azcan in caftan
> Of tan with henna hackles, halt! (60)

It is the little American poet, an "inchling," who, dismissing this "ten-foot poet" of the universal with derisive words – "Fat! Fat! Fat! Fat! I am the personal. / Your world is you. I am my world" (60) – asserts the rights of the unique and the personal (the province of lyric) against larger poetic forms. Other personae, human and inhuman, speaking and nonspeaking, are scattered throughout *Harmonium* and subsequent volumes, but they are most spectacularly on parade in Stevens' chief theoretical poem, "Notes Toward a Supreme Fiction." The personae in "Notes" include the young "ephebe," or pupil-poet, who writhes in silence and fear in his attic room while the powers of the world – lion, elephant, and bear – roar outside; "the MacCullough," the head of the clan of that name, who can speak as the representative voice of many; a nameless man "in his old coat, / His slouching pantaloons, beyond the town, / Looking for what was, where it used to be"; an old seraph, bored as much by the repetitions of nature (spring) as those of culture (the bandeaux of the daughters identical with the bandeaux of their mothers); a planter who loved all his environments – his primal land of origin, the land where he subsequently lived out his life, and an opulent imagined land "là-bas"; Ozymandias (borrowed from Shelley) and his spouse Nanzia Nunzio, attempting an impossible nakedness; a "blue woman" who determines to see nature without projecting her own nature upon it; and "Canon Aspirin" who aspires to both heights and depths, while realizing that his sister's deliberate "pauvred color" may be as true as his "violet abyss" (329–52). Each of these personae embodies some aspect of Stevens himself or of the world as he perceives and conceives it. Nature can be either the round planet itself (the beloved "Fat girl" and "soft-footed phantom" of "Notes") or a wholly sinister devouring mother, as in the late lyric "Madame La Fleurie"; there, the poet fears that his former view of nature as a beflowered and benevolent maternal principle was utterly mistaken: now "His grief is that his mother should feed on him, himself and what he saw, / In that distant chamber, a bearded queen, wicked in her dead light" (432). Although Stevens' personae may not speak aloud, the poet's use of free indirect discourse representing what they would say if they were to speak (as with the blue woman) adds to his resources of voice.

If we grant Stevens his premise – that evolving perceptions demand changing embodiments – then we will move willingly within his fluidities of self-reference and their expressive voices, individuated by diction, decor, and decorum. We will become uneasy when he is uneasy, bewildered when he is bewildered, coarse when he is coarse. Coarseness of voice interestingly arrives in Stevens when he is most viscerally repelled by the physical world and its offerings. In one such poem, for instance, the Stevensian man with the guitar reappears, temporarily named "Jaime," but the phonemes of his Hispanic name are grotesquely transcribed on the page as "Ha-eé-me," just as his action, "jugar" (the Spanish for "to play" the guitar), is deformed in the poem's title to what appears to be a misheard noun, "Jouga," perhaps activating a pun on "conjugal" and the marital yoke (in French, *joug*). As the poem proceeds, the erotic bond between Jaime and his wife-as-guitar (or guitar-as-wife) is jeeringly and luridly described:

> The physical world is meaningless tonight
> And there is no other. There is Ha-eé-me, who sits
> And plays his guitar. Ha-eé-me is a beast.

Or perhaps his guitar is a beast or perhaps they are
Two beasts. But of the same kind – two conjugal beasts.
Ha-eé-me is the male beast . . . an imbecile,

Who knocks out a noise. The guitar is another beast
Beneath his tip-tap-tap. It is she that responds.   (295)

Stevens can imagine no end to this debased conjugal union except for a merciful
obliteration of its guitarist in sleep, leaving the tropical erotic world to produce
its own sound, bare of human music: "And after a while, when Ha-eé-me has
gone to sleep, / A great jaguar running will make a little sound" (295).

What are the rewards of reading Stevens if we not only allow an independent fictive existence to his personae – the fearful ephebe, the bestial
Jaime, the devoted planter, the austere blue woman – but also track them
back to their emotional sources in the poet? One reward is a felt exhilaration in the sheer fertility of Stevens' imagination, as out of himself he
generates so many allegorical selves and voices. As he says, gratefully,

[O]ut of what one sees and hears and out
Of what one feels, who could have thought to make
So many selves, so many sensuous worlds,
As if the air, the mid-day air, was swarming
With the metaphysical changes that occur,
Merely in living as and where we live.   (287)

For Stevens, the phrase "metaphysical changes" denotes all the thoughts
and feelings that cast their colors on the physical world, transforming it as it
assumes the different weathers of the heart. The seasons and the weather, in
Stevens as in Keats, parallel the inner storms – and inner glories – of human
existence. Seasonal changes offer a way of writing in which there would be
no personal intervention at all: no "I," no "he" or "she," no "one," no
"we," no "you." The season of autumn offered such an opportunity to
Keats, as he evoked the almost imperceptible waning of a day and a season
until, at the close, "gathering swallows twitter in the skies." Keats's poem is
perfectly "impersonal" in its voicing (the utterer addressing autumn never
specifies his own identity in any way). Yet "To Autumn" is suffused by a
complex of human emotions, from the ecstatic to the sorrowful; it is as
though the season, in Keats's montage of tableaux, memorializes itself.
Stevens adopted this impersonal or nearly impersonal voicing for some of
his most moving poems, in which the natural world reveals itself by itself,
with human interpretation muted.

Impersonality can be used to convey stark deprivation, as in the proverbi-
ally named "No Possum, No Sop, No Taters." There, Stevens represents,

through an almost invariant syntax, the kind of despair he had violently articulated in prose as a young man: "I'm in the Black Hole again. . . . The very animal in me cries out for a lair. I want to see somebody, hear somebody speak to me, look at somebody, speak to somebody in turn" (*SP* 128). In the poem, Stevens writes:

> The field is frozen. The leaves are dry.
> Bad is final in this light.
>
> In this bleak air the broken stalks
> Have arms without hands. They have trunks
>
> Without legs or, for that, without heads.
> They have heads in which a captive cry
>
> Is merely the moving of a tongue.
> . . . .
>
> It is deep January. The sky is hard.
> The stalks are firmly rooted in ice.   (261)

Yet, in another mood altogether, the impersonal "one" can be the vehicle of the joyous poem of the sleight-of-hand man, vivid with Stevens' never-failing wonder before the gorgeous and energetic phenomena of the natural world:

> One's grand flights, one's Sunday baths,
> One's tootings at the weddings of the soul
> Occur as they occur. So bluish clouds
> Occurred above the empty house and the leaves
> Of the rhododendrons rattled their gold,
> As if someone lived there. Such floods of white
> Came bursting from the clouds. So the wind
> Threw its contorted strength around the sky.   (205)

Although he practiced a constant displacement of his lyric "I" into a "one," or a "he," or a persona, Stevens said, truly, that "The poem is the cry of its occasion" (404). We need, then, to ask of each poem, "Of what occasion is this the cry?" We are invited to conjecture what sort of occasion might compel a poet to say "Bad is final in this light," and to see himself as lacking vital body parts (hands, legs, even a head). What causes the cry that he senses stirring his tongue to remain captive; why does he feel rooted in ice? Or, by contrast, what occasion might provoke a poet to say that this is the wedding day of his soul (while not dignifying the experience beyond the pleasurable sprucing up bestowed in rural life by the weekly bath)? The more one becomes accustomed to the furniture of Stevens' poems, the more easily one can imagine the emotional occasion of which a certain poem is the cry. And, because a reader's understanding changes with age, different Stevens poems open themselves over time to the reader's consciousness. The red of the Stevensian sun, the green of the grass, the blue of the sky, the shapes of the clouds, the threat of the tropics and their barbaric vegetation, the desiccation of the bleak winter, the interesting cusps of the seasons (as autumn turns to winter, as winter turns to spring) – all these become familiar presences, and the poet's variations on them induce a constant refreshment.

Even though we recognize the strategic dryness of presentation motivating Stevens' use of, say, the impersonal "one," we can read the signs of intense feeling under his pronominal detachment. In "The Snow Man," for instance, although we begin with the apparent invocation of an impersonal necessity – "One must have a mind of winter" – and end with the abstract formula of "Nothing that is not there and the nothing that is" (8), we nonetheless intuit how bitterly the speaker of the poem feels the absence of the flowerings and leafings of spring, as he tries so hard, in his bare place, "not to think / Of any misery in the sound of the wind. . . ." He is so miserable, longing for his vanished deciduous forms, that he is unable to relish any of the evergreen manifestations of ornament and plenty and radiance surrounding him: "the boughs / Of the pine-trees crusted with snow; / . . . the junipers shagged with ice, / The spruces rough in the distant glitter / Of the January sun. . . ." Like the deciduous trees, the speaker is denuded: he is "nothing himself." He cannot affirm the beauty of the evergreen somethings before him; he can only try to banish his nostalgia for warmth and spring, seeing "Nothing that is not there and the nothing that is." It is a first step in stoicism; it will be some time, even after practicing the austerity of seeing nothing that is not there, before he can call what *is* there "something" rather than "nothing"; see "The Plain Sense of Things" for his achievement of that position.

If we were to conjecture the probable occasion of "The Snow Man," we might say:

There was once a land full of leafy trees and sunny warmth and spring breezes, and the man who lives there thinks these conditions to be permanent. Then the leaves begin to fall, the days become chilly, the breeze sharpens into a wind, and the temperature sinks. At first the man is shocked, and then grief-stricken, and then angry; but as the days wear on, and the leaves on the ground are scraped along by the wind, and the sun grows increasingly distant, he slowly realizes that he will have to exist within this altered world. He begins to try to quell his yearning for the past and to attempt to live immersed in the present. Then the cold deepens further, and snow falls, encrusting (to his initial dismay) the trees, while ice roughens the boughs of the evergreens. The man asks himself when he will cease to desire the remembered warmth; he realizes that to cease desiring he will have had to expel spring and summer and autumn from his mind; he will have had to acquire "a mind of winter" before he can behold the ice and listen to the wind and be immune to any thought of misery. He formulates his recognition into a universal law: "One must have a mind of winter . . . / And have been cold a long time / . . . not to think / Of any misery. . . ." But it would be a long time – and require the present self-annihilation rendering him "nothing himself" – before he could see or hear something wintry and call it beautiful.

"The Snow Man" provides all the information we need to imagine a probable scenario antecedent to its utterance. But our intuition of the mourned past and the icy present that generated the poem does not explain the strategies by which Stevens constructs his lyric. If the poem is the cry of its occasion, it has to enact, not merely state, the occasion of which it is the cry. The exhaustion of the man who has been cold a long time, the despair of the man who is stifling his misery, must be made expressive in the voicing of the poem. Stevens makes his speaker's paralysis evident in the atonality and automatic repetitiveness of the syntax: "One must have . . . To regard . . . And have been cold . . . To behold . . . and not to think . . . in the sound . . . In the sound . . . Which is the sound . . . the same wind . . . the same bare place . . . For the listener, who listens. . . ." Yet the speaker still has his eyes, which register – even as they once registered the green leafiness of spring, so desolately lost – the snow and ice and evergreen boughs and the effect of the glittering sun in the January sky. And his winter notations escape, in their "rough," "shagged," glitter[ing]" energy, the inert repetitiveness of the rest of his utterance. Nature is itself, and beautiful, in every season; and although the speaker *sees* the winter scene, he has not yet been able, by refusing nostalgia and misery, to delight in its species of color and beauty.

It is not only the two dictions of the poem that convey to us dumb misery set against snowy evergreens in the sun's dazzle. There are rhythms, too, that reflect the speaker's mind – the short lines of deprivation, the longer lines of the new winter sights, and the longest line of all, the last, which finds a strikingly immobile and tautological way to complete its predecessor: "And, nothing himself, beholds / Nothing that is not there and the nothing that is." This is plenitude, even if it is a fixed plenitude of nothings: the nothings "line up" with each other so that the beholder, the summer absence, and the winter presence all bear the same name, "nothing," as though perception has at last been aligned with circumstance. If we imagine the poem rewritten in personal terms – "I have been looking for a long time at the frost on the pine trees, watching the cold glitter of the January sun, and trying not to think of my misery at the loss of summer or the harshness of the sound of the wind; and I stand in the snow, as if turning to snow myself, no longer knowing who I am, trying not to think of the past but not able to see any value in the present" – we can see that the personal narrative does not exhibit the implacable force of Stevens' imagined law-of-wintry-being. The impersonal voicing becomes more inexorable, and more moving, than the personal narrative might have been.

The impersonal voice, when it substitutes for the lyric "I," not only helps Stevens to preserve personal reticence but also aids him in his desire to speak universally. If Stevens' first youthful conundrums concerned the loss of faith, his later ones concerned the possible relation between the singular poet and the people surrounding him. In "The Man with the Blue Guitar" he asked whether the poet could speak for the masses: "A million people on one string? / And all their manner in the thing[?]" (136). Doubting whether the voice of the idealistic poet aiming at sublimity could articulate the voice of common life and death, he decides to combine, or alternate, those two separate voices in a duet that will combine poetry and truth, Goethe's *Dichtung und Wahrheit*:

> A few final solutions, like a duet
> With the undertaker: a voice in the clouds,
>
> Another on earth, the one a voice
> Of ether, the other smelling of drink, . . .
> . . . .
> The imagined and the real, thought
>
> And the truth, Dichtung und Wahrheit, all
> Confusion solved. . . .   (145)

This solution – two voices speaking in antiphonal and antithetical equilibrium – is one never abandoned by Stevens, who always aims "by a peculiar speech to speak / The peculiar potency of the general, / To compound the imagination's Latin with / The lingua franca et jocundissima" (343) – enacting here his compound aim by naming the imagination's Latin in English and the common tongue in Latin. The device of two voices is brought to its extreme point in the late lyric "The Hermitage at the Center," in which two opposing utterances cascade down the page together. The first lines of the poem's five tercets, read in succession, make up an evocation of old age, of twice-told tales, of a tottering wind, of a dying universe. The following two lines of the tercets, read successively, make up, by contrast, a praise of the eternal freshness of maternal nature, as spring birds substitute "Their intelligible twittering / For unintelligible thought" (430). Although at first the old man who speaks "The Hermitage at the Center" (as he walks in the park near its duck pond) cannot reconcile his own imminent death with the perpetual freshness of nature, he is able to conclude by presenting simultaneously his two undeniable if antithetical intuitions; the last look of the poet will always be directed toward the inamorata-Muse and her ever-young progeny:

> And yet this end and this beginning are one,
> And one last look at the ducks is a look
> At lucent children round her in a ring.   (430)

As always, the rhythm of the speaking voice in Stevens matches its content: the poem subsides in two pentameters of which the irregular first, with its spondaic single last look, is resolved in the equable liquid cadence of the regular pentameter that follows:

```
      x  _  _  _ x  x  _  x x _
      And one last look at the ducks is a look
      x _ x  _ x  _   x _ x _
      At lucent children round her in a ring.
```

One knows how the speaker feels by the way he voices his rhythms in these two lines – the lingering regret of the last dying look is relieved by the speaker's love of the regular, perpetual, and beautiful fertility of the terrestrial muse.

But the duet of the two voices, of natural perpetuity and human mortality, is not Stevens' only way of being faithful to the antitheses of human experience. He wanted above all to represent the "central" (his preferred name for the universal): "My solitaria / Are the meditations of a central mind" (265). Often he used the universal "we" for this purpose, nowhere more successfully than in "The Auroras of Autumn," his long poem acknowledging, painfully, the inhuman indifference of nature (represented by the "ice and fire and solitude" [356] of the aurora borealis). Necessity, by its relentless law of incessant change, eventually destroys everything in which we have placed our faith, our hope, and our love. As he describes the ravages of Necessity, Stevens (using the universal "we") assumes the intensity and certainty of the voice we associate with prophecy:

> It leaps through us, through all our heavens leaps,
> Extinguishing our planets, one by one,
> Leaving, of where we were and looked, of where
>
> We knew each other and of each other thought,
> A shivering residue, chilled and foregone,
> Except for that crown and mystical cabala.   (360)

This "we" of universal emotional reference is sufficiently general to apply to everyone: who has not lost what was once thought permanent? Elsewhere, Stevens' "we" is more philosophically abstract: "these opposite things [life and death] partake of one, / At least that was the theory, when bishops' books / Resolved the world. We cannot go back to that" (195). Or, in another instance, an aesthetic generalization will employ the "we" to signify America's difference from England: "We regret we have no nightingale. / We must have the throstle on the gramophone. / Where shall we find more than derisive words?" (167). Yet all these thoughts, although phrased collectively, have deep personal reference for the poet, whether he is contemplating the destruction of his beloved "planets," or his youthful loss of faith, or his inability to participate in a nineteenth-century European tradition. Believing as he does that his readers experience the same contemporary predicaments and occasions as he, he feels confident that the cry of the poem can be felt to surge from them as well as from himself.

Stevens' "impersonal" voice is often that of a storyteller, embedding his allegorical personae in a plot. His early long poem "The Comedian as the Letter C" sketched ironically, through his persona Crispin, his journey toward personal and aesthetic fulfillment. Although he never again wrote a long narrative, he did not abandon the attractions of sequential plot and its concomitant, a narratorial voice. The Stevensian plot may have as few as two events: "Large Red Man Reading" opens as the celestial sun-poet reads from his sky-tabulae, with the result that the ghosts of human beings return from the wasteland of the stars to hear him remind them of the preciousness of the simplest human things. Or it can be a plot-of-three-locations, such as that of the planter in "Notes Toward a Supreme Fiction," with his three islands, past, present, and dreamed-of. Or it may be a plot that can have no end, such as Nanzia Nunzio's undressing before Ozymandias, who laconically refutes her claim to eventual nakedness: "the spouse, the bride / Is never naked. A fictive covering / Weaves always glistening from the heart and mind" (342). Each of these small narratives gives Stevens a new occasion from which the cry of the poem can issue, from which the heart and mind can weave an ever-glistening web.

Stevens' wish to remain "outside" his plot as narrator exists in tension with his sympathy for his lyric protagonist, and when he relaxes this tension, moving closer to his subject, the voice of the poem takes on a revealing tenderness. He says, with curious indirectness, of his planter, "An unaffected man in a negative light / Could not have borne his labor nor have died / Sighing that he should leave the banjo's twang" (340). The planter's nature was a receptive one, he lived in a positive atmosphere, he worked at his planting, and he loved the music he made – or so a positive formulation would have put it. The touching negatives of understatement here preserve Stevens' "objectivity" – but we recognize the empathy underlying them. We hear in Stevens a comparable fellow-feeling for the protagonist of the plot in "Chaos in Motion and Not in Motion" when, after a truly terrifying narrative of the speed-up of life's chaotic motion in old age ("People fall out of windows, trees tumble down, / Summer is changed to winter, the young grow old" [311]), the poet's voice breaks down in a blend of irony and sympathy:

> And Ludwig Richter, turbulent Schlemihl,
> Has lost the whole in which he was contained,
>
> Knows desire without an object of desire,
> All mind and violence and nothing felt.   (311)

Sudden tones of personal compunction such as these change Stevens from impersonal narrator to fellow-sufferer, even if one beset by wry irony.

A memorable aspect of the Stevensian voice is its love of axioms. In 1906, reading the *Pensieri* of the nineteenth-century Italian poet Giacomo Leopardi, Stevens wrote, "They are paragraphs on human nature, like Schopenhauer's psychological observations, Pascal's 'Pensées,' Rochefoucauld's 'Maximes' etc. How true they all are! I should like to have a library of such things" (*SP* 160). As his daughter comments, "[M]y father did accumulate 'a library of such things,' as well as writing his own 'Adagia'" (*SP* 160). Such brief abstract sayings, because of their impersonal voicing and their confident style, seem the condensed fruit of much thought; they struck the young Stevens as "true." The wish to say something "true" led him to perform a similar compression on his own musings (which, left to themselves, often expanded into long poems). Stevens' axiomatic voice begins early, often in a couplet, as in "Le Monocle de Mon Oncle":

> The honey of heaven may or may not come,
> But that of earth both comes and goes at once.   (12)

Much of "The Comedian as the Letter C" turns on two such axiomatic declarations, phrased scholastically: "Nota: man is the intelligence of his soil" (22) and "Nota: his soil is man's intelligence" (29). "Thirteen Ways of Looking at a Blackbird" is full of brief theses, such as the sinister one about marriage: "A man and a woman / Are one. / A man and a woman and a blackbird / Are one" (75). The Stevensian *pensées* continue down to the last poems. "An Ordinary Evening in New Haven" closes with one of the poet's most persuasive reflections:

> It is not in the premise that reality
> Is a solid. It may be a shade that traverses
> A dust, a force that traverses a shade.   (417)

Such concise assertions succeed when they seem both original and true. They declare a kind of logic ("It is not in the premise that") while remaining human in their speculative formulation ("It may be"). They are both traditional in reference ("Remember, O man, that thou art dust, and unto dust thou shalt return"; the Homeric shades in Hades) and provocative – can a shade traverse a dust, can a force traverse a shade? But how else can one express the flitting of sorrow across a face, or a will that steels itself before death?

The change that Stevens most feared – that the natural world would cease appearing symbolic of his feelings and that poetic voice would consequently forsake him – appears to have come upon him at times toward the end of his life. "The Course of a Particular" and "The Region November," two lyrics of disheartening apathy (which, like all dejection poems, contradict their own premise) appear among the posthumously published works. In the first, "the leaves cry," but although the poet would, in the past, have taken up their cry into his own sensibility and emotions, he now "holds off and merely hears the cry. / It is a busy cry, concerning someone else." This is so because "though one says that one is part of everything, / . . . being part is an exertion that declines" (460). The poet no longer has the energy to read the world as symbolic of his own nature, and his voice is threatened by silence. In "The Region November," the wind (summoned as a powerful vocal source in *Harmonium*) now works without poetic effect:

> It is hard to hear the north wind again,
> And to watch the treetops, as they sway.
>
> They sway, deeply and loudly, in an effort,
> So much less than feeling, so much less than speech,
>
> Saying and saying, the way things say
> On the level of that which is not yet knowledge. . . .   (472–73)

The effort of the trees remains below the level of intelligible utterance, just as in "A Clear Day and No Memories" – when the Stevensian dead soldiers, parents, lovers have become so remote as to be forgotten – the air "has no knowledge except of nothingness / And it flows over us without meanings" (475). It is difficult to find a voice for the inertia, apathy, and absence of consciousness that attend old age; Stevens is one of the few poets who lived long enough, and wrote late enough, to wrest audible expression from such hard desolation.

When, in this final period, Stevens finds reason to rejoice, the rejoicing often takes on a tempered tone. Deprived in so many ways of the kind of life he had longed for, Stevens came to acknowledge his lack of a true home, a domestic one surrounding the hearth, the *foyer*. He lives suspended in "a world without a foyer, / Without a remembered past, a present past, / Or a present future, hoped for in present hope" (473). In this emotional solitude, the poet is saved by what he calls "local objects":

> Little existed for him but the few things
> For which a fresh name always occurred, as if
> He wanted to make them, keep them from perishing. . . .
> . . . .
> These were that serene he had always been approaching
> As toward an absolute foyer beyond romance.   (474)

Romance ought to have provided a domestic foyer, but in that quarter Stevens had been crucially disappointed, and, after his marriage failed, he was harshly critical of his own early illusions.

He finally looked for, and found, joy where he could in his "local objects"; and these stinted but restorative moments give the late voice its unfeigned poignancy. He is reduced, in "Not Ideas About the Thing But the Thing Itself," to being joyful that he has lived through one more winter, that the "scrawny cry" he hears outside his window comes not from a delusional dream but from a real bird. This harbinger is "A chorister whose c preceded the choir" of other birds, announcing the coming of "the colossal sun, / Surrounded by its choral rings, / Still far away" (451–52). The gradual approach of certainty in the speaker's voice, felt as the poem unfolds its tentative lines, climaxes in its prophecy of "the colossal sun," only to decline in the wistful "Still far away." Bravely and yet mitigated by simile, the poem closes with the speaker's tempered claim: "It was like / A new knowledge of reality" (452).

Perhaps impoverished reality, in old age, could provide only a "scrawny cry," but Stevens was still capable of imaginative extrapolation to the iconic form of voice, issuing from a gold-feathered bird in an envisaged bronze decor "Beyond the last thought" (476). As the speaker contemplates the bird's "foreign song," he learns from it (as he tells himself in the second person) that happiness is not a product of the philosophical reason, but of the delighted senses as they contemplate "mere being":

> You know then that it is not the reason
> That makes us happy or unhappy.   (477)

He ends with five impregnable declarative sentences of descriptive fact, each depending on its glowing verb of individual being:

> The bird sings. Its feathers shine.

> The palm stands on the edge of space.

> The wind moves slowly in the branches.
> The bird's fire-fangled feathers dangle down.   (477)

These five sentences imply, by their austerity of their syntactic form, that it is purity of observation, raised to iconic height by the light of that "third planet" (695), the imagination, that is the highest good. The ecstatic quiet of seeing and hearing, of contemplating the intransitive motions of the inexhaustible iconic components of being – tree, bird, song, wind, fire – is sufficient for happiness. In this last exhibit of voice, praising the voice of plenary being, Stevens lays aside the duet with the undertaker to let us hear, beyond the last thought, a song "without human meaning, / Without human feeling" (476). The fascination of the ever-present foreign song of abstract being guarantees the perpetual antiphonal responsive voice of Stevens' poems, as they bear "Some affluence, if only half-perceived, / In the poverty of their words, / Of the planet of which they were part" (450).

NOTE

1. Alexander Pope, "Essay on Man," *The Poems of Alexander Pope*, ed. John Butt (New Haven: Yale University Press, 1963), vol. I, 218.

11

BEVERLY MAEDER

Stevens and linguistic structure

I

Wallace Stevens began writing poetry seriously around 1913 and had accumulated enough to publish his first volume, *Harmonium*, in 1923, followed by an expanded edition in 1931. During this formative time artists of all kinds were embracing new subjects such as the modern urban landscape, the depths of the unconscious, or "primitive" art objects. Avant-garde writers, artists, composers, and choreographers were experimenting widely and radically with form and style, breaking all the rules of outward decorum that were still considered the norm. Painters swapped visual beauty for jagged shapes or abandoned figurative painting for abstraction; composers burst beyond harmony into dissonance or devised new tonal systems and free forms; and poets abandoned regular stanza form for the expressive irregularities and freedom of "free verse." A curious and cultivated man, Stevens was and would remain attuned to such developments. Contrary to many of his contemporary poets, such as William Carlos Williams, T. S. Eliot, and Ezra Pound, however, and contrary to his trailblazing predecessor, Walt Whitman, Stevens earned his linguistic and poetic freedom within a certain formal discipline.

Although Stevens said he was "for" free verse,[1] in his own practice he favored shapes that were visually regular: overall structures arranged into a series of couplets, quatrains, or – as he would reconfirm in many of his later poems – tercets. It is only in *Harmonium* that he would experiment with varying the number of lines in stanzas. This he does in "Infanta Marina," for instance, where the expansion of the Infanta's thought is represented or enacted in the increase in the number of lines from two in the first stanza to six in the fourth. The middle stanza of "Domination of Black" also experiments with a self-reflexive expansion of the stanza, as five successive lines begin with anaphoric "Turning" or "Turned" (7). Such experimentation lays the foundation for later work in which Stevens would keep line numbers stable but loosen the meter and give full rein to enjambment and caesura.

In terms of prosody, while enjambment and caesura are particularly visible, what the reader "hears" is the loosening of metrical beat in favor of what Stevens would call a "voice intoning" (720). In early attempts such as "Sunday Morning" and "The Comedian as the Letter C," Stevens' lines are modeled on the five-beat iambic blank verse that has so marked the English heritage. The dictates of this heritage were merely the starting point for Stevens, however, for over the years he developed more flexible and fluid ways of creating movement, especially in his longer poems. He allowed himself ever greater deviations in the number of feet or the fall of the stress, as is obvious if we compare "Extracts from Addresses to the Academy of Fine Ideas," written in 1940, to the poems of *Harmonium*, written twenty years earlier. By *Transport to Summer* (1947), he would abandon a more or less iambic meter for a freer accentual pattern, a line in which any number of intervening unstressed syllables conjoin with irregularly placed stressed syllables to create a rhythmic flow rather than a metric pattern. Thus in "Notes Toward a Supreme Fiction" near the end of "It Must Change," we find the metrically iambic line "The lake was full of artificial things" followed by a tercet in which each successive line is freer from the iambic foot: "Like a page of music, like an upper air, / Like a momentary color, in which swans / Were seraphs, were saints, were changing essences" (343). Of course, the enjambment between the last two lines quoted also enacts a refusal to repeat the strict metrical beat of the "artificial things" line, while it rhythmically illustrates "momentary color" and "changing essences." Although Stevens took advantage of the modernist tendency to create significant shape by caesura and enjambment, his development of accentual rhythm that varies, expands and contracts a basic five-stress line or sometimes a tetrameter (as in "The Man with the Blue Guitar," for instance), shows how a modern poet can steer a middle course between "free verse" (as in E. E. Cummings or Williams) and the metrical symmetries of English poetry.

II

Consequential as these elements of form are, Stevens' main formal innovations – and the ones that cause bafflement to the first-time reader – have more to do with the way he brings language as his very *materia poetica* into focus. How can we understand the sound and the sense of the "junk-shop, / Full of javelins and old fire-balls" and the "rigid room" (197) of the star-gazing speaker in "Dezembrum"? In "The Idea of Order at Key West," how can we understand the intricate grammatical and spatial relationship set up in "And when she sang, the sea, / Whatever self it had, became the self / That was her song" (106)? Whether caustically iconoclastic or epistemologically speculative, such poems make us aware of a certain linguistic and poetic self-consciousness. "Dezembrum" suggests that we should explore the semantic side of Stevens' poetry, the word choices he makes and the metaphors he uses. These are what seem to connect his poetry to things and thoughts in the world. On the other hand, "The Idea of Order at Key West" impels us to look at how his very grammar and syntax work to produce a sequential ongoingness that is the hallmark of Stevens' poetic practice. These are what linguists call the paradigmatic or vertical axis of word choice, on the one hand, and the syntagmatic or horizontal axis of syntax or word order, on the other. Of course, they cannot exist separately any more than space can be said to exist without time, or vice versa. Indeed, in what follows, a special place will be reserved for words in English that are weak in semantic content but that bind other words and parts of sentences together in special ways. These I will call "function words," such as prepositions, modal verbs, and certain usages of the verb *to be*, words that are necessary to syntax but do not seem to add sense. They are the very stuff of the ongoing development of many poems, but they are also central to the poems' tentative, speculative edge.

Stevens' early poem "The Apostrophe to Vincentine" can be read as a parable of how a poem's creative process is generated by the materiality of its words, just as some modern painting can stress originating in the visible brush strokes or blotches of paint on bare canvas. Vincentine is said to have been "figured" by the speaker (stanza I), perhaps imagined in the abstract or calculated as by arithmetic. Yet the story conveyed in the poem tells us, on the contrary, that she never existed as an abstract idea, since her first existence lies in the very *figure*/metaphor represented by the speaker-painter. Vincentine goes through four phases, one in each stanza. She is first "nameless" and "nude" on a background of color and placed between the heavens and the earth (recalling the Creation according to Genesis) (I). Once become "flesh," she is clothed metaphorically in a dress of "whited green" (II). Taking liberty with grammatical case, Stevens adapts the adjective or noun "white" as a verbal past participle "whited," making explicit the metaphor of the painter as poet – the painter mixing one pigment with another, the poet combining words. In stanza III Vincentine comes "walking" (twice), then "talking" (once). These moments of humanization and autonomy are set off by rhyme and distinctive line length. Stanza IV recounts the artist-creator's moment of empathy and the transforming vision he has of her, as his consciousness expands into "Illimitable spheres of you" (42–43) before the final apostrophe to the inspiring figure.

The poem's form demonstrates that Vincentine's autonomy is ostensibly, even ostentatiously, produced by the poet's self-conscious pattern of words. For instance, although Vincentine is said to be "nameless" (I), her name precedes the story of her creation in the title. From a common sense point of view, this is because her story is told in retrospect, after her name is known. But on the level of the poem's material words or discourse, it is the sound of the signifier "Vincentine" that provides the poet with the material for his rhymes – "between," "lean," "clean," "green," in twelve lines out of twenty-eight. More important, the speaker enacts the step-by-step transformation of the title's "Heavenly Vincentine" (42) from stanza I to the apotheosis of "Turned heavenly, heavenly Vincentine" (43) of the final line. The statement that the creature is "Turned" introduces the literal representation of the name apostrophized in stanza I, but now semantically fulfilled and syntactically complicated by a quasi-tautology – saying that heavenly Vincentine is heavenly. Yet the poem fulfills the Latin etymology of Vincentine's name: *vincere*, to win or earn victory in the poet-painter's wonder at his own work. The parable of the poem alerts us as to how a word-name such as "Vincentine" can set off sound patterns, self-reflexively enact an etymology, and acquire different syntactic functions as the poet moves the word and relates others to it from one stanza to the next. They show Stevens taking a hard look at words themselves and taking cues from the acoustic and visual materiality of words, not just from their denotation and connotation.

The most audible manifestations of Stevens' emphasis on the material of language can be found in the rambunctious experimentations that he deploys in his first book, *Harmonium*. Here, in his most biting iconoclastic mood, Stevens sometimes uses onomatopoeia and dissonance as a means of critique, as when he writes in "The Doctor of Geneva" of the bells that "clanked and sprang / In an unburgherly apocalypse" (19). But more often he weaves his delight in sound into a celebratory gesture. In two of his early lighthearted poems he uses the signifier – the sound as well as the visible look of the word – of "Oklahoma" to introduce not only the pleasure of being and moving but also the pleasure of saying (for the speaker) and hearing (for the reader) sound. Thus in "Life Is Motion" Bonnie and Josie emit a preverbal "'Ohoyaho, / Ohoo' . . ." in celebration of "flesh and air" (65) and the joy of bodily movement. In a second Oklahoma poem, "Earthy Anecdote," onomatopoeia enacts the bucks' repeated "clattering" and "swerv[ing]" (3), celebrating bodily movement and the movement of language, while the noise the poem's visual form makes "swerves" self-reflexively. Such sound-play is rarely an isolated point but contributes to a poem's ongoing structure, much as in "Ploughing on Sunday" when the onomatopoetic "Tum-ti-tum" (16) picks up the repeated /t/ of the cock's "tail" to carry forward a movement that plays with the changing functions of wind, rain, and sun in a secularized universe. Nor would Stevens forget these playful, ear-opening and eye-arresting experiments in his poetry of the 1930s and even 1940s, particularly in self-referential poems that allude to the poet's own work with "lingua franca et jocundissima" (343).

Stevens also focuses on his language as *materia poetica* when he makes baffling semantic choices. Among these are words that are made strange by deviating from their normal grammatical usage, such as the description of "the paltry nude" who "scuds the glitters" and goes her way "in the scurry and water-shine" (4–5). *Harmonium* is a gold mine of both playful and ironic uses of foreign words, hybrid words, or exotic-sounding ones: "Barque of phosphor" (18); a "black barouche" (48); a "flambeaued manner" (62); "equipage" (76); "Vocalissimus" (77); and titles such as "Cy Est Pourtraicte, Madame Ste Ursule, et Les Unze Mille Vierges," the body of which creates a three-way contrast among the title's medieval bookishness, the pseudo-innocence of the poem's language about the scene described, and the implicitly sexual connotation of the "quiver" that is "not writ / In any book" (17). Stevens would later take some distance from the exotic flourishes he included in his early poems, perhaps precisely because they seemed too much akin to *fin-de-siècle* dandyism or a facile mode of parodic critique. Indeed, in his 1949 "An Ordinary Evening in New Haven," the exotic-sounding "black cassimere" seems a gentle critique of his past, one that is combined here with the significant "effete green" (411). This does not detract, however, from the fact that inventions and exoticisms continue to strew the titles and paths of his poems, though with less frequency, and that they are more than playful tricks of prestidigitation.

Particularly instructive here is Stevens' continued use of French words. Stevens read French all his life, copied excerpts from French texts into his own commonplace books, and corresponded with Parisian book and art dealers who wrote to Stevens in French (though Stevens replied in English). French words epitomize a double function that exotic words have in his work. On the one hand, as Stevens wrote to a friend in 1953, using French brought him "pleasure" (L 792). That pleasure certainly includes Stevens' attachment to French literature and culture, from Voltaire to symbolist poetry, from Crispin-Candide to Baudelaire's "semblables" (258–61) who recur satirically in "Dutch Graves in Bucks County." But the primary pleasure for the reader, as it was for Stevens, is the sensuous pleasure of the very sounds they contribute to individual poems. Listen to how "English" is enriched by the nasal play of "Le Monocle de Mon Oncle" or the new diphthong in "grisaille" (gray, overcast weather) in "Add This to

Rhetoric." "[A]s you paint, the clouds, / Grisaille, impearled, profound" (182) also points to a second effect French and other foreign words have in Stevens' repertory. The defamiliarizing French word for grayness and gray weather then spawns a strange "native" word, "impearled," to add luster to the painting (a self-referential metaphor, of course, for poetry too). In Stevens' repertory of *materia poetica*, the exotic term brings home the distinction the poem makes between two material worlds: the given world of nature, the one that "merely grows," on the one hand; and the made world of art, artifice, and language, the one that "is posed" (182), on the other. *Homo faber* paints with "grisaille" and thus heightens our perception of how language itself is not only a purveyor of sensuous pleasure but also a shaper of new vision.

Stevens' early robust experiments with foregrounding language as a thing itself as well as a vehicle also include violent shifts in register, especially characteristic of some of *Harmonium*'s most ironic poems. The inner clash of "concupiscent curds" in "The Emperor of Ice-Cream" and the conflict between the plain language of the "dresser of deal" and "horny feet" and the ponderous, quasi-biblical phrasing of "Let the lamp afix its beam" (50) create an instability of tone that may baffle the reader, just as it may show an uncertainty about how to honor the dead in a now godless world. In "A High-Toned Old Christian Woman" the noble architectural metaphors of church "nave" and "peristyle" are quickly superseded by "Squiggling like saxophones" and other jazzified instances of a "jovial hullabaloo among the spheres" (47). Here the joy of the poet's language joins in an attack on the woman of the title, with the stated aim of making her "wince." In an example such as "Tea at the Palaz of Hoon," an ironic tonal discrepancy occurs between the sounds of the title's haunting "Hoon" in his Spanish "palaz" and the pompousness of Hoon's own "Not less because in purple I descended" (51). Word choice in these cases means less the search for the right word or *le mot juste* than the experimental combination of surprising signifiers, whose strangeness of sound, tone, register, and connotation combine to draw attention to, and stimulate pleasure in, the poem's constructedness or artifice.

III

At the heart of Stevens' work with word-worlds was his perception, as he wrote in "The Pure Good of Theory," that "It is never the thing but the version of the thing" (292). That "It" is a "version" of a thing is underscored by the salience of the linguistic madeness of Stevens' poems in the examples we have just looked at. It is also implicit in Stevens' work with metaphor. Metaphor, according to Aristotle's *Poetics*, establishes relationships between things that "resemble" each other. In the same family we can include simile, with its explicit "like" or "as." In Stevens' understanding of what a poet has to do, he reserved a special place for metaphor. "It is only au pays de la métaphore / Qu'on est poète" (920) – it is only in the land of metaphor that one is a poet, he wrote in a notebook. Besides giving several lectures that had metaphor at their center (most collected in *The Necessary Angel*), Stevens made metaphor the title or stated theme of eighteen poems in his *Collected Poems*. In most of Stevens' poems, things resemble each other only partially and provisionally.

Metaphors are closely linked to our ways of understanding the world. The metaphor of the Garden of Eden as a place of fulfillment prefiguring paradise is one of the most potent metaphors in this respect, as is the romantic metaphor of nature as a receptacle for the divine spirit that infuses all things. Stevens felt that the belief systems encompassing these tropes had become defunct, but their powerful influence on his thought and writing is evident. As we have just seen, inherited metaphors for a central, transcendent force enter Stevens' early work sometimes to be simply ironized, as in "A High-Toned Old Christian Woman." But if metaphor is necessary, and if the particular metaphors of his own culture pervade the language he works with, and are indeed imbricated in it, then how can a poet go beyond irony and free himself from these "wormy metaphors" (131)?

A degree of poetic freedom can come from relativizing individual metaphors. "Sunday Morning," for instance, scatters metaphors related to the belief in paradise throughout the poem: the sepulcher in Palestine, death as the "mother of beauty," the garden "where ripe fruit never falls," a divine source as the object of orgiastic worship, a vision of "casual flocks of pigeons" sinking "on extended wings" (55–56). Critics have agreed to disagree about the hierarchy of the metaphors in this poem. The fuzzy boundaries between the speakers and the weakness of the narrative architecture make it difficult to say whether any of these images takes priority over the others and whether any one can displace our traditional trope of paradise. The trope is situated in a new relativizing context that avoids confirming any given alternative.

A different kind of displacement can be seen in a late poem "The River of Rivers in Connecticut." Here the elderly poet revisits the classical metaphor of Stygia and the "last" river that the dead must cross to reach it. The Styx is at first a foil against which the poet describes another river, on "this side of Stygia." The river of the living here and now is said to be "fateful," like the Styx, yet, unlike the Styx, its banks are inhabited by "no shadow" and the river itself is "Flashing and flashing in the sun" (451). In the second half of the poem, Stevens' speaker casts off explicit comparisons and wrests more freedom for his own inventiveness, primarily by testing out multifarious general epithets, many of which are metaphorical. Calling his poetic river of life an "unnamed flowing" relates the river only tangentially to the (unnamed) Styx of the first stanzas; the final exhortation to "Call it" "The river that flows nowhere, like a sea" (451) frees it entirely from the Styx or so greatly exceeds the Underworld metaphor that the Styx becomes irrelevant. As Stevens' speaking voice is emboldened by images of "vigor" and even by the internal contradiction of "flowing" yet flowing "nowhere" that he attributes to the river, the new life-sustaining "River of Rivers" becomes a metaphorical creation on its own, generated by, yet free from, the originary metaphor.

As may be clear by now, the hallmark of Stevens' poetic use of metaphor is the transforming process he submits metaphors to. An opening metaphor is a catalyst, like the "jar in Tennessee" (60) in "Anecdote of the Jar." It sets off an ordering movement in the wilderness. It can be, and often is, related to an "old" metaphor, such as the Styx or Keats's Grecian urn here, for instance. But we find Stevens' language freshened by the work and wordplay he does with it in the course of the poem as the jar becomes "Like nothing else in Tennessee" (61). "Nomad Exquisite" (note the defamiliarizing combination in this title) provides us with an interesting example. Its topos of prolific, fertile tropical nature – the "dew of Florida" – might be worked in a Coleridgean or Wordsworthian vein as a metaphor (or perhaps synecdoche, the part for the whole) for the Creator or a primal creative force as well as for poetic inspiration itself. However, the "I" observer here is not necessarily involved in the scene as "the beholder." Moreover, this "beholder" is put into a surprising parallel with the "eye of the young alligator" by a construction formed by "As . . . As," while the speaker stands out in the final couplet's "So, in me, come flinging / Forms, flakes, and the flakes of flames" (77). In a sense, it is the tension produced by the leap of imagination through another beholder and the "young alligator" that produces a vivified linguistic movement. In addition, the careful construction with "As . . . As . . . So" could signify cause and effect, comparison, or simultaneity, or all at the same time, as would be typical of Stevens' deftly articulated ambiguities, so that the speaker seems to create a slight but perceptible distance between the romantic cluster of metaphors of poetic inspiration and his own creation. Finally, his celebration in "Forms, flames, and the flakes of flames" is less an intelligible "hymn" than a play with alliteration (/f/ and /fl/) and synesthetic association (shape, color, heat, cold).

If these shifts seem infinitesimal, the asymmetries and even disruptions that exist among metaphors and variants of metaphors in a Stevens poem can also lead to a series that eludes synthesis. In a minor way, "Asides on the Oboe" eludes any unified version of the "impossible possible philosophers' man" (226), even after a long variation. He is a reflection of ourselves, "responsive / As a mirror," yet "a mirror with a voice," dictating a higher law, replacing outworn images of divinity; he is "the glass man, without external reference," yet connected to the (World War II) experience of "death and war" (227). Or in "Crude Foyer," the succession of word-images relating the "foyer" (270), the mind, and the eye seems to fashion and refashion the beginning metaphor without coming to a definitive form. As Stevens writes in one of his epigrammatic "Adagia" (and varied in "Man Carrying Thing"), "Poetry must resist the intelligence almost successfully" (910).

The key notion here is that of a process of permutation that Stevens builds into his poetic structure. As we have just seen, such variation often exists in a dispersed manner across a given poem, often transited by careful but ambiguous grammatical structures. These structures can be involuted, particularly when Stevens piles up his prepositions: *in, on, for, of.* They can also foreground linearity, however, as when they concentrate metaphors in rapid juxtaposition or apposition of individual words, phrases, or sentences. "The Motive for Metaphor" is a showcase for the apposition of metaphors on large and small scales. A retrospective poem, the first three stanzas establish seasonal metaphors of spring and fall and approximations and attenuations for the "half dead" self surrounded by "quarter-things," all undecided, yet predictable. The major shift comes with the phrase "Desiring the exhilarations of changes," followed by a simple colon. The grammatically ambiguous appositional phrase it introduces seems almost to enact itself. This is "the motive for metaphor." This very phrase introduces more rapid apposition and transforms the shape and content of the poem. Synecdoches for the smithy at his forge are piled up on the principle of association and graded from longer to shorter expressions, finally apposing mere adjectives to each other in the last line's "vital, arrogant, fatal, dominant X" (257). The energy takes on an impulsive, even violent edge not only because the variations are abrupt, but also because expressions are broken by enjambment ("the hammer / Of red and blue") or punctuated by dashes (" – / Steel against intimation – the sharp flash" [257]) to create a disjointed movement of the hammer and the poet's words.

The permutations within "the vital, arrogant, fatal, dominant X" have numerous potential senses and effects. They may ironically fulfill the "changes" previously announced, cross out what precedes, complement but not quite finish the series of "the ABC of being," stand on the edge of a new series XYZ, among other things. In the shifts from "vital" to "fatal" and from "arrogant" to "dominant," the acoustic and visual materiality of the rhyming syllables propulses the semantic invention on through life and death to a final struggle. But the "X" is in some ways a new nameless avatar for the poet's desire or "motive." Because of the syntax of apposition, especially the articulation around the colon, it is not clear whether the poem produces any proposition "about" metaphor or "about" the poet, the two ostensible subjects of the poem. Instability of definition seems to belong to the grammatically energetic, ongoing momentum, the rhythmic fiber of the poem. In compressed form, "The Motive for Metaphor" typifies Stevens' propensity, especially in his longer poems, to modulate metaphors toward a conclusion that is, after all, inconclusive and tentative.

IV

The inconclusiveness of Stevens' metaphoric developments, then, is the outcome not only of changing semantic content but also of highly self-conscious methods of syntactic construction. As one of Stevens' titles says, "Someone Puts a Pineapple Together," and this putting together in Stevens' poetry is done with characteristic function words and sentence shapers. Indeed, his poems are exceptionally full of such relatively "empty" usages and words. Worth mentioning here are the verb *to seem*; similes with *like* or *as*; the hypothetical *as if*; the modal *might*; the conditional and future in the past *would*; sentence fragments; optatives (desires) and questions; and numerous different usages of the verb *to be*. Rather than revealing poor craftsmanship or a dilution of sense, such a signature style exposes the subtlety of the functional core of language. As Helen Vendler was one of the first to point out,[2] these words and usages situate Stevens' poems in the realm of possibilities and potentialities rather than certainty.

"Description Without Place," for instance, seems to begin by integrating subjective perception into a statement of general truth: "It is possible that *to seem* – it is to be, / As the sun is something *seeming* and it is" (296; emphasis added). What the equation between being and seeming will generate is a meditation on how the work of description of all sorts also creates this seeming, which is our knowledge of the world, how we think it might be. A more sensuous Stevens, however, insists on how something looks to an observer or, more generally, how it appears to him. Similes and the verb *to seem* can take on their strongest semantic senses then. In "Not Ideas About the Thing But the Thing Itself," the combination of *seeming* and simile stresses an initial hesitation about a sensorial stimulus, a bird's cry, that imbues the poem's occasion. A bird's cry at dawn could be taken for granted, if the poem did not say that the "scrawny cry from outside / *Seemed like* a sound in his mind" (451; emphasis added). Mental deductions follow until they finally come to rest in an expanded metaphor of the bird as "chorister." The closing simile comes to override the specifics of the occasion: "It was *like* / A new knowledge of reality" (452; emphasis added). The "like" here, along with the earlier "Seemed," foregrounds how experience lies in impressions and approximations, not in empirical reality. What is more, in this closing poem to *Collected Poems*, as in many earlier poems, the contingency of the life of the senses does not prevent the poet from savoring the approximations he unfurls. Rather, *seeming* and simile allow him to revel in the very process of approaching possible revelation through language, despite the transitoriness any revelation implies.

Seemingly conclusive and definitive affirmations are almost always transitory since, in Stevens' world, flux is the condition of the world and of the human being in it. "The Poems of Our Climate" encapsulates our dissatisfaction with forms of conclusiveness in the image of "the never-resting mind" (179). In this sense, Stevens' poetry is often speculative and foregrounds thought as a process, a process in which *as if*, *might*, and *would* can alert us to an imaginative and intellectual activity that is mulling over fragments or alternatives in a hypothetical mode. Thus, "It is as if / We had come to an end of the imagination" (428), the main hypothesis of "The Plain Sense of Things," is a preliminary to embracing its own contradiction and the series of beautiful images that follow. Stevens' most insistent use of *as if*, "Study of Images II," similarly doubts poetry's ability to achieve what it calls the "right joining" of things and sounds and thought. The poem laments that it is "As if, as if, as if the disparate halves / Of things were waiting in a betrothal known / To none" (396). Yet this lament supersedes the misshapened images of the poem's opening with a series of – albeit idealized and more abstract – metaphors for harmony. Such structures of hypothesis, then, may open the way for demonstrations of poetic power, images, and permutations that reaffirm poetry's own presence, yet without reaching a final assertion. The conditional or future in the past *would* can also prepare for an open end. "Waving Adieu, Adieu, Adieu" presents a series of static and invalid metaphors for dying in a "world without heaven" (104) with a heavily insistent *would*; they are only obliquely counterpointed at the end. In a late poem, "The Poem That Took the Place of a Mountain," the elderly poet thinks back over his poetic career as one in which he looked for "the outlook that *would* be right, / Where he *would* be complete in an unexplained completion" (435; emphasis added). Symptomatically, it remains unsaid what the "outlook," later figured as the "exact rock," actually brought him. Any one defining version, we now realize, would be inadequate to the changing nature of one's perspective, one's needs, and one's desires. Intellectually, a final assertion would miss the very point of speculation, which seems to consist of permutational movement rather than its outcome.

Indeed, the end of a Stevens poem seems to be primarily a material and formal necessity, the end of writing on the finite page. The end of "Thinking of a Relation Between the Images of Metaphors" implies this most provocatively. The several "variation[s]" on the dove and the fisherman lead up to the performative "state the disclosure." Its final form is expressed with *might* (three times) and *would*, and ends: "The fisherman *might* be the single man / In whose breast, the dove, alighting, *would* grow still" (310; emphasis added). This reduction of multiplicity to singleness and separateness to union states a hypothetical possibility, not a final definition. Moreover, the stillness of ceasing to sing is a corollary to coming to the end of the poem, the poem's cessation, while the hypothetical proposal for singleness and union leads the reader to see any final stillness as a temporary and transitory pause in the movement of desire. A Stevens poem, then, provides a finite form for the embodiment of infinite becoming.

There are also three grammatical constructions that prevent the very material of his speculations from coalescing into definitive statements: the sentence fragment, the optative mode of wish or volition, and the question. Although several of the short poems touched on above include these strategies, it is in the longer poems that we see them most clearly contributing to the sense of temporariness that marks Stevens' poetry. Cantos XVIII to XXI from "The Man with the Blue Guitar" provide apt examples, especially as this long poem's raison d'être is to try out variations or improvisations on its theme, which is the guitar player's resistance to playing "things as they are" (135). Canto XVIII begins with a noun clause, "A dream (to call it a dream) in which / I can believe" (143), but fails to become or generate a main predicate. The dream has no affirmed status or "existence" in itself but is simply posed as an object of speculative analogies. In a converse manner, canto XIX begins with what looks like a form of a subordinate clause, "That I may reduce the monster to / Myself" (143), but this can also be read as an optative, a statement of volition: may I reduce the monster. This is also, then, an utterance that is purely speculative, the expression of a desire that can take only speculative shape. Canto XX opens with two questions about life and belief. Although this canto does not pursue the questioning to the end, as canto XV does, nonetheless the questions it formulates remain open, since the only response is the conditional and grammatically strange "believe would be a friend" (144). Canto XXI consists of two apposed noun phrases, of which the first is a brief "A substitute for all the gods" (144), the second a longer one just as incomplete. Such utterances constitute stages of syntactic development that never complete themselves as propositions. In the context of the whole poem, they perform moments of incompletion that attune us to other ways that the poem performs an ongoing and intellectually interminable process.

When we think of syntax in Stevens' poetry we may think primarily, however, of the pervasiveness of the polymorphous verb *to be*. As the linguist Emile Benveniste pointed out decades ago,[3] the formal linguistic entity *to be* has numerous different usages in Indo-European languages, only a few of which state being or existence. Of course, the verb *to be* can be used to express absolute existence, as when you say something just "is," or "there is" something. This is what Stevens at first seems to say at the end of "The Snow Man," in which a hypothetical observer "beholds / Nothing that *is* not there and the nothing that *is*" (8; emphasis added). As it has frequently been pointed out, even "nothing" is a something for the verb "is" to state existence about. However, even this cannot be affirmed, for the final "nothing that is" potentially (and simultaneously) could be a shorthand for "the nothing that is there" – "there" forming a locative expression for that particular place of wind and leaves, beheld by that particular observer, and self-referentially "there" in this particular poem's preceding words. So in its undecidableness, Stevens' poem seems to question the stability, solidity, and reference of existential statements even while it seems to be saying that something "is." The clause *it is* (or *it was*) occurs more frequently in Stevens than any other combination derived from *to be*. Working as building blocks in poems, sentences with *it is* may state sheer existence, but as a momentary passage. This is particularly clear in "The Latest Freed Man," in which the last twenty lines of the poem make seven statements beginning with "It was," with all but one anaphorically at the beginning of a line. The "It" has no actual referent but merely serves to introduce the verb and its complement, as in "It was everything being more real," "It was everything bulging and blazing and big in itself" (187). The repetition of "It was" puts the poem on a metonymical path, where one object leads to another, all contributing to the speaker's gradual awakening as sunlight floods his room. The fullness of the awareness of the "freed man" ends with "the chairs," but the list of new objects is potentially all-encompassing. Perception and zest for life pervade such statements, always as part of a process. As is the case of some longer poems that foreground "it is" and "it was," such statements mark moments of a process of tentative speculation.

Within Stevens' repertory of forms of *to be*, the shiftier usages of *to be* are legion, and many of them serve the tentativeness of Stevens' poetic form, either within individual sentences or in short sequences. These include most notably "A *is* B" (the copula, A = B, with B as a noun or attribute); or "*there are* X somewhere" (actually a locative or "existence" situated in a place). Such seemingly innocuous usages stand out in the loosely connected "Thirteen Ways of Looking at a Blackbird," which uses or even focuses on *to be* in seven of its thirteen variations on the blackbird. The blackbird is pictured in a different situation and articulated in a different grammatical context in each fragment. These variations give us glimpses of winter landscapes (cantos I, VI, and XIII), but also of a geometrical world turned metaphysical when the blackbird "mark[s] the edge / Of one of many circles" (76), or of a train ride turned fairy tale in which a "glass coach" becomes an "equipage" (76), among other situations. The framing cantos I to IV and XIII contain usages prevalent in the Stevens corpus that seem to create stilled pictures or define a state of things, while playing with their very madeness as art. Indeed, Stevens draws attention to how artificial or stunningly functional they are through a whole series of tricks. The impression of functionality is cumulative, but three examples from these framing cantos will give the idea (emphasis added):

1. "The only moving thing / *Was* the eye of the blackbird" (74). This initial copular equation plays with the pun on "moving" as signifying movement and emotion, the paradox that the bird's eyes do not move, and the implicit contrast between the movement evoked and the staticity of both the mountain scene and the verb "was." This play is emphasized later in the spurious deduction, "The river *is* moving. / The blackbird must *be* flying" (76), where *is* enters into a new relation with "moving" as the auxiliary for the present continuous tense.
2. "A man and a woman / *Are* one. / A man and a woman and a blackbird / *Are* one" (75) hints at the mystery inherent in the union between two human beings, while it also playfully foregrounds the potential for syllogisms (A *is* B, B *is* C, therefore A *is* C) to say nonsense. At the same time, the underscoring of "are" in this context also exemplifies the function – more than the "meaning" – of *to be* as the stuff of linkage and relation in the poem's development. (Indeed, the philosopher Jacques Derrida would claim that the copula cannot state existence but can only establish linguistic relations.[4])
3. "It *was* evening. . . . / It *was* snowing / And it *was* going to snow" (76) accumulates a copular description with "was" as an auxiliary for past and future tense. Here we find Stevens punning on the function word itself and demonstrating its – and perhaps his – versatility.

From on the ground, as it were, and from a bird's-eye view, the *being* of the framing cantos reveals the verb *to be* as the basic stuff for constructing images and then moving on, as one statement outdistances another.

V

Stevens' style creates a seamless whole with his subject. The "subject" itself is a double one. On the one hand, it is the shifting world of the senses and of what we see, of the outward world in all its banality and potential for surprise. Along with this it is the blundering spirit, the "never-resting mind," dissatisfied with the common versions of the world unseen and resistant to the common visions of public events. On the other hand, Stevens himself claimed that his subject was poetry. He resisted pressures made on poets to shape their poetry to fit the demands of the era and to adopt a more accessible and, at times, more politically engaged language. The strategies he developed in his formal expression demonstrate his commitment to linguistic freedom and are discernible in his loosening of meter within the bounds of stanzaic form; his expansion of English semantics, metaphors, and word-combination; and his syntactic devices for keeping possibility open. "Poetry constantly requires a new relation" (914). That new relation requires constant process and transformation through the creative work of the language of poetry.

NOTES

1. Wallace Stevens, "Letters to Ferdinand Reyher," ed. Holly Stevens, *Hudson Review* 44 (1991): 390.
2. Helen Vendler, *On Extended Wings: Wallace Stevens' Longer Poems* (Cambridge: Harvard University Press, 1969); "The Qualified Assertions of Wallace Stevens," *The Act of the Mind: Essays on the Poetry of Wallace Stevens,* ed. Roy Harvey Pearce and J. Hillis Miller (Baltimore: Johns Hopkins Press, 1965), 163–78.
3. Emile Benveniste, "The Linguistic Functions of 'To Be' and 'To Have'" (1960), *Problems in General Linguistics,* trans. Mary Elizabeth Meek (Coral Gables: University of Miami Press, 1966), 163–80.
4. Jacques Derrida, "The Supplement of Copula: Philosophy before Linguistics," *Textual Strategies: Perspectives in Post-Structuralist Criticism,* ed. Josué V. Harari (Ithaca: Cornell University Press, 1979), 82–120.

12

BONNIE COSTELLO

Stevens and painting

Migratory passings to and fro

Wallace Stevens felt profoundly the need for the arts in a time of faltering faiths. In his 1951 lecture at the Museum of Modern Art in New York, he says: "The paramount relation between poetry and painting today, between modern man and modern art is simply this: that in an age in which disbelief is so profoundly prevalent or, if not disbelief, indifference to questions of belief, poetry and painting, and the arts in general, are, in their measure, a compensation for what has been lost" (748). The arts preserve and renew our humanity by bringing feeling to experience and by creating a record of "what we felt / At what we saw" (128). They offer a form of resistance to contemporary upheaval, not an escape, but a way of collecting ourselves and pressing back with expressive orders. Painting in particular – with its direct appeal to the eye and its palpable being in the world, with its visible history of orders formed and reformed – embodied Stevens' sense of this project: to confirm our humanity through imaginative response to reality. Throughout his career Stevens contemplated the relation between poetry and painting; he saw in this relation not only a common artistic aim, but also a paradigm for an ultimate relation: "The world about us would be desolate except for the world within us. There is the same interchange between these two worlds that there is between one art and another, migratory passings to and fro, quickenings, Promethean liberations and discoveries" (747).

As this remark suggests, Stevens' relation to painting was not fixed or singular; movements in painting and the experience of particular works prompted his poetry in a variety of ways. Certain artists stimulated Stevens' imagination, and their names turn up in letters, essays, and even poems. He liked the classicism of Claude Lorrain, the silvery atmosphere of Jean-Baptiste Camille Corot, the struggle for realization in Paul Cézanne, the decreative energy of Pablo Picasso, the comic-tragic disposition of Paul Klee, the virility of Pierre Tal-Coat. Critics have found links between Stevens' poetry and artistic movements such as impressionism, symbolism, cubism, and even surrealism and abstract expressionism. But as Stevens writes: "The subject of modern relations [between poetry and painting] is best to be approached as a whole" (748) in terms of the imagination as a power that might replace the power of faith.

From New Jersey epicurean to American modernist

For the young bachelor Stevens, wandering galleries or enjoying the pleasures of nature on his weekends away from the law office, pictures were worlds and the world conveyed itself as a picture. He left a record of his aesthetic sensibility in journal entries such as this one of February 27, 1906, which responds to works of American impressionism and to Corot, the master of the Barbizon school of painting in France:

> Saw a little [Jean Charles] Cazin at the American Art Gallery to-day called "Departure of Night," that I liked: a step or two of road, a roadside house of white, a few trees and just the sky-full of *clair d'aube* – with three stars, as I remember. He had caught even in so small a painting the abandoned air of the world at that hour, that is, abandoned of humans. If there had been a light in the house – it would have been quite different. One could imagine the dewy air and the quiet. There was an [Jozef] Israels that I thought well of: a girl knitting by the sea. I liked her bare feet + the ordinary sand + the ordinary water. But what I liked best was that she was not dreaming. There was no suggestion even of that trite sorrow. It was a capital point – exquisite prose instead of dreary poetry. It was as if she had confidence in the ordinary sand + the ordinary water. And there was a gray-green Corot. One noticed, incuriously, an inch of enamored man and an inch of fond woman in the foreground, and one approved. Fortunate creatures to be wandering so sweetly in Corot!
>
> (L 88–89)

These impressions carried over so that his experiences of the landscape itself appeared to be marked by the painter's brush: "A half-misty, [Henri] Fantin-La Tourish night" (L 92), begins another entry of the same year, comparing the effects of nature to those of the nineteenth-century impressionist. This habit of imagining the world in aesthetic and compositional terms was lifelong. In 1949, a window in a fruit shop becomes the locus of a still life: "beauteous plums, peaches like Swedish blondes, pears that made you think of Rubens and the first grapes pungent through the glass" (L 647).

Stevens worried in the early days that he might be but a "New Jersey Epicurean" (L 87), a mere weekend consumer of the art world, and certainly his attraction to the arts was at first more about daydreaming and the indulgence of the senses than about any rigorous intellectual engagement

with painting's challenge to conventional reality. But modernism was underway, with the visual arts in the lead, and Stevens would not only partake
of, but also join in, its "Promethean liberations and discoveries." In 1913,
New York City's "Armory Show" brought together a broad array of innovative work from Europe, generating shock in the popular media but excitement
in the arts community. At Harvard, Stevens had met Walter Arensberg, whose
passion for collecting avant-garde works would later bring Stevens in touch
with such innovators as Albert Gleizes, practitioner and apologist for cubism,
and Marcel Duchamp, Dadaist anti-master of found art and conceptual art.
Throughout his life Stevens made regular stops at the Metropolitan Museum
of Art, the Museum of Modern Art, and various galleries in New York. When
Stevens settled in Hartford, he would reside just a few blocks from the
Wadsworth Atheneum which, under the directorship of A. Everett (Chick)
Austin, would bring new art from abroad and support innovative work at
home (the museum produced the plays of Gertrude Stein, for instance, and
was the first to buy work by Joseph Cornell). By the 1940s, Stevens had begun
collecting art himself, with a strong preference for French work (part of his
broader love for French culture). He corresponded with the Paris art dealer
Paule Vidal, who supplied him with suitable items, though, as he lamented to
her, "I have a taste for [Georges] Braque and a purse for [Camille] Bombois"
(L 545). (He in fact did acquire a small drawing by Braque.) Stevens also
subscribed to several art journals, read widely in art criticism, theory, and
biography, and even wrote a few essays for exhibition catalogues.

Clearly Stevens' interest in the visual arts went well beyond an epicure's,
and it profoundly shaped his poetry. His art-historical frame of reference
is broad: masters of Italian Renaissance art, of Dutch genre painting, and
French classicism and romanticism all find mention in Stevens' work. But
"he has not / To go to the Louvre to behold himself," Stevens reminds us in
"Prelude to Objects." The imperative of the modern artist is to "Design / The
touch. / Fix quiet. Take the place / Of parents" (179–80). Stevens' firm belief
that the artist must "construct a new stage" (219) for his own historical
moment led him back repeatedly to the example of modern painting.

Like many of his contemporaries in the New York art world – such as Arthur
Dove, Georgia O'Keeffe, Charles Sheeler, Alfred Stieglitz – Stevens believed
that art should reflect not only its time, but also its place. The landscape of
America had always required a distinctive aesthetic as part of its liberation
from England: "John Constable they could never quite transplant / And our
streams rejected the dim Academy" (125). American culture's Germanic roots
might turn up as kitsch ("Granted the Picts impressed us otherwise / In the taste
for iron dogs and iron deer" [125]), but Stevens, along with many, sought
a distinctly American modernism, prompted by innovation in Europe but

shaped to the national reality. Indeed, America's "earthy" character seemed particularly suited to the fascination with the primitive that was driving modernist art in all arenas. "The Comedian as the Letter C" describes a quest for this native aesthetic.

> The responsive man,
> Planting his pristine cores in Florida,
> Should prick thereof, not on the psaltery,
> But on the banjo's categorical gut,
> Tuck tuck, while the flamingos flapped his bays.   (31)

Harmonium and avant-garde experimentation

Modern poets were particularly innovative in their treatment of the image, and they looked to the visual arts for inspiration and example. Through their association with painting, poets found a way to break poetry's reliance on statement and formal convention and to recenter their project around a principle of expressive design. Stevens was attracted to the many visual arts movements that emphasized how things are seen rather than what is seen. Impressionism, the dominant American aesthetic during Stevens' young adulthood, encouraged his penchant for recording effects and atmospheres, moods and changes in himself and in the environment. Impressionism rejected the idea that painting should reflect objective knowledge of a fixed reality and concerned itself more with the conditions under which the individual viewer sees reality. Its emphasis on painting outside, from life, and capturing through techniques of brushwork and palette the fugitive effects of light, weather, and movement across the surface of a scene can be felt in many early Stevens poems, especially those he dedicated to his fiancée, Elsie Kachel, in what he called "The Little June Book." "Shower" is typical in its impressionist emphasis on color rather than on the precise contours of objects: "Pink and purple / In water-mist / And hazy leaves / Of amethyst; / Orange and green / And gray between, / And dark grass / In a shimmer / Of windy rain" (512).

"Sea Surface Full of Clouds," a late poem in *Harmonium*, is perhaps Stevens' most extreme experiment in impressionist serial landscapes, in which the same object – the ocean seen from a cruise ship in November "off Tehuantepec" – is presented with variant adjectives and metaphors to reflect changes in the speaker's mood and perhaps also the mood of the sea and sky. Despite an abundance of color words, the scenic, pictorial element of the poem is almost irrelevant. Rather, the transfiguring power of the imagination overtakes the base, producing first playful eccentricity, then grotesque excess in the representation. If the poem owes something to the project of impressionism, it pulls away from the impressionist emphasis on pleasure to create increasingly disturbing, unnatural effects. Surrealism was becoming fashionable at the time he wrote this poem, and the odd conjunctions of objects, pressing against the boundaries of sense ("the sea as turquoise-turbaned Sambo, neat / At tossing saucers" [85]), may owe something to that movement.

One can only speculate about the stimulus for certain images in Stevens' poetry. Is the "green freedom of a cockatoo / Upon a rug" (53), along with the other vibrant colors of the opening of "Sunday Morning," inspired by the post-impressionist movement called fauvism and by Henri Matisse's experimentation with lush interior color and design? Perhaps, but Stevens might also have borrowed the peignoir, oranges, and exotic bird from Edouard Manet's *Woman with Parrot* hanging in the Metropolitan Museum of Art. Stevens joins other modernist writers (Henry James, Ezra Pound, T. S. Eliot, William Carlos Williams) in creating here a "portrait of a lady," not in imitation of visual arts techniques but in a verbal analogue, more focused, ultimately, on the feelings and ideas of the subject than on her physical appearance.

Other poems of *Harmonium* embrace some of the structural experimentation emerging in modern painting, especially cubism. A key element in cubism is the breaking up of illusion created from one-point perspective. Moving beyond impressionism's attention to subjective experience of transient surfaces, cubists broke from illusionary space and attempted to represent the object from many angles simultaneously. They presented a prismatic reality, liberated from the contingencies of the single beholder. Language does not lend itself to this spatial, geometric complexity, although some poets of the modernist movement attempted to find an equivalency between geometry and grammar. Stevens instead sought a serial equivalent to cubism's multiple perspectives. His "Thirteen Ways of Looking at a Blackbird" is more verbal than visual, its "ways" having more in common with rhetorical riddles than with geometric angles of vision. Yet some of the conceptual drive of cubism, especially its concern with structure and multiplicity in form, likely motivated this poem of assembled fragments. A similar concern with relative space informs some of the segments of "Six Significant Landscapes." The "significance" here has more to do with design than with semantics. The poem plays with scale, with the relative value of substance and shadow, with geometric form and other visual elements of painterly experimentation. In this case Stevens, like other modernists, was attracted to Eastern traditions in art, particularly Chinese Buddhist painting, which decenters the human in the landscape. Although the sequence is image-based, the metaphors are not derived from visual similarity. "The night is of the color / Of a woman's arm" (58) does not invite us to picture either element of the comparison, but to make a conceptual link. We might rename this "six irrational landscapes," since they disobey the rational, unitary organization of space in favor of an expressionistic, perspectival dynamic.

Composing as theorizing, theorizing as composing; the performative relation between images and ideas

Ultimately it was in the *idea* of painting, and the ideas generated in the *discussion* of painting, that Stevens discovered his richest resources for poetry. Many artists find it useful in defining the ambition of their art to call on another art as analogy. For the romantics, music – the nightingale, the Aeolian harp – seemed especially powerful. Pound often thought of sculpture, W. B. Yeats of dance, when conceiving art's ontology. Although Stevens' poetry includes references and analogies to these arts, painting seemed to typify the power of the imagination and its role in a secular, often desolate world. Indeed, Stevens keeps an association with painting constantly before the reader: through frequent references to the eye and the composing mind; through painterly subject matter; generic associations and titles (a landscape with a boat, a vase of flowers, a nude on a couch); through scattered references to painterly technique (etching, chiaroscuro, grisaille); through the emphasis on color, hue, shape, line, plane; and even through direct, indexical references to painters (Nicolas Poussin, Claude Lorrain, Jean-Baptiste Camille Corot, Franz Hals).

Yet the experience of reading a poem by Stevens is nothing like the experience of looking at a painting (or looking at anything other than words). Although certain paintings may well have prompted certain images in Stevens' poetry, he almost never describes a work of art or responds to it directly (as W. H. Auden or Williams describes Pieter Brueghel's *Landscape with the Fall of Icarus* or Yeats describes a Chinese carving of lapis lazuli). He does not try to "paint" with words or directly transpose techniques of modern art. Stevens' jar in Tennessee undoubtedly owes something to Marcel Duchamp's "readymades," but the more important reference for this poem as it tries to define a role for modern art is Keats's "Ode on a Grecian Urn." Indeed, although Stevens was endowed with a rich visual imagination, one does not experience a strong engagement of the visual faculty in reading his poetry. Beyond the barest outline of craggy shore and bronze horizon, he does not offer mental pictures. On the contrary, Stevens sometimes actively blocks visual thinking, reminding us that his is "a world of words to the end of it" (301). Color abounds, but more as word than as visual impression: red often puns with "read" as if to remind us of textual primacy; blue and green operate more as symbols of the imagination and nature than as visual stimuli.

Stevens brings the world of painting to mind as analogy for artistic endeavor. Modernist painting proved art's power to go beyond sensibility and affect. Poet and painter alike aspire to create a "mundo," or world, not apart from experience but a part of it. Both painter and poet do more than copy; they "compose." Both "construct" and, by expressing their being in this way, they help us to realize our own reality. As with other modernists, Stevens' composing activity is inseparable from a theorizing activity: to construct is to present an idea about the relationship between the imagination and reality, about the purpose of modern art and the condition of modern man. Stevens was also building on the sense that modern art was deeply embedded in theory, that modernity involved a constant reexamination of the nature of reality, and that each work of art was not only an assertion of being, but also a philosophy of being. No figure was more important to Stevens in this connection of being and seeing than Paul Cézanne, whose urgent desire for "realization" (which Stevens derived from the painter's letters as well as from his work) inspired the poet throughout his career. "On my death there will be found carved on my heart . . . the name of Aix-en-Provence" (*L* 671), he noted, locating himself in Cézanne country.

One can link Stevens and Cézanne in terms of color schemes – the insistent blues and yellows – or particular poems that employ the painter's subject matter ("The Well Dressed Man with a Beard," "The Poem That Took the Place of the Mountain," "Study of Two Pears"). But more generally the poet draws from the artist's struggle to unite perception and composition, world and will. In his commonplace book Stevens records Graham Bell's admiration of "the look of hard and unrelenting authenticity" in the artist's rendering and for "Cézanne's peculiar determination to pin down his sensation, and the exactness and intensity of notation resulting from this" (*SPBS* 53). Stevens adds, "I note the above both for itself and because it adds to subject and manner the thing that is incessantly overlooked: the artist, the presence of the determining personality. Without that reality no amount of other things [verisimilitude, technical mastery, evocative power] matters much" (*SPBS* 53–55).

Stevens was writing in a time of powerful theorizing about the arts, when questions about the real and the actual were bound up with questions of style. He shared these questions with painters even as his medium required different responses. "No poet can have failed to recognize how often a detail, a propos or remark, in respect to painting, applies also to poetry. The truth is that there seems to exist a corpus of remarks in respect to painting, most often the remarks of painters themselves, which are as significant to poets as to painters. . . . Does not the saying of Picasso that a picture is a horde of destructions also say that a poem is a horde of destructions?" (741). Stevens had used this very quotation from Pablo Picasso in his poem

"The Man with the Blue Guitar" (1937). The image was likely triggered by Picasso's early (pre-cubist) painting of *The Old Guitarist* ("I sing a hero's head, large eye" [135]). But it is Picasso's statement and other theories of the relation between art and reality that propel this meditation. Modern painters, and Picasso in particular, were fond of evoking music, and Stevens' poem, which plays on the permutations of a few phrases, has many of the features of musical improvisation, the other art along with poetry that inhabits time rather than space. "The Man with the Blue Guitar" is a *performance* of theory about the nature of modern art and the creative imagination in a time of lost faith and social crisis. Stevens likely saw in Picasso's painting a figure for man in an anti-heroic age, his gaze turned inward rather than upward, lean in his poverty yet asserting his being and his identity through art. As a performer, he represents the artist in society who must do more than please himself, who must reckon with others and address the community. Stevens only mentions the painting, in passing and rather late, concerning himself instead with the articulation of this new humanism, its feeling and force as much as its formulation. But, like the modern painter, the poet creates an entwining of "things as they are" (137) and "the imagined" (151) world; his endlessly dialectical and reciprocal language works to move us from art as illusion to art as realization. For both, value remains focused on process rather than product. That Stevens' poem has in turn been the stimulus for modern works – such as Robert Motherwell's collage *The Blue Guitar* or David Hockney's series of etchings *The Blue Guitar* – testifies to these "migratory passings to and fro."

If Stevens in "The Man with the Blue Guitar" is prompted more by Picasso's theory than by anyone's painting, we should not then conclude that Stevens' poem is simply a form of art theory or philosophy in verse. With language as his medium rather than color and lines, Stevens creates a texture of rhetorical forms, rhythms, and tonalities rhyming and clashing to express a new humanism, in which impoverished man, man breathing and living in change in his "banal suburb" (149), becomes a Promethean hero. We feel a centripetal–centrifugal pull here between indexical reference and abstract compositional design:

> Dew-dapper clapper-traps, blazing
> From crusty stacks above machines.
>
> Ecce, Oxidia is the seed
> Dropped out of this amber-ember pod,
>
> Oxidia is the soot of fire,
> Oxidia is Olympia. (149)

We do not dwell pictorially on crusty stacks or amber pods, partly because the sonic surface of the language dominates our attention. Sound is his medium, as paint is Picasso's. More in lexical texture and variegated syllables than in statement or semantics, the words build this double sense of man as both poor and regal, of language as both referential and internally patterned. Reiterative and permutational in sound and sense, the passage composes a "fluent mundo" (351) rather than a copy of the world or a statement about it.

Decreation as modern creation; nostalgia for classicism

Paradoxically, this new construction of reality requires decreative acts. Stevens, writing through two world wars, perceived this as a truth for art as much as for culture as a whole. The poet must disassemble the norms of experience, "things as they are," or as they have been conventionally perceived. The man with the blue guitar, as the prototype of the modern artist, is a "shearsman of sorts" (135). In contemplating this idea of a " 'hoard / Of destructions'" (141), we might think of the radical disassembling and reassembling of representational space characteristic of cubism and collage. Stevens shared the pervasive idea in modernist painting that experiential truth is fragmentary, relational, and complex and that modern form must embody prismatic reality. The cutting and clashing of an older classical unity means this dialectical poem never arrives at a synthesis, but pushes forward in its tensions, a unity in discordant chords.

"The Man with the Blue Guitar" explores immediate debates of its time, especially about the validity of surrealism, much in discussion because of an exhibition at New York's Museum of Modern Art in 1936. In "The Irrational Element in Poetry," Stevens identifies Picasso as an example of the modern "obsession of freedom" (789), the refusal to allow things as they are to dictate experience. Yet surrealism in such artists as Salvador Dali added a layer of the irrational rather than establishing a freedom for the imagination to change things as they are. Stevens writes in "Materia Poetica": "The essential fault of surrealism is that it invents without discovering. To make a clam play an accordion is to invent not to discover. The observation of the unconscious, so far as it can be observed, should reveal things of which we have previously been unconscious, not the familiar things of which we have been conscious plus imagination" (919). The discords of modernity must work not merely to add but also to discover and create.

However Stevens may have been attracted to this theory or that in modern art, it is the constant search and questioning, rather than any particular formulation, that absorbed him: "In painting, as in poetry, theory moves very rapidly and things that are revelations today are obsolete tomorrow, like the things on one's plate at dinner" (L 647). In many poems he expresses nostalgia for that classical unity, even as he acknowledges that modernity must push it aside. "A sunny day's complete Poussiniana, / Divide it from itself" (198), he writes in "Poem Written at Morning," evoking Nicolas Poussin, the French seventeenth-century painter of ideal pastoral scenes with religious and mythological significance. These perfect, harmonious illusions are replaced by radical metaphors that draw attention to the artist's freedom. Stevens shares the modernist painter's sense that truth is complex and faceted, that it cannot be encompassed in a single, unified scheme such as classical painting offered.

In "Botanist on Alp (No. 1)," Stevens employs a painterly title to suggest a series of perspectives or compositional studies (the numbering also playfully suggesting that each construction is another "alp" in the artist's chain of realities). The speaker – a botanist because he studies nature, but also because he studies "leaves" or departures from the past – is dismayed that the old classical unities of Claude Lorrain no longer support reality. "Panoramas are not what they used to be. / Claude has been dead a long time . . ."

> But in Claude how near one was
> (In a world that was resting on pillars,
> That was seen through arches)
> To the central composition,
> The essential theme. (109)

The modern reality seems a scattering of disassociated fragments by comparison. "What composition is there in all this . . . ?" (109) wonders the botanist; yet the poem hints at a new artistic order in the ascendancy, perhaps something more like Cézanne's images of Mt. Ste. Victoire. If the modern artist's moment is a decreative one in which no particular unity can become identified with reality, in which the mechanics of illusion (here represented by "the funicular") are exposed and disabled, the "hoard of destructions" might nevertheless lead to a realization that brings man and nature dynamically together.

Poetry and the genres of painting: nude, still life, landscape

In all modern work one must distinguish between content and subject matter, the latter often a mere pretext for formal exploration. For Stevens, the purpose of the poem is the imagination's struggle with reality, its desire for reality and its desire to realize the urges of the will. By frequently borrowing painting's nominal subject matter – ladies with flowers or land-scapes with boats – Stevens shares this essential content.

Stevens turns repeatedly to one of the enduring subjects of painting, the female nude, embodiment of classic beauty and object of male gaze. In "The Apostrophe to Vincentine," he takes on the stance of Pygmalion imagining into being a Vincentine marble statue; in "The Paltry Nude Starts on a Spring Voyage," he reimagines Botticelli's Venus on a half shell as a modern "discontent," "Eager for the brine and bellowing / Of the high interiors of the sea" (4). "Peter Quince at the Clavier," in which the poet-player recalls the biblical story of the elders gazing at the unsuspecting Susanna, has medieval and Renaissance painterly sources. The female nude as it has been depicted in art since classical times stands in Stevens' mind for muse, for the earth's body, for the object of desire with which the imagination seeks a marriage.

A subgenre in the history of the nude is the odalisque or supine nude, familiar from Giorgione (Giorgio da Castelfranco) to Matisse. In "So-and-So Reclining on Her Couch," Stevens turns this figure into a focus for theory. Adopting the stance of an artist contemplating his model, he offers three projections of the relationship between the image and its maker. One might think of this series as representing turns in a creative process or as chapters in the story of art. Stevens takes on the language of propositional, Euclidean instruction, although in an experimental, even playful, rather than didactic mood. The repeated terms "suspension" and "floats" with reference to the vision of the woman suggest the peculiar ontology of art's creations: they are of the mind and yet external to it, of the world and yet not subject to its same conditions.

Projection A presents the force of classical illusion where the image seems autonomous and the beholder free from the confines of perspective: "She floats in air at the level of / The eye" (262), as if a body given rather than made, transcending the time and place of her origin and her reception. If she is at some level a "mechanism" (something mechanically projected), she becomes an "apparition" (something present yet otherworldly and mysteri-ous). Her eyes "dripping blue" suggest the innocent gaze or naive illusion, but they also indicate wet paint, taking us out of her ontological suspension and back into the world of creative process. The "motionless gesture" of Projection A vanishes, replaced by another "suspension," that of the absent presence of the creating hand, the "invisible gesture" retained in the object. Here we have a form of romantic expressionism. Projection C floats in modernist "contention," "the flux / Between the thing as idea and / The idea as thing" (263), between the image as an interpretation of reality and the image as a reality in its own right. In this final projection, in which the desire of the artist and his creative presence are unconcealed, Stevens finds a place to "confide[]," to locate his faith. Just here the poem turns from art to reality, to the "unpainted shore" beyond projections. The fresh acquaintance of the world as something other than the projection of his desires turns the speaker's attention away from the artist's model. She has performed her role and is excused: "Good-bye, / Mrs. Pappadopoulos, and thanks" (263). Stevens loves to play with names, and we can speculate as to the model's identity: she is Greek not only to evoke classical statues but also because she participates in a classical discourse about the relationship of thing and idea; she is Mrs. Pappadopoulos because she models as spousal inspiration and double to the (for Stevens) virile (and patriarchal) creative force of the artist.

Although Stevens' poems are not for the most part pictorial, they do, as in the above example, tend to imagine the creative process in terms of looking and painting, and the two activities are themselves identified. "By metaphor you paint / A thing" (198), he writes in "Poem Written at Morning." By the late 1930s, Stevens had begun to turn toward the overlooked, toward the humble genre of still life. Within this space of insignificant aesthetic and domestic objects – vases of flowers, pink carnations, dishes of peaches, and so on – the poet found a way of exploring and resisting the pressure of reality: "Both the poet and the mystic may establish themselves on herrings and apples. The painter may establish himself on a guitar, a copy of *Figaro* and a dish of melons. These are fortifyings, although irrational ones. The only possible resistance to the pressure of the contemporaneous is a matter of herrings and apples or, to be less definite, the contemporaneous itself" (788–89). Stevens could have been referring here to any number of cubist paintings or collages in which the newspaper is wedged in beside a bit of fruit and an instrument. Perhaps he was thinking, in part, about Picasso's collage of 1912, with its headline torn from *Le Journal*: "LA BATAILLE S'EST ENGAGÉ" (the battle has commenced).

"Study of Two Pears" presents just this desire of the artist to establish himself, where the compositional space takes primacy over representational space, where objects and substance dissolve into relations of color and contour. Although Stevens evokes modern painting in his analysis of forms, he does not create a visual composition, but rather explores the interplay between seeing and conceptualization. The title contains a pun, reminding us that there are always two pairs or a pair of pears, one in nature and one as idea. The play of denial and assertion in the stanzas keeps this duality in suspension:

> They are not flat surfaces
> Having curved outlines.
> They are round
> Tapering toward the top.   (181)

In a Cézanne still life, the representational illusion is brought into a surface dynamic formed of geometric distortions and conspicuous brushwork marking the construction of the image. The largely monosyllabic lexicon of the poem may convey the deliberately crude rendering of modern brushwork. But the simplicity of the words masks a rather complex study. Are we looking at actual pears, or at a composition of pears? And is this ambiguity perhaps built into the creative, indeed the perceptual process? The weak linking and passive verb constructions – "are . . . / Composed," "are touched," "are modelled" – leave the question open. "The pears are not viols, / Nudes or bottles" (180), writes Stevens – and for a minute they *are*, just as cubist painting blends organic forms, human forms, and the shapes of musical instruments. But "viols" plays on "vials," so that we are not sure of the referent – bottles or violins? Like the painter, Stevens plays with container and contained. The poem explores temporality as well, removing the object from ordinary reality. Although the description suggests something static ("They are yellow forms / Composed of curves"), the participles – "Bulging," "Tapering," "Flowering" – suggest the continuing sense of movement that arises for the beholder. The still life encompasses many seasons, merging nature's organic process with art's creation and perception. Thus the eye moves up from the base where redness connotes ripeness to the top where a dry leaf hangs. Yet the colorful "Flowering over the skin" (181) recalls the earlier flowering of the tree that brought forth the pears and perhaps the flowering of the artist's composition. The poem is a process of beholding and composing, a process surrendered as the eye turns finally to the "shadows of the pears," and the image is reduced to "blobs" (181).

In "Someone Puts a Pineapple Together," Stevens returns to the themes of "Study of Two Pears." But he relinquishes the doomed goal of fixing an image of reality. "Someone Puts a Pineapple Together" reminds us explicitly of its ties to the genre of still life – "It is something on a table that he sees" (693) – but there is nothing "still" in this poem. Where "Study of Two Pears" seems wary of metaphor, even as it creeps in, continuing to distinguish the pears from the observer's subjective will, in "Someone Puts a Pineapple Together," "The profusion of metaphor has been increased" (693). The thing observed is acknowledged as a tangent of himself and becomes a swarm of metaphors evoking a core reality, "An object the sum of its complications, seen / And unseen" (696). The faceted surface of the pineapple suggests for Stevens the way that an object might be known as a prism of perceptions. Unlike the minimalist vocabulary of "Study of Two Pears," this poem thrives in its eccentricities, creating outlandish duplications of the pineapple as owl, as bottle with green genii, and as yesterday's volcano. The poem celebrates the "Promethean liberations" that find reality in expressive abstraction.

This distinction between seeing as the restraint of will and seeing as the release of will is present dialectically in many poems of *Parts of a World*, especially in "Landscape with Boat." There are two painters here: one, an oxymoronic "anti-master-man, floribund ascetic" (220), negating the forms of the past (his own and his culture's) to get at an untouched, primitive reality; and the other, an imaginative man who sees reality from his own imperial perspective, his eccentric metaphors showing reality as a tangent of himself. Although Stevens sides with the latter, he empathizes with the former. The poem asks us to consider them together. The anti-master-man, looking for the thing itself, cleansed of all human tint or gesture, is trapped in a paradox: even his ideal of the "single-colored, colorless, primitive" (220) requires an act of supposition and composition. Stevens registers this ambiguity in the verb "brushed" – in brushing away thunder he creates an impression, indeed paints an impression, leaving his brushwork. He "wanted the eye to see / And not be touched by blue" (220) in the sense of feeling and of adulteration or "touching up" as in painting. Stevens registers his labor in the repetitive sentence structures and redundant vocabulary that almost mimic a painter's application of paint. The ascetic is literally and figuratively "at sea."

But the end of the poem offers an alternative, a forceful if also comical and festive composition created not from a neutral center but from a "sofa on a balcony" (221). From this vantage point the world is indeed "touched," but subjective colorings become substances in their own right, "emerald / Becoming emeralds" (221), the subjectivity of the beholder merging with reality. As if to register this achievement, Stevens evokes all the senses at the end of the poem (where the earlier ascetic seemed caught in a sense-less void). Nature itself is an artist, a creator of illusions of which we are the instrument ("the eye so touched, so played / Upon by clouds" [220–21]), and the landscape is a mirror of the senses. In this half of the poem we are struck by the lexical and syntactic variety as well as by the play of color and image in contrast to the ascetic's repetitions.

> He might watch the palms
> Flap green ears in the heat. He might observe
> A yellow wine and follow a steamer's track
> And say, "The thing I hum appears to be
> The rhythm of this celestial pantomime." (221)

Here, then, is an achieved composition, a "landscape with boat," a work not so much of solipsism as of "capable imagination" (226), however irrational or even nonsensical.

Necessary angel; rhopography and megalography

In the migratory relations between Stevens' poetry and the art of painting, one instance, "Angel Surrounded by Paysans," stands out as a paradigm of what is likely a common, but mostly silent, method in Stevens' poetry: the allegorical or metaphorical transmutation of images from painting. This example may affect the way we think about Stevens' abstraction. The image source for this poem leaves no direct trace in the poem itself. The poem has little visual interest; it builds on the rhetorical structure of a question, answered by another question. Yet in his letters Stevens explicitly identified the poem with a still-life painting in the Cézanne tradition which he had acquired from the dealer Paule Vidal: "Now that I have had the new picture at home for a few days, it seems almost domesticated. Tal Coat is supposed to be a man of violence but one soon becomes accustomed to the present picture. I have even given it a title of my own: *Angel Surrounded By Peasants*. The angel is the Venetian glass bowl on the left with the little spray of leaves in it. The peasants are the terrines, bottles and the glasses that surround it. This title alone tames it as a lump of sugar might tame a lion" (*L* 649–50).

We began this discussion of Stevens and painting by noting that the "migratory passings to and fro" between poetry and painting were associated, in his mind, with the passings between the imagination and reality. Nowhere is this liminal movement, in all its layers of association, more realized than in this closing poem of *The Auroras of Autumn*. The subject is august, even semi-religious, yet the objects that have generated the meditation could not be more humble. Stevens unites an interest in the ordinary detritus of life (here pots and vases), which art historians, following the Greek, call "rhopography," with a desire for the momentous and spiritually significant, or "megalography." "Angels Surrounded by Paysans" explores a presence/absence dynamic undoubtedly drawn from Tal-Coat's mixtures of solid and transparent surface. The crude, energetic brushwork suggests a freedom from the strictures of appearance such as the poem celebrates. Yet the subject matter of still life might itself be important here. Stevens remarks in his letter that he has "domesticated" this painting by bringing it home and giving it a title, but still life is already concerned with the domestic. The lion-like virility of Tal-Coat's sensibility has entered into the shallow, intimate space of the table. Stevens has also retained that threshold spirit of still life: peasants gathered and a welcome at the door, a transfiguration of the commonplace.

What Stevens found in Tal-Coat, and what he celebrates in the poem, is the power of the imagination, the way art "apparels" the ordinary world in human feeling and significance. The angel is at once at the center of the peasant group, as if one of them, and also apart, standing at the door, as if an expected Old Testament Elijah. The angel is an embodiment of a new humanist faith. Art responds to the human need for repetition – it begins in an act of mimesis: "in my sight, you see the earth again" (423), not just "things as they are" but things made eloquent, without turning from what they are. The modern artist Tal-Coat has released his images from the "stiff and stubborn" delineations of rational space and declared Promethean liberations that are not mere escapism. The instinct of repetition behind pictorial representation is echoed in the repetitions of the poem – "liquidly in liquid lingerings," "an apparition appareled in / Apparels of such lightest look" (423). Such repetitions remind us that the apparition is not other-worldly, that the "apparel" is not added on like a "tepid aureole" (Stevens puns on the pots here, the "ware of ore"). The spatial paradox of a figure surrounded, yet also at the threshold, is repeated in the rhetorical paradox and circularity in which a question that is also a statement ("There is / A welcome at the door to which no one comes?") is answered by another question ("Am I not," which closes with a vanishing "I am gone?"). The circuitry keeps alive the passings to and fro between the imagination and reality, poetry and painting.

13

JACQUELINE VAUGHT BROGAN

Stevens and the feminine

I

The subject of Wallace Stevens and the feminine proves to be extremely important in understanding a poet who, from the meditating woman of his early "Sunday Morning" to the composing Penelope of his late "The World as Meditation," produced a variety of female characters even as he explored some of his most important philosophical, metaphysical, and even spiritual questions. It is not surprising that as a poet, living in what he called the "epic of disbelief" (101), Stevens would take recourse in a traditional poetic trope – that is, that like Petrarch or Dante before him, he would often employ a female muse when exploring his most pressing and nearly ineffable questions. As the world and, especially, quite conservative parts of the United States faced the tumultuous changes from the traditional and religious values of the nineteenth century to the more skeptical and agnostic ones of the twentieth, such a poetic gesture might have provided something of the familiar, an aesthetic comfort zone that allowed for poetic production, even while Stevens struggled to create a modern poetry that would suffice in these changing and troubling times.

Yet invoking a female muse, as he does in "To the One of Fictive Music," was itself a problematic gesture during Stevens' times, for the world not only witnessed the Great War, the Great Depression, and World War II, but also markedly different and changing attitudes toward women. The turn of the century saw, for example, the rise of "the new woman," both in the United States and in Europe. Mina Loy, an experimental poet who immigrated to the United States in the 1910s, advocated "free sex," and Isadora Duncan, famously performing a new ballet in France at the same time, scandalously danced with notably bare (or "free") feet. Taken together, these two women might be said to embody the sometimes desired, sometimes feared modern woman who frequently advocated radically new mores for the relationship between men and women.

Certainly not all women of the early twentieth century were so extreme; nonetheless, by the early 1920s women in several countries had achieved suffrage, were entering the workforce in record numbers, and, in several instances, were in control of literary production as editors of major presses and journals. These accomplishments underscored a new and positive appreciation of women. At the same time, these very changes stirred up deepened hostility toward, and anxiety about, women that resulted in their being projected as threatening, even emasculating beings.

Such a conflict inhabited Stevens' poetry throughout his poetic career. The positively described, creative female "singer" of the early "The Idea of Order at Key West" is countered by the lesser-known woman of "Good Man, Bad Woman," who, the poet tells us, "can corrode your world, if never you" (559). In later years a similar conflict manifests itself in the difference between the Penelope of "The World as Meditation," "Whose mere savage presence awakens the world in which she dwells" (442), and the far more threatening "bearded queen, wicked in her dead light" (432) of "Madame La Fleurie." In fact, for many male writers at the time (including, among others, Ezra Pound and Ernest Hemingway), an anxiety about the changing roles of men and women led occasionally to the extreme emphasis on what Stevens himself would insist must be the "masculine nature" and "virility" (685) of the modern writer, as he puts it in "The Figure of the Youth as Virile Poet." In that essay, he even goes so far as to say that "The centuries have a way of being male" (675).

Yet, in the same paragraph in which that sentence appears, Stevens introduces what he calls "a kind of sister of the Minotaur" (675) – a surprising female figure – as the new and necessary condition for the modern imagination. That essay was written during World War II. The extreme "pressure" or violence of that global war prompted Stevens to abandon his earlier allegiance to strictly masculine structures and expressions in favor of more inclusive ones. In fact, in his well-known poem "Of Modern Poetry," written and published in 1940, Stevens overtly states that in order for "modern poetry" to "suffice," "It has to face the men of the time and to meet / The women of the time. It has to think about war" (218–19). As examples of what such a subject matter might be, Stevens rather surprisingly concludes, it "may / Be of a man skating, a woman dancing, a woman / Combing" (219) – that is, possible figurations including both genders as equally worthy of poetic expression. It is this critical change in his poetics that eventually allowed him to write what he called "the finally human" (444) – that is, the great high poetry of his later years in which the masculine and feminine become one.

II

Given these larger political and poetic contexts, it becomes necessary when considering Stevens and the feminine to distinguish Stevens' attitudes toward women in real life from both his treatment or presentation of female characters in his poems and the increasingly complex but important emergence in his poetry of what might be called the "feminine within." The latter is a psychological, even Jungian term that represents a concept that would prove crucial in Stevens' evolving attempts to create in poetry a defense against what he called "a violence without" (665), by which he meant the "pressure of reality" (654) or global violence that was the consequence of World War II. Since Stevens' attitude toward women in real life is more rightly the concern of his biographers – several of whom have exposed his admittedly strained relations with women in real life, especially with his wife, Elsie[1] – I will focus on the latter two of these three possible categories: his presentation of female characters and the emergence of the feminine within.

"A High-Toned Old Christian Woman" is a good place to start when examining Stevens' treatment of female characters in his poems. Although at times Stevens would condemn, however playfully, the "arrogantly male, / Patron" (39) of "Last Looks at the Lilacs" or that "Damned universal cock" (60) of "Bantams in Pine-Woods," we must admit that it is not merely religion that Stevens is mocking or denigrating in this frequently anthologized poem. This woman is not only "high-toned" and "old," but she is also specifically a widow whose ideas are presumably naive and outdated. Most important, she is pitted in the poem (with no hope of receiving respect) against the injunctions of the speaker who forcefully articulates his own supposedly superior – and, shall we say? – sexist poetics. The poem concludes with these irrefutable lines: "This will make widows wince. But fictive things / Wink as they will. Wink most when widows wince" (47). Notably, the "This" of that final assertion alludes to the opening claim of the poem, "Poetry is the supreme fiction, madame." But as the address to a madame underscores, the poem is not addressed to another (even if imaginary) male listener or friend. The female gender, as well as religion, is the object of mockery in this poem; making an old widower wince would not have been as witty.

Although Stevens chose not to include in his final collection many poems that depicted women in denigrating or overtly sexist ways – for example, "For an Old Woman in a Wig," "Good Man, Bad Woman," "Lulu Gay," and "Lulu Morose" – he did include a number that did. Consider, for example, the woman of "The Emperor of Ice-Cream," dead, lying on a deal

dresser, with her "horny feet" (50) protruding, or the "lady dying of dia-
betes" in "A Thought Revolved," who is told in these trying circumstances
to "rejoice, rejoice!" (171). Just by their titles alone, a number of poems
imply a belittling attitude toward women: "The Paltry Nude Starts on a
Spring Voyage," "The Ordinary Women," "Another Weeping Woman,"
"The Virgin Carrying a Lantern," "Infanta Marina," or, more abstractly,
"O, Florida, Venereal Soil." "Farewell to Florida" specifically bids goodbye
(good riddance?) to a traditionally feminized landscape, whose "mind,"
Stevens says, "had bound me round," in favor of the "North," characterized
as "a slime of men in crowds" so that he can "be free again, to return to the
violent mind / That is their mind, these men" (97–98). Other poems that
suggest a continuing tendency to be reductive in the presentation of females
include the sarcastic "United Dames of America," the mocking poem entitled
"The Woman That Had More Babies Than That," and the biting "Madame
La Fleurie," to name only a few.

One of the ways in which Stevens presented women in a reductive manner
can be found in the very silence of his female characters – they rarely speak.
This might seem innocuous until we remember that during this time women
were demanding and achieving voice in personal, artistic, professional, and
political realms, especially in the United States. It is quite telling, then, that
one of the few exceptions to the silent women in Stevens' poetry – the
"purple woman with a lavender tongue" who "Said hic, said hac, / Said
ha" (558) – is from a poem, "Metropolitan Melancholy," excluded from his
final collection. Another is the woman quoted in "Like Decorations in a
Nigger Cemetery," who is immediately dismissed with the poet's sarcastic
aside that those "words / Are a woman's words, unlikely to satisfy / The taste
of even a country connoisseur" (127). In general, women in Stevens' poetry
almost never speak, whereas his male characters do. In fact, for a poet so well
known for writing metapoetry – or poetry about poetry – it is neither "poetry"
nor "writing" that Stevens mentions most often in his poems, but rather
"man" or "men." As a look at the concordance to Stevens' poetry reveals,
the words "man" and "men" appear five times more than "woman" and
"women."[2]

A corollary of this poetic repression is that women in Stevens rarely move.
Consider the enormous difference between his earliest and most famous
female and male characters – the woman of "Sunday Morning," reclining in
her chair, and the ever-traveling Crispin of "The Comedian as the Letter C."
The woman of "Sunday Morning" ultimately has many sisters, from the
early "Romance for a Demoiselle Lying in the Grass" to the late "So-and-So
Reclining on Her Couch." The implicit sexual titillation of these reclining
females is made overt in "New England Verses," in the section entitled "*The*

Female Nude": "Ballatta dozed in the cool on a straw divan / At home, a bit like the slenderest courtesan" (89) – or, in other words, like a prostitute. The corresponding masculine section entitled "*The Male Nude*" is markedly different in tone, even if the male figure is mildly chided by the poet: "Dark cynic, strip and bathe and bask at will. / Without cap or strap, you are the cynic still" (89). Too often, women in Stevens remain precisely figures – empty ciphers for masculine rumination and scripting, including even the supposedly more appealing women found in "Sunday Morning" and "The Idea of Order at Key West."

"Sunday Morning," admittedly in contrast to many of the poems discussed thus far, presents a woman, at least initially, in a positive light. In contrast to the old high-toned Christian woman discussed above, the woman in Stevens' most serious poem of his early years appears intelligent as she contemplates sophisticated questions. She even speaks and is cited directly two times by the speaker (whom I take to be Stevens). As she ponders the limitations of Christian faith and the constraints of several possible alternatives to that faith, she specifically asks: "But when the birds are gone, and their warm fields / Return no more, where, then, is paradise?" (54). Later, while considering the merits and satisfactions of this changing earth (as does Keats in "Ode on a Grecian Urn"), she is quoted as saying, "But in contentment I still feel / The need of some imperishable bliss" (55) – an almost courageous admission, given the canonical status of Keats's poem and its well-known ending. She certainly does not find that contentment in "truth" and "beauty" as Keats had earlier posited. Instead, her "imperishable bliss" lies, however ironically, in what may well be the poem's most memorable lines: "Death is the mother of beauty, mystical, / Within whose burning bosom we devise / Our earthly mothers waiting, sleeplessly" (55).

It is critical to note, however, that these words, presented in the poem as the most insightful and intelligent response to the woman's questions and needs, are spoken not by the woman (however intelligent she initially seems to be), but rather by the speaker. In the next lines (which begin the penultimate section), the speaker quickly replaces the woman with "a ring of men" who "Shall chant in orgy on a summer morn" (55), adding, "They shall know well the heavenly fellowship / Of men that perish and of summer morn" (56). Granted, in the final section Stevens returns to the woman: "She hears, upon that water without sound, / A voice that cries, 'The tomb in Palestine / Is not the porch of spirits lingering. / It is the grave of Jesus, where he lay'" (56). Nonetheless, we should note once again that this supposed "truth" or revelation is not uttered by the woman, but rather by some mysterious, unidentifiable "voice," who is clearly a mask for Stevens himself and for his own theological position. In fact, this final revelation, which undercuts the entire Christian tradition associated with Sunday mornings, clears the way for the last eloquent lines of the poem – lines that are clearly Stevens' own and that considerably outdistance the woman's efforts in revising Keats's ideas in his canonical poem. At the end of "Sunday Morning," we have no "contentment" in the sublime, and certainly not in "truth" or "beauty." Instead the poet tells us we must accept only the "Ambiguous undulations" that "pigeons make / . . . as they sink, / Downward to darkness, on extended wings" (56). Finally, it is not the woman who debunks the allegedly naive Christian faith (even if she is not in church that Sunday and even if she is asking serious questions), but rather the poet, who is clearly the singular and superior intelligence of the poem.

Similar to this woman is the purportedly idealized female singer of "The Idea of Order at Key West." Much as in "Sunday Morning," by the end of the poem this woman emerges once again as only a springboard for the speaker, whom I take, once again, to be Stevens himself. Admittedly, in contrast to many of the women in Stevens' poetry mentioned thus far, the female singer in this poem is neither denigrated nor mocked. Furthermore, she is dynamic, walking and singing by the shore:

> And when she sang, the sea,
> Whatever self it had, became the self
> That was her song, for she was the maker. (106)

As alluring and even enduring as she may seem to be, in the next stanza, as Stevens abruptly breaks into the poem with his direct address to a male friend – "Ramon Fernandez, tell me, if you know" – she evaporates. With this unexpected intrusion, it becomes apparent that she has been, all along, merely a cipher for Stevens himself and the way in which he sings. As a muse, she is totally dismissed and is replaced by the masculine "rage for order" (106) that Stevens really has in mind. Subsequently, lights "Mastered" the night, "portioned" out the sea, "Arrange[d]" and "deepen[ed]" night, so that the words, in a kind of phallic domination, ironically create the "fragrant portals," or the feminine principle, which is ultimately erased and silenced in the poem. As in "Sunday Morning," it is not the woman singing we hear at the end. It is Stevens himself, who appears once again to be the supreme poet, blessing "The maker's rage to order" the world and evoking the deepest aspects "of ourselves and of our origins / In ghostlier demarcations, keener sounds" (106).

Whether consciously or not, Stevens appears, repeatedly, though most especially in his early years, to dismiss his female characters, even in their most positive poetic manifestations. I suspect this was learned from a larger cultural bias against women when Stevens began writing, a bias that prompted him, most acutely in the first half of his career, to repress what we might call the "feminine within" – that is, the "other" half of his own psyche and poetic voice. At the conscious level, for many years Stevens was committed to creating the "major man" (334ff.), the poet whose "virility" in his poetry could compensate for the loss of religious faith in the modern world while also providing a psychologically necessary defense against the escalating violence of the century's global wars. However, sometime in the middle of World War II Stevens began to question the efficacy of masculine structures and their modes of domination and mastery. Whether consciously at first or not, this led to a concurrent questioning of his own commitment to a masculine poetics and to a willingness to be open to the female aspect of his voice that he had for so long repressed.

III

As already mentioned, we find this important change overtly stated in the early wartime poem "Of Modern Poetry." But we find it most curiously expressed in an essay written during the middle of World War II entitled "The Figure of the Youth as Virile Poet." In the first part of the essay, Stevens articulates what we might call a gender-specific, masculinist poetics. He goes so far as to say that the "character of the poet" must be seen as "virile" – otherwise, "the masculine nature that we propose for one that must be the master of our lives will be lost" (685). For reasons already noted, at the time this essay was written, many other writers were emphasizing the "masculine" nature of authors and authorship. Yet Stevens appears excessive here in his insistence on a youthful, virile, male poet who would, notably, "master" our lives. (I am reminded of the ending of "The Idea of Order at Key West" with its "maker's rage to order.") Within this context, the surprising evocation in the fifth section of this essay of a "feminine" figure for the imagination proves quite remarkable and, even more, unpredictable:

> When we look back at the face of the seventeenth century, it is at the rigorous face of the rigorous thinker and, say, the Miltonic image of a poet, severe and determined. In effect, what we are remembering is the rather haggard background of the incredible, the imagination without intelligence, from which a younger figure is emerging, stepping forward in the company of a muse of its own, *still half-beast and somehow more than human, a kind of sister of the Minotaur.* This younger figure is the intelligence that endures.   (675; emphasis added)

Notably, this "sister" is essentially androgynous, since in the next sentence Stevens asserts that this figure is also "the imagination of the son still bearing the antique imagination of the father" (675).

It seems clear that Stevens is allowing, even if subconsciously, the female principle to emerge at last. However, it also appears that at the conscious level "she" is not entirely accepted as yet, since she is essentially (and ambiguously) described as a monster, being both "half-beast" and "somehow more than human." Ironically, at the very point later in the essay that the figure of the youth as the virile poet supposedly speaks or finds his own voice, Stevens has him say,

> No longer do I believe that there is a mystic muse, sister of the Minotaur. This is another of the monsters I had for nurse, whom I have wasted. I am myself a part of what is real, and it is my own speech and the strength of it, this only, that I hear or ever shall. (680)

What is most provocative about this passage, especially since it is in such conflict with the semantic intent, is that even as he rejects the "sister of the Minotaur" at the supposed moment of self-identification, he reinstates her as "nurse."

Stevens' ambivalence toward this female figure for the imagination does not end with this monstrous image, but rather with an extremely complicated (even logically contradictory) evocation of the "virile poet" in conjunction with the "sister of the Minotaur" as the new, necessary figure for the imagination in the new era – an era dominated, as Stevens insisted, by the violence and chaos of World War II. After saying near the conclusion of the essay, "We have been referring constantly to the simple figure of the youth, in his character of poet, as the virile poet," Stevens ends with the following lines, once again spoken by this imagined, new, virile poet:

> Inexplicable sister of the Minotaur, enigma and mask, although I am part of what is real, hear me and recognize me as part of the unreal. I am the truth but the truth of that imagination of life in which with unfamiliar motion and manner you guide me in those exchanges of speech in which your words are mine, mine yours. (685)

Thus, at the very end of this extraordinary essay, Stevens articulates a desired union between the metaphorically masculine and feminine parts of the imagination. As such, the conclusion of this essay represents the precise moment when Stevens' earlier derision of the feminine has reached something of a crisis under what he describes as the "pressure of reality" (656), or the violence of war. For, as I think we might agree, however right the "sister of the Minotaur" feels in this passage, she is genuinely beyond rational explanation. Instead, she appears utterly irrational – that is, an otherwise unpredictable textual eruption that begins to give expression to what has been repeatedly repressed in his poems over many years. In the 1942 "Notes

Toward a Supreme Fiction," she emerges as Stevens' "Fat girl," a "more than natural figure," a "more than rational distortion. . . ." She becomes "The fiction that results from feeling." The implied male lecturers at the Sorbonne will get it straight one day, "Pleased that the irrational is rational" (351).

This crisis is overtly dramatized again two years later in an important section of the 1944 "Esthétique du Mal," written as the violence of the global war expanded exponentially. In the tenth section of this pivotal poem, Stevens distinguishes between two sets of female figures in his poetry. On the one hand, he writes,

> It is true there were other mothers, singular
> In form, lovers of heaven and earth, she-wolves
> And forest tigresses and women mixed
> With the sea. These were fantastic. (283)

These "other mothers," immediately linked in the text to the monstrous "she-wolves" and "tigresses," are the "fantastic" manifestations of his own feminine voice, or anima, repressed as we have seen throughout most of his early poetic career. It is both culturally and poetically predictable that this uncomposed and, therefore, potentially destructive aspect of his creative energy is perceived by – or figured by – Stevens in this section of "Esthétique du Mal" as a threatening woman. On the other hand, the following lines suggest a conscious awareness of a problem in his figurations of women and implicitly introduce the possibility of resolution in poetic tropes similar to that of the androgynous "sister of the Minotaur":

> He had studied the nostalgias. In these
> He sought the most grossly maternal, the creature
> Who most fecundly assuaged him, the softest
> Woman with a vague moustache and not the mauve
> *Maman*. His anima liked its animal
> And liked it unsubjugated, so that home
> Was a return to birth. . . . (283)

As in "The Figure of the Youth as Virile Poet," his desire to overcome the "fantastic" distortions noted above seems quite apparent here in his Jungian evocation of an androgynous figure – that "softest / Woman with a vague moustache. . . ."

Increasingly, over the next few years, especially in the post-World War II volumes *Transport to Summer* (1947) and *The Auroras of Autumn* (1950), Stevens begins to express the feminine within. The change from his earlier masculine poetics to a far more inclusive one is most elegantly voiced in "Angel Surrounded by Paysans," included in the latter volume, where we come across a masculine character, "a man / Of the mind," who finally *speaks* with what I see as Stevens' previously repressed, though increasingly desired, feminine voice. In contrast to "The Idea of Order at Key West," there is no control here, no mastering, no portioning of the night; we are moved by the feminine lightness of the glance and dress and by the gentleness of the feminine tone:

> Am I not,
> Myself, only half of a figure of a sort,
>
> A figure half seen, or seen for a moment, a man
> Of the mind, an apparition apparelled in
>
> Apparels of such lightest look that a turn
> Of my shoulder and quickly, too quickly, I am gone? (423)

The angel is, in fact, a "necessary angel," one who is questioning rather than "ordering," one who is, admittedly, too easily gone and subject to change – but, therefore, also a sign of our best and necessarily mutable linguistic orderings. Most important, he (she?) is also finally heard through the door (instead of being held off beyond the portals), heard, even if only whispering. This poem, which ends the last volume of poetry that Stevens wrote before the section called *The Rock* in his *Collected Poems*, achieves something of a resolution (emphasizing far more the solution or mixing than the earlier tone of resolve), one that comes to find its greatest plenitude in the final lyrics of his late period.

"Final Soliloquy of the Interior Paramour," included in *The Rock*, presents the occasion in Stevens' oeuvre in which the masculine and feminine principles are finally fully integrated. As the word "paramour" from the title suggests, there is a romance, even an intimacy (communion, communication), in this poem that is dependent precisely upon difference – that is, upon the presence of differing masculine and feminine aspects of the self. The most telling signs of this are the plural pronoun "we" and that most feminine of articles, the "shawl," which, Stevens says, is "Wrapped tightly round us, since we are poor" (444). Even though Stevens' characteristic tone of dominance is absent in this poem, the recognition and recovery of his own, internal feminine voice does not undermine his poetic authorship, as Stevens obviously feared it would in "Farewell to Florida" and other early poems. Instead, the recovery of this voice gives recognition to this now fully accepted muse as an integral, feminine part of himself. It allows him to give expression to what is beyond control, beyond order, beyond dominance in our lives and thereby to endow with significance that little that we can order in words. As opposed to his sarcastic positioning in "A High-Toned Old Christian Woman," in this poem Stevens articulates a different "supreme fiction" or spiritual possibility. "We say God and the imagination are one . . ." – a possibility that, with its elliptical ending, spreads outward, rather than "Downward to darkness," as in "Sunday Morning." In essence, the discovery here of the feminine voice, which was so silenced in his early poems, opens up the space in Stevens for the magnificent tones and visions of many other poems of his later years, poems that most critics regard as his most important and most successful.

Among these is "The World as Meditation," in which Stevens shifts completely the poetic process of creation from his previous insistence on males to the female Penelope. In contrast to "The Idea of Order at Key West," in which it turns out the "maker's rage to order" is actually nothing but his own, in this late poem the female Penelope remains the central and only figure for the creator/poet who essentially creates herself even as she creates her perfect mate, Ulysses, through imaginative recreations of, and responses to, the rising sun:

> She has composed, so long, a self with which to welcome him,
> Companion to his self for her, which she imagined,
> Two in a deep-founded sheltering, friend and dear friend. (442)

There is no poetic "mastering" or dominance here, but rather a tantalizing questioning of poetic possibilities:

> But was it Ulysses? Or was it only the warmth of the sun
> On her pillow? The thought kept beating in her like her heart.
> The two kept beating together. It was only day.
>
> It was Ulysses and it was not. Yet they had met. . . . (442)

"Finally," we might say. As opposed to the way the female is intellectually supplanted in "Sunday Morning," Penelope remains the thinker and the composer in the poem. She represents the possible poet who encapsulates an axiom Stevens had earlier articulated in "The Noble Rider and the Sound of Words." There, he says, "It is not only that the imagination adheres to reality, but, also, that reality adheres to the imagination and that the interdependence is essential" (663). She even fulfills the possible figure offered at the end of his earlier "Of Modern Poetry," since it is while "she combed her hair" that "She would talk a little to herself . . . / Repeating his name with its patient syllables" (442). The poem is also intensely sexual, I might add, but in a way that allows Penelope to experience the sexuality herself, rather than being reduced to an object of desire, as in the earlier reclining women discussed above: "She wanted nothing he could not bring her by coming alone. / She wanted no fetchings. His arms would be her necklace / And her belt, the final fortune of their desire" (442). Finally, it appears, at the end of his life Stevens came to be fully open to that "feminine within."

Admittedly, such a development as I have sketched here could appear itself reductive. Certainly in "Madame La Fleurie," also a late poem, we see the monstrous and bearded inversion of mother earth in the "bearded queen" (432) who is devouring him. Similarly, the mother in "World Without Peculiarity" becomes a hating "thing upon his breast" (388). Yet, in general, the development described above is accurate. As Stevens says in "Artificial Populations," a poem written the year he died, "This artificial population [rosy men and women of the rose] is like / A healing-point in the sickness of the mind" (474). Even more to the point is "Farewell Without a Guitar," written just four years before his death, in which Stevens overtly describes his changed relationship to both the masculine and the feminine:

> The reflections and repetitions,
> The blows and buffets of fresh senses
> Of the rider that was,
>
> Are a final construction,
> Like a glass and sun, of male reality
> And of that other and her desire.   (462)

Although the rather poignant "rider that was" refers nostalgically to the masculine "noble rider and the sound of words" of 1941, it is possible to say that from "To the One of Fictive Music" (1922) to the end of his life, much of Stevens' poetry was written in response to that significant "other." Yet, the female figure of this poem, so nebulously and delicately evoked, is not a high-toned old Christian woman – nor even the singer of "The Idea of Order at Key West," for that matter – but precisely a part of himself that he could never fully come to know except as "she" finally came to be voiced and embraced in his poetry. At the end of this poem, Stevens imagines an altogether new "male reality," one that includes "that other and her desire." It is no wonder, then, that earlier in the poem Stevens has said "Farewell," since "Spring's bright paradise has come to this" (461).

If, as he would finally conclude in another late poem, "Not one of the masculine myths we used to make" (439) is either true or ethical, Stevens' late poetry suggests that he came to appreciate the feminine within in ways that he could not have imagined in his early years. As opposed to the bravado of his pre-World War II poems, the tone of most of his late poems accomplishes, or perhaps even transcends, genuine humility. Put differently, if after World War II Stevens wished he had written another section of "Notes Toward a Supreme Fiction" called "*It Must Be Human*" (L 863–64), by the end of his life what he did call "The finally human" (429) in yet another late poem definitely had come to embrace the "feminine."

NOTES

1. See in particular the chapter entitled "The Woman Won, the Woman Lost," in Milton Bates's *Wallace Stevens: A Mythology of Self* (Berkeley: University of California Press, 1985), 49–82. There Bates exposes how Stevens' wife was his initial poetic muse when writing poems the two of them would share, but how she became displaced, both as muse and in heart, as he began writing more public and sophisticated verse.

2. John N. Serio and Greg Foster's *Online Concordance to Wallace Stevens' Poetry* (http://wallacestevens.com/concordance/WSdb.cgi, 2004) lists the following results for word frequency and rank:

Word	Frequency	Rank
man	365	38
men	229	54
woman	73	131
women	40	163
poetry	39	164
writing	3	200

14

DAVID R. JARRAWAY

Stevens and belief

The question of belief is arguably a major preoccupation throughout much of Wallace Stevens' work. To gain an initial foothold on this important theme, we might turn to a late essay entitled "The Relations Between Poetry and Painting," for it is there that Stevens remarks that in the modern age "in which disbelief is so profoundly prevalent or, if not disbelief, indifference to questions of belief, poetry and painting, and the arts in general, are, in their measure, a compensation for what has been lost" (748). Poetry, in particular, is an especial sort of compensation, since according to Stevens it is mystical and irrational together, and it prompts him to ruminate: "while it can lie in the temperament of very few of us to write poetry in order to find God, it is probably the purpose of each of us to write poetry to find the good which, in the Platonic sense, is synonymous with God" (786). In short, he declares in an important "Memorandum" to a letter from 1940, "The major poetic idea in the world is and always has been the idea of God" (*L* 378).

Such emphatic declarations about belief are hardly surprising for Stevens. From his early youth and on into an adulthood that bore witness to his own marriage within the Lutheran Church, the baptism of his only daughter by Episcopal rite, and a purported conversion to Roman Catholicism on his deathbed, Stevens would be drawn to and sustained by a faith whose outward and visible signs mattered less – "I hate the look of a Bible" (*L* 102), he once declared – than the inward and spiritual grace they were intended to impart. In a moment of candor from his seventy-second year, therefore, Stevens could admit: "I am not an atheist although I do not believe to-day in the same God in whom I believed when I was a boy" (*L* 735).

Yet it would be a mistake to think that the modern poet might offer himself and his work as a replacement for the loss of faith as Matthew Arnold once suggested. To the contrary, Stevens remarks, "we do not say that the poet is to take the place of the gods" (842). To do so would be an argument for humanism, and Stevens is quite emphatic that "the more I see of humanism the less I like it" (*L* 348). In that important "Memorandum" mentioned previously, however, Stevens does speak of adapting the idea of God "to our different intelligence" (*L* 378). If there is to be a future in the idea of belief, one implication of such a remark coming from a poet might be that intelligence could afford itself a different take on the whole question if it were to be examined from a rhetorical rather than from a rational, theological, or metaphysical perspective.

This alternative approach to thinking about belief would thus entail an effort to seek out new motives for metaphor, so to speak, neither inscribed in the classical (God instituted for man) nor the romantic (man substituted for God) conceptualizations of faith. Moving beyond the structural opposition of such notions that often preoccupy Stevens in his early poetry, it should not surprise us to discover Stevens midway through his poetic career writing about the romantic in "a pejorative sense," as he phrases it, "some phase of the romantic that has become stale" (915). Hence, moving beyond the binary opposition of classical mimesis (man corresponding to God) and romantic poesis (God corresponding to man), we conceivably find a poet motivated by the dismantling of generic forms of godlike correspondences. More and more, he becomes inspired by a metaphysics having to do with the rhetorical production of such correspondences, a rhetorical (or semiotic) generation of modernist forms that comes gradually to replace their classic and romantic counterparts.

Indeed, as we watch Stevens on his way to a rhetoric of belief, at the same time we perhaps view the structuralism of his modernism on the way to a "third idea" (841), as he calls it, a rhetoric whose post-structuralism is thoroughly postmodern. By displacing the quest for faith onto the question of belief, the poet enables us to trace a continuous pattern of spiritual rebirth spiraling through much of his later work. Here, as we shall see, Stevens' adapting his idea of God to a differing rather than an identifying or corresponding intelligence allows his artistic idiom to become productive rather than reductive, generative rather than generic, provisional rather than revisionary – the idiom of a "Metaphysician in the Dark," as it were, such as the one in "Of Modern Poetry."

When Stevens ruminates about belief in God, then writes in his "Adagia" about poetry as "that essence which takes its place as life's redemption" (901), we can hypothesize, following the 1940 "Memorandum," that in fact some of his earliest efforts at writing poetry revolved around the idea of eliminating God, then, more vexatiously, finding substitutes for God. These undertakings, as Stevens could only know with hindsight, were arguably the agendas of his first two books, *Harmonium* (1923) and *Ideas of Order* (1936), respectively. Indeed, we might say even further that *Harmonium* tends to foreground the elimination of God for the purposes of originating metaphorical play. Correspondingly, *Ideas of Order* focuses more on the substitution of God as a means of ultimately terminating metaphorical play. The fact that each book attempts to undo the other, however, reveals just how deeply divided Stevens' earliest writing actually is in its conventionally theological and thoroughly structuralist phase through to the mid-1930s.

In a 1902 journal entry, Stevens writes that "the true religious force in the world is not the church but the world itself: the mysterious callings of Nature and our responses" (L 58). Thus, the initial *Harmonium* volume is perhaps intended to forward much of that argument with a general brief against the mythology of transcendence and its ritualization of death countered by the drollery of such poems as "The Worms at Heaven's Gate," "Cortège for Rosenbloom," and "The Emperor of Ice-Cream." In these, Stevens offers praise for the meaning that lies within earthly immanence in contrast to spiritual transcendence. In the "Materia Poetica" we are informed that it is the relation of art to life, and not the reverse, that is important in face of the absence of belief in God (916). Hence, in a poem such as "Nomad Exquisite," the narrator cannot seem to catch hold of enough of nature's "angering for life" (77). But if *Harmonium* aims emphatically to resolve the conflict between immanent and transcendent belief, it is perhaps the most widely read and interpreted poem in the volume, "Sunday Morning," that reveals that a too-worldly poetry might have its shortcomings too: "And shall the earth / Seem all of paradise that we shall know?" (54).

It is thus interesting to speculate that the program that Stevens set for himself in his second volume, *Ideas of Order*, was one of immanent transcendence, a synthesis of both physical and metaphysical experience. But with its overall conception in terms of a cycle of romance – the "gorgeous wheel" (99), for instance, in "Sailing After Lunch" – it is fairly clear that the transcendent perspective of ascent is unmistakably the metaphorical radical in the new work. "Mud Master," for instance, moves much beyond the dilemma of determining the superiority of intelligence over soil or soil over intelligence in "The Comedian as the Letter C" back in *Harmonium*. By scaling a falling shaft of light, the Mud Master transcends reality and lays claim to a metaphysically superior realm beyond *both* soil and self.

Indeed, with a text such as "The Idea of Order at Key West" and its clamant rage for artistic form, one really begins to wonder whether real life could actually matter at all. For Stevens in search of substitutes for outworn faith, the new book is perhaps a significant religious achievement after the manner of T. S. Eliot's *Four Quartets*, where a similar preoccupation with a godlike form ostensibly conduces to mystic stillness. But with the several references to turning and returning in Stevens' own "Anglais Mort à

Florence," we wonder if the exclusivity of form in *Ideas of Order* has not become a liability as it counters the excessive realism of *Harmonium* – a debility, in fact, to Stevens whose quest for a differing faith through poetry has now become somewhat synonymous with a mechanical uniformity.

With the symbolic devolution of an outwardly assertive *Harmonium* to an inwardly motivated *Ideas of Order*, Stevens' early work would appear to have enclosed belief within a contradictory verbal structure and possibly stymied any new thinking on the question. Yet Stevens' continuing to revolve the principles of mimetic reality and poetic imagination, and in particular the interrelations between them, affords us a realization that suddenly must have become apparent to him in view of the complementary closure of his first two books. Fortuitously, Stevens seems startled to discover that the determination of things could not possibly be made intelligible unless there were other things to compare them to. That is to say, a poetry that ended up in an identity of self-relation as *Ideas of Order* appeared to have was terminal. But one that opened itself up to difference was a project that could break through the vicious circle of mechanical self-perpetuation.

Reality, therefore, was a necessary angel. Without it, there could be no way for the imagination to distinguish itself in its presupposing both distinction from and relation to otherness. Imagination, accordingly, would be doing its job not by detaching itself from the world but by transforming it through metaphor and thereby effecting an escape from some of reality's most paralyzing clichés. In all of this rumination, however, Stevens is utterly insistent that it is not a case of choosing one element of the relation over the other. Rather, the poet recognizes that a "universal interdependence" (657) exists between the imagination and reality and that always his artistic choices must be guided by the acknowledgment, as he states in his essay "The Noble Rider and the Sound of Words," that they are "equal and inseparable" (657).

With this brand-new sense of the co-dependent relativity of the imagination and reality emerging from roughly the period of "The Man with the Blue Guitar" (1937), Stevens gives a fairly clear impression of just how far behind his current projects were prepared to leave the previous formalism of the 1920s and early 1930s. The new poetry now springs from "the fluctuations between reality and imagination" (*L* 364) and acknowledges that each verbal site involves an aspect of itself in every other – what Stevens refers to as "a dithering of presences" and "a complex of differences" (858). As such, the new poetry gives no sense of a closed symbolic economy rhetorically centered in a transcendent imagination previously. In an important letter to Hi Simons from 1940 commenting closely on his new book,

Stevens writes: "Imagination has no source except in reality, and ceases to have any value when it departs from reality. . . . There is nothing that exists exclusively by reason of the imagination, or that does not exist in some form in reality. Thus, reality = the imagination, and the imagination = reality" (*L* 364). Hence, in what appears to be a rather startling set of post-structuralist formulations, Stevens explodes the notion of a mutually exclusive subject and object, inside and outside, or presence and absence underwriting his present work.

The interplay of revolving thought now from some middle ground thus allows Stevens to surmount the metaphysical logic enclosing the descent to reality at the beginning and the ascent to the imagination at the end of his previously stalled artistic agenda. But repositioning his project at the meta-physical site of some middling beast's interlude – the "lion in the lute" (lude?) (143) referred to in "The Man with the Blue Guitar" – would also be a way of revolutionizing theology's conventional "logic" beyond a belief that Stevens had formerly laid out between the rhetorics of descent (the temporalization of space) and of ascent (the spatialization of time) back in his first two books. Hence, " 'to sit and to balance things / . . . to the point of still, / . . . To know that the balance does not quite rest, / That the mask is strange, however like' " (148) – such post-theological knowledge suggests that belief could never be static and that, like poetry, must constantly be de-forming and later re-forming itself within the play between the imagin-ation and reality. The utterly central implication for belief in Stevens' third book, therefore, is that truth is not strictly theological as it could only be in his earlier formalist rhetoric. Instead, truth moves beyond the products of logic to become more process-like, a function of change in the universal give-and-take that is, to borrow Mark Taylor's errant theoretical term, "a/ theological." As Stevens writes in another letter from this period, "The only possible order of life is one in which all order is incessantly changing" (*L* 291–92).

The allusion to that strange mask in "The Man with the Blue Guitar" above provides us with a vital link to Stevens' next collection of verse, *Parts of a World*, published in 1942. Commenting on the mask two years previ-ously, Stevens states: "You do not pierce an actor's make-up: you go to see and enjoy the make-up; you do not bother about the face beneath" (*L* 362). Such a remark underscores perhaps the most radical idea in "The Man with the Blue Guitar," namely, the "absence in reality, [in] / Things as they are" (145). For the question of belief, the absence in reality theoretically destabil-izes the metaphysical ground of truth traditionally located in some beneath or beyond. Accordingly, reality's absence turns the logical or transcendental signification of truth loose to the play-acting of appearances merely. Apart from imparting a certain faceless mystery to Stevens' blue guitarist and thus making him the first of several figurations for the Metaphysician in the Dark in Stevens' work noted earlier, the much larger import of reality's frank absence points to the programmatic questioning of the very notion of belief based on logical or structural – theorists today might say "logocentric" – premises throughout his fourth collection of poems.

Stevens' important separation between a logocentric or metaphysical belief and one based on something quite other would appear to be represented in the new work perhaps with the contrast between Mrs. Alfred Uruguay in the poem by that name and Lady Lowzen in "Oak Leaves Are Hands." In the former case, we find a figure of pure negation – she says "no / To everything, in order to get at [herself]" (225) – approaching some state of the real atop a mountain, despite the falsifying bell the donkey she rides wishes for her. In the latter, Lady Lowzen takes a completely opposite tack: she "Skims the real for its unreal" (243). But inspecting further, we find that Lady Lowzen's position is only the inversion of Mrs. Uruguay's, not its subversion, for she too operates on a principle of negation. And so we are invited to look to the "figure of capable imagination" (226) back in "Mrs. Alfred Uruguay" as a way out of this impasse of negation and as a more appropriate model of belief.

One such figure is perhaps offered to us with "The Man on the Dump." If nearness is the necessary condition for the presencing of self and, by implication, the centering of belief as in the previous two poems, here we notice that one beats and beats (tin cans, lard pails) "for that which one believes" because "That's what one wants to get near" (185), yet to no avail. So many of the images in this poem thus tend to be holders of things – paper bags, corsets, boxes, chests – because logocentric belief is impossible without some kind of total self-containment – an idea that Stevens develops more generally in many of the other titles included in *Parts of a World*: "The Glass of Water," "A Dish of Peaches in Russia," "Man and Bottle," and so forth.

The questioning of belief rooted in various forms of egocentrism as we have just seen thus explains a certain ravaging or dismemberment of body parts throughout *Parts of a World*: hands, heads, and perhaps most important of all, eyes. The eye, of course, is the eye of logic or reason in the Western metaphysical tradition, overlooking the safety and security of stable self-presence, the first-person "I" on which it plays and with which it equivocates. Of the five senses, sight rules supreme, if the others matter at all, since in the commonsense view of human affairs, seeing is believing. Thus, in "Arcades of Philadelphia the Past," the image of the eyes held in the palm of the hand makes fairly clear that super vision is the privileged power in the mental economy: "the eyes are men in the palm of the hand" (207). But the entire metaphysical project of centering absolute knowledge within the rational self, and belief on the consequence of protective self-reflection, is suddenly no more with the opening lines of "On the Road Home": "It was when I said, / 'There is no such thing as the truth'" (186). In other words, as soon as it is admitted that there are "many truths" and that these are not "parts" of one single absolute and totalizing Truth, only then is there a shift to a different sense of reality in Stevens' latest work. Only then is the cat out of the paper bag previously, or in this poem, the fox "out of his hole" (186), and only then does the question of belief really begin to change.

With the displacement of belief away from metaphysical ideas of order and onto process and change, we might now turn to Stevens' most famous poem from 1942 (though added at the end of his next collection, *Transport to Summer* [1947]), "Notes Toward a Supreme Fiction" – a long poem that, once past its middle section significantly entitled "It Must Change," dares to ask in its third and final part: "What am I to believe?" (349). Now that we are long past the notion of any kind of absolutizing truth – "The the" (186) is as close as we come in "The Man on the Dump" – Stevens' new poem draws our attention to its title in the very first instance: "Supreme Fiction." In its simplest terms, then, "Notes" is a text privileging a fiction stranger than truth: metaphysical absence. As such, it arguably succeeded in delivering Stevens permanently from the impasse of order that quite possibly threatened to paralyze his artistic career. Thus, by turning the question of belief into an infinitely renewable problematic, "Notes Toward a Supreme Fiction" gave Stevens the artistic and the spiritual assurance that fiction as well as faith – now that he was beginning to write about each in fairly much the same terms – were themselves infinitely renewable.

In beginning the very first line of the prologue of "Notes Toward a Supreme Fiction" in the form of a question – "And for what, except for you, do I feel love?" (329) – and by leaving the referent for the pronoun "you" deliberately vague, Stevens uses a strategy right from the start that is calculated to vex the reader's hankering for "single, certain truth" with doubt and indeterminacy cast in "uncertain light" (329). The metaphysician now is truly in the dark with such an introduction and is offered the strictly momentary certitude of poetry's willful changefulness to provide him with any kind of peace. But all of this can only be made "implicit" in the title, as Stevens states in an important letter to Henry Church. "I have no idea of the form that a supreme fiction would take," Stevens remarks; "the essence of poetry is change," and the essence of change is not that it provides stable truths but rather "that it gives pleasure" (*L* 430). Thus, the second and third of the poem's major divisions, "It Must Change" and "It Must Give Pleasure," respectively, are very much anticipated in the poem's title and opening lines.

In the third section, Stevens' revolving the question of belief becomes the project of "the difficultest rigor" (344) and the focus for the remainder of the poem. To this difficult end, the first thing to go in erecting a faith in fiction must be its access by way of the logical and sensible – common sense, in a word, so favored by the seeing "I" noted earlier. Stevens' counter-model in this project is the biblical Jerome, a further variorum figure of the Metaphysician in the Dark. This is because Jerome captures that irrational moment in the interpretation of his fictions, particularly that "unreasoning" (345) that is so problematic to the seeing that is commonly believing. Such unreasoning, however, Stevens has been foregrounding throughout much of "Notes Toward a Supreme Fiction." Reasoning "with later reason" (346), as he calls it, works not according to the more accustomed logic of Western metaphysics. Following the darker mystical tradition of Hebraic interpretation signaled by Jerome, Stevens' "later reason" defamiliarizes logical (or theological) sameness and leads alternatively to a mysterious absence beyond reason. This absence in reality, once again, is underscored in the poem's first section, "It Must Be Abstract," where we are initially adjured to see the sun again, but "with an ignorant eye" (329).

In sum, therefore, by moving out from under the finite paradigms of presence in classicism and romanticism, Stevens' modernism offers us their opposite. His poetry thus becomes a model of infinite absence, hence a rhetoric of limitless expressiveness. But his modernist rhetoric is limitless only if the imagination can keep reality open. Infinitely revolving the language through which the forms of thought are constructed, Stevens' poetry nudges itself toward a "violet abyss" (349), and it is arguably that very postmodern presentiment that makes poetry's own existence possible. Approaching this fictional abyss, as "Notes Toward a Supreme Fiction" suggests, through a constant stripping away of different versions of reality – in a letter, Stevens uses the example of removing layers of varnish and dirt accumulated over generations on the surface of a painting in order to get at this first idea (L 426–27) – we now understand it is the process of repeated contextualization that constitutes the believer's art, rather than some ultimately representable product, which theoretically cannot nor should not exist. The "vast repetitions" concluding the text have a final good only in this sense: "the going round / And round and round, the merely going round, / . . . is a final good" (350).

The image of the abyss as absence just noted in Stevens' "Notes" offers itself in much post-structuralist theory – one thinks of Heidegger or Derrida here – as a kind of limit or margin against which writing renews itself at the intersection between past and future, tradition and change, form and force, representation and repetition. Paradoxically, its apparent nothingness is actually powerful and productive, revealing how a regressive transport back in time can actually constitute a progressive movement forward. Like spiritual dearth, the death of God, even absence itself, abysmal nothing becomes an ever-fecund source for renewable faith.

Precisely these rhetorical contours of supreme absence by which the "no-longer" measures the extent of the "not-yet" provide us with a good entry point into Stevens' fifth collection, *Transport to Summer*. The bilateralism of its rhetorical structure thus allows us to appreciate how important the no-longer of past effort might still be helpful in allowing Stevens to chart the not-yet of future belief. For this reason, the metaphysics of presence continues to die a slow death in further containment poems such as "A Woman Sings for a Soldier Come Home," "The House Was Quiet and the World Was Calm," and "The Bed of Old John Zeller," among others. The many paradoxes of the violet abyss opened up by the consideration of its status as supreme fiction in "Notes," and thus as a model for new belief, appear to indicate that we never really quite come clear of the forms or laws of expression. In openly questioning that belief, then, freedom is a function of constraint inasmuch as constraint is a condition of freedom.

Put another way, the question of belief forms itself to the structure of desire as a mutual relation between things no-longer and things not-yet. In this doubly dynamic sense, the question of belief in the very first instance resists the repression of time coincident with the faith in transcendence that Stevens endeavors to work through in his earlier poetry, as we have seen. Since traditional faith is foundationally the eternization of the timeless moment that we find Stevens repeatedly calling into question, post-formalist (or postmodern) belief privileges the timely moment and thereby honors the play of differences by which it seeks the motive for metaphor through desire's fulfillment within time rather than beyond it.

Desire, then, in its strictest sense is an infection of time, and its force lies precisely in its inability to bring itself to any kind of culmination. This amounts to its ability to inhabit disconnection and fragmentation, to bear within itself the destiny of its own non-satisfaction. An example from Stevens' new work might be the disjunctively titled poem "God Is Good. It Is a Beautiful Night," in which the image of a severely fragmented poet is presented: a head and zither here, a book and shoe there, and a rotted rose someplace else. We then witness some sort of attempt to integrate the whole, as when the head reading the book, and speaking, "becomes the scholar again, seeking celestial / Rendezvous" (255). But still the zither remains rusty and the poet's music thin, since the truly venerable song must refuse precise formulation and exact containment. When the subject of that elusive song does, in fact, turn out to be God, as in "Less and Less Human, O Savage Spirit," God *is* Good as a postulate of faith only because it resists all the atemporal, conventional, logocentric approaches to its proof as dogma. "[God] must be incapable of speaking" (288), therefore, only in the sense that His existence in language is never conceptually determinate but infinitely interpretable through time and, consequently, ontologically undecidable.

Accordingly, God's absent presence that unfolds in the infectious temporality of being's desire becomes "the deepnesses of space" (295) solemnized by a pilot's noble death in "Flyer's Fall." That "nothingness of human afterdeath," as the text puts it, thus becomes the very generative matrix of belief: but a belief "without belief," that is, without any total transcendent truth; hence, a belief "beyond belief," a belief in "Darkness" (295), outside the dirty fates of convention. For the Metaphysician in the Dark, the question of belief all comes back once again to the perspectivism of seeming-truth, constituted by the temporal force rather than the eternal form of the poet's (or believer's) desire, and hence by the individual manner of his style or address. Whether a seeming of words or worlds, the making can never be universal and intrinsic, only particular and relative, as in the case of the concluding rubies in "Description Without Place," the reality of whose intense color is strictly an event of relation to the other: "Like rubies reddened by rubies reddening" (302). With the absence of center or logos for the metaphysician, so contemporary a/theologians would argue, there can be no specially appointed time or place for faith to transpire. Like Stevens, we should conclude, therefore, that there is only description without place. And like the question of belief, description without end, since "In a description hollowed out of hollow-bright, / The artificer of subjects [is] still half night" (302).

Earlier, we mentioned that the motive for metaphor prompted by the question of belief is a responsiveness to the play of differences. Clearly, a quite other sense of metaphor than one synonymous with figurative comparison or likeness has overtaken Stevens' work by "Credences of Summer," and in an essay composed about the same time, entitled "Three Academic Pieces," he is provoked to clarify exactly what that new sense of metaphor might be. In its more conventional and restricted economic sense, Stevens tells us, metaphor tends toward some ultimate form of meaning expressive of equivalence or "identity" (687). The question of belief undoubtedly makes clear to him the contradiction in such a theory in that the successive interchanges within the ever-increasing transport of verbal meaning to some terminus of totalizing identity would find metaphor doing away with itself entirely. But rather than suspend the operation of metaphor altogether, the poet would prefer to refigure it, open it out to a more general economy. He calls this more elliptical economy "resemblance." Divorcing it from a process of mere mechanical imitation or identification – "We are not dealing with identity. . . . [I]dentity is the vanishing-point of resemblance" (687), he states emphatically – Stevens connects "resemblance" to the activity of incessant creation to be found in nature, whose own prodigies of "metamorphosis" serve as an analogue to the "activity of the imagination" (687).

Resemblance, therefore, gives us a take on metaphor in its productive rather than its reductive sense. Stevens, recurring to a central term from "Description Without Place," refers in the essay to such formativity as "intensification," that is, "a sense of reality keen enough to be in excess of the normal sense of reality" (691), just as the intermediacy of metamorphosis could be said to exceed the immediacy of identity. "[I]t is not too extravagant," Stevens concludes, "to think of resemblances and of the repetitions of resemblances as a source of the ideal" (693) and, by implication, as a source for belief as well.

"Credences of Summer," perhaps the most ambitious contribution to the *Transport to Summer* volume, invokes this multiplicitous sense of resemblance from the point of view of belief in its very title. In response to that question, once again, the credences of the poem speak to a range of competing vocabularies for belief – vocabularies urged on by desire's double-dynamic of the no-longer and the not-yet noted earlier. And such is never more the case than when we creep ahead to the eponymous text of Stevens' next collection and wonder whether "The Auroras of Autumn" has not come to take the place of "Credences of Summer." Ushered into an act of choice between competing vocabularies within the two poems, the Metaphysician in the Dark is thus empowered by Stevens' theory of resemblance. What authenticates the act of choice, according to "The Auroras of Autumn," is the "velocities of change" (357). Hence, empowerment for the Metaphysician in the Dark lies "where the truth [is] not the respect of one," according to "Someone Puts a Pineapple Together," "But always of many things," and it is truth's metaphorical velocities that perhaps give him "a purpose to believe" (695).

The exact contrast to the Metaphysician in the Dark here is offered, once again, by "The Auroras of Autumn" in the person of the "scholar of one candle" (359) in canto VI. The scholar can see the multifarious shifts of force, the "Arctic effulgence" (359) of the auroras, flaring on the frame of everything he imagines Being to be. But such force – that "ever-never-changing same" called "Again" (308) in the "Adult Epigram" from *Transport to Summer* – fills the scholar with panic. Stevens' point, however, so playfully worked out in the previous "Credences of Summer," is frankly that life is not reducible to the single form or frame. In "The Auroras of Autumn," therefore, change makes of life a veritable drama of alterity, in the canto's memorable image of "a theatre floating through the clouds, / Itself a cloud... of cloud transformed / To cloud transformed again, idly, the way / A season changes color to no end" (359). If the scholar of one candle fails us in his desire to presence the productive absence of nothing in canto VI, then the figure of the father in canto IV gives us better reason to hope. For there we find this father figure immersed in a constantly iterated "space," no doubt the space that the "violet abyss" of "Notes Toward a Supreme Fiction" had left open between desire and its fulfillment. Moved by an excess of force, therefore, the master of nothing joins Stevens' necessary angel from the final section of "Notes" and "leaps from heaven to heaven more rapidly" in the proper pursuit of transformative resemblance than "bad angels leap from heaven to hell in flames" (357).

When we move more fully, via "The Auroras of Autumn," into Stevens' final collections of poems, *The Auroras of Autumn* (1950) and *The Rock* rounding out *The Collected Poems* (1954), the velocities of change give us the sense that the question of belief is perhaps less a state of mind than it is a discursive exercise: an "act of the mind" (219) that we might extrapolate from "Of Modern Poetry" back in *Parts of a World* – a thought-event, as it were. The sense of unlimited possibility of meaning for such a thought-event is fit exercise for the capable imagination, but an imagination, Stevens reminds us in "Imagination as Value," not integral to any romantic sensibility, that is, "imagination as metaphysics" (727). Rather, it is one that exercises "the power of the mind" (726) over things – the things that we find so abundant in the poet's last work: "Things of August," "The Plain Sense of Things," "Not Ideas About the Thing But the Thing Itself," and so forth. Moreover, if the believer's imaginative will-to-power is construed as "a certain single characteristic," he tells us, "it is the source not of a certain single value but of as many values as reside in the possibilities of things" (726). Within just such a plurivalent source we consequently might expect to find the question of belief opening itself up to that new site and that new space different from the up/down, inside/outside, real/apparent metaphysical foundationalism of duplex thought brought to a close in his first two books. Here, in "A Primitive Like an Orb," Stevens tags this new site a "miraculous multiplex" (379), suggesting that belief, like the imagination from which it springs, has at last become an eventful thing of infinite possibility.

In further prose statements, Stevens describes such acts of the imagination as a process of defamiliarization by which operation "the typical function of the imagination . . . always makes use of the familiar to produce the unfamiliar" (744), or otherwise "import[s] the unreal into what is real" (735), thereby converting the normal into the abnormal. That the potential for such conversion exists in language marks the prologue to what is possible as far as belief is concerned. However, words carried to the furthest point of such a declension – that is, to their furthest point of familiarity – deliver us up to spirituality's "inert savoir" depicted in the opening stanzas of "The Plain Sense of Things": "as if / We had come to an end of the imagination" (428). The plain sense of the title might indeed mark the end of the imagination if it were literally possible for words to become coincident with things – the Real Thing, as we like to say.

But we live in the mind for the most part, Stevens would say, and such an identifiable familiarity is only one of degree, and, as such, a question of the extent to which artifice has proceeded within us (728–29), or put the other way, the extent to which the so-called Real Thing in its being presenced is actually being shielded from a more defamiliarizing absence. At some point, in other words, even the normal, which might appear to represent the imagination at its most deprived, was once an extension of the abnormal. Like belief converted to truth or dogma, then, the normal too easily absents itself from its imaginative provenance in metaphor and plainly risks capitulating to "an inevitable knowledge, / Required, as a necessity requires." "Yet [even] the absence of the imagination," the text tells us, "had / Itself to be imagined" (428). Thus, in its inert savoir, the poem as an act of the mind doubles as the multiplex condition for the continuance of the very metaphoricity that, in the end, must imagine or explain itself, hence the "sense" in the present poem's title that must be made plain. And it is in this ironic "sense," the sense in which there is no plain sense, that a tremendous hope for the future of belief lies.

In the end, then, the true Metaphysician in the Dark must jettison the commonsense myth of transparency with its semblance of unconstructed inertness at the very heart of metaphysical belief and begin working instead from "The Hermitage at the Center" or "Vacancy in the Park," that is, from the absence at the center of the imagination's metaphoricity previously. In the former text, Stevens makes it the subject of "unintelligible thought" (430), in an effort to reverse the logocentric inevitability in the poems just mentioned, or in implicated pieces such as "Our Stars Come from Ireland" and "The Irish Cliffs of Moher." The exchange here thus becomes the "unexplained completion" in "The Poem That Took the Place of a Mountain" as well. There, the "exact rock" of the textual space must be filled with "inexactnesses," since the view of total presence is one that the imagination's program of abnormal defamiliarization can only edge toward, but never entirely approximate as the original site of metaphor's – and dare we say, the question of belief's – "unique and solitary home" (435).

In emulation of this state of rhetorical approximation, Stevens leaves us in his final book the figure of George Santayana in "To an Old Philosopher in Rome," a friend and mentor from Stevens' Harvard years. Close to death now in the poem, as Stevens himself was in real life, Santayana merits the highest praise because he stops upon the threshold of "as if," rather than within the enclosed certainty of any metaphysical thought, the threshold, that is to say, between "The extreme of the known in the presence of the extreme / Of the unknown" (432). As a last gesture toward the Metaphysician in the Dark, therefore, Santayana is heroic in the autumn of his life because he continues to question that which eludes the ascertainable structures of faith. His credences thus come to affirm a complicated and amassing harmony, imaged perhaps in the convent bells whose "peculiar chords" continue, in Stevens' riddling phrase, "clinging to whisper still" (434). "[S]till" as both adjective and adverb in this final tribute becomes Stevens' rather ingenious way of keeping open the question of belief at the edge of "wakefulness" (433) and our imaginative response to it as well.

GUIDE TO FURTHER READING

WORKS BY WALLACE STEVENS

The Collected Poems of Wallace Stevens. New York: Knopf, 1954.
The Contemplated Spouse: The Letters of Wallace Stevens to Elsie, ed. J. Donald Blount. Columbia: University of South Carolina Press, 2006.
The Necessary Angel: Essays on Reality and the Imagination. New York: Vintage, 1951.
Opus Posthumous, ed. Milton J. Bates. New York: Knopf, 1989.
The Palm at the End of the Mind: Selected Poems and a Play, ed. Holly Stevens. New York: Knopf, 1971.
Secretaries of the Moon: The Letters of Wallace Stevens and José Rodríguez Feo, ed. Beverly Coyle and Alan Filreis. Durham: Duke University Press, 1986.
Selected Poems. London: Faber and Faber, 1953.

BIOGRAPHICAL STUDIES

Bates, Milton J. *Wallace Stevens: A Mythology of Self.* Berkeley: University of California Press, 1985.
Brazeau, Peter. *Parts of a World: Wallace Stevens Remembered; An Oral Biography.* New York: Random House, 1983.
Crockett, John. "Of Holly and Wallace Stevens in a Purple Light." *Wallace Stevens Journal* 21.1 (1997): 3–33.
Filreis, Alan. *Wallace Stevens and the Actual World.* Princeton: Princeton University Press, 1991.
Gaddis, Eugene R. "Poets of Life and the Imagination: Wallace Stevens and Chick Austin." *Wallace Stevens Journal* 28.2 (2004): 261–78.
Lensing, George S. *Wallace Stevens: A Poet's Growth.* Baton Rouge: Louisiana State University Press, 1986.
Lombardi, Thomas Francis. *Wallace Stevens and the Pennsylvania Keystone: The Influence of Origins on His Life and Poetry.* Selinsgrove, Pa.: Susquehanna University Press, 1996.
Longenbach, James. *Wallace Stevens: The Plain Sense of Things.* New York: Oxford University Press, 1991.

Richardson, Joan. *Wallace Stevens: The Early Years, 1879–1923*. New York: William Morrow, 1986.

———. *Wallace Stevens: The Later Years, 1923–1955*. New York: William Morrow, 1988.

Sharpe, Tony. *Wallace Stevens: A Literary Life*. New York: St. Martin's Press, 1999.

Stevens, Holly. "Bits of Remembered Time." *Southern Review* 7 n.s. 3 (1971): 651–57.

———. *Souvenirs and Prophecies: The Young Wallace Stevens*. New York: Knopf, 1977.

STEVENS AND *HARMONIUM*

Blackmur, R. P. "Examples of Wallace Stevens." 1931. *Language as Gesture: Essays in Poetry*. New York: Harcourt, Brace, 1952. 221–49.

Buttel, Robert. *Wallace Stevens, The Making of "Harmonium."* Princeton: Princeton University Press, 1967.

Litz, A. Walton. *Introspective Voyager: The Poetic Development of Wallace Stevens*. New York: Oxford University Press, 1972.

MacLeod, Glen. *Wallace Stevens and Company: The "Harmonium" Years, 1913–1923*. Ann Arbor: UMI Research Press, 1983.

Rehder, Robert. *The Poetry of Wallace Stevens*. New York: St. Martin's Press, 1988.

STEVENS IN THE 1930s

Burnshaw, Stanley. "Stevens' 'Mr. Burnshaw and the Statue.'" *Stanley Burnshaw: The Collected Poems and Selected Prose*. Austin: University of Texas Press, 2002. 348–57.

Cleghorn, Angus J. *Wallace Stevens' Poetics: The Neglected Rhetoric*. New York: Palgrave, 2000.

Filreis, Alan. *Modernism from Right to Left: Wallace Stevens, the Thirties and Literary Radicalism*. New York: Cambridge University Press, 1994.

———. "Modern Poetry and Anticommunism." *A Concise Companion to Twentieth-Century American Poetry*, ed. Stephen Fredman. Oxford: Blackwell, 2005. 173–90.

Monroe, Robert Emmett. "Figuration and Society in 'Owl's Clover.'" *Wallace Stevens Journal* 13.2 (1989): 127–49.

Nelson, Cary. *Repression and Recovery: Modern American Poetry and the Politics of Cultural Memory, 1910–1945*. Madison: University of Wisconsin Press, 1989.

Wald, Alan. *Exiles from a Future Time: The Forging of the Mid-Twentieth-Century Literary Left*. Chapel Hill: University of North Carolina Press, 2002.

STEVENS AND THE SUPREME FICTION

Bates, Milton J. "Stevens' Soldier Poems and Historical Possibility." *Wallace Stevens Journal* 28.2 (2004): 203–209.

Leggett, B. J. *Wallace Stevens and Poetic Theory: Conceiving the Supreme Fiction*. Chapel Hill: University of North Carolina Press, 1987.

Litz, A. Walton. "Space and Time in 'Notes Toward a Supreme Fiction.'" *Wallace Stevens Journal* 17.2 (1993): 162–67.

Peterson, Margaret. *Wallace Stevens and the Idealist Tradition.* Ann Arbor: UMI Research Press, 1983.

Ransom, James C. "Teaching the Long Poem: The Example of 'Notes Toward a Supreme Fiction.'" *Teaching Wallace Stevens: Practical Essays,* ed. John N. Serio and B. J. Leggett. Knoxville: University of Tennessee Press, 1994. 74–83.

Vendler, Helen. "'Notes Toward a Supreme Fiction': Allegorical Personae." *Wallace Stevens Journal* 17.2 (1993): 147–61.

STEVENS' LATE POETRY

Baechler, Lea. "Pre-Elegiac Affirmation in 'To an Old Philosopher in Rome.'" *Wallace Stevens Journal* 14.2 (1990): 141–52.

Bates, Jennifer. "Stevens, Hegel, and the Palm at the End of the Mind." *Wallace Stevens Journal* 23.2 (1999): 152–66.

Berger, Charles. *Forms of Farewell: The Late Poetry of Wallace Stevens.* Madison: University of Wisconsin Press, 1985.

Harrison, Robert Pogue. "'Not Ideas About the Thing But the Thing Itself.'" *New Literary History* 30 (1999): 661–73.

Leggett, B. J. *Late Stevens: The Final Fiction.* Baton Rouge: Louisiana State University Press, 2005.

McCann, Janet. *Wallace Stevens Revisited: "The Celestial Possible."* New York: Twayne, 1995.

STEVENS AND HIS CONTEMPORARIES

Gelpi, Albert. "Stevens and Williams: The Epistemology of Modernism." *Wallace Stevens: The Poetics of Modernism,* ed. Albert Gelpi. Cambridge: Cambridge University Press, 1985. 3–23.

Kenner, Hugh. *A Homemade World: The American Modernist Writers.* New York: Knopf, 1975.

Lentricchia, Frank. *Modernist Quartet.* Cambridge: Cambridge University Press, 1994.

Perloff, Marjorie, "Pound/Stevens: Whose Era?" *The Dance of the Intellect: Studies in the Poetry of the Pound Tradition.* Cambridge: Cambridge University Press, 1985. 1–32.

Schulze, Robin G. *The Web of Friendship: Marianne Moore and Wallace Stevens.* Ann Arbor: University of Michigan Press, 1995.

Steinman, Lisa M. "Lending No Part: Teaching Stevens with Williams." *Teaching Wallace Stevens: Practical Essays,* ed. John N. Serio and B. J. Leggett. Knoxville: University of Tennessee Press, 1994. 169–78.

Walker, David. *The Transparent Lyric: Reading and Meaning in the Poetry of Stevens and Williams.* Princeton: Princeton University Press, 1984.

STEVENS AND ROMANTICISM

Abrams, M. H. "Structure and Style in the Greater Romantic Lyric." *From Sensibility to Romanticism: Essays Presented to Frederick A. Pottle,* ed. Frederick W. Hilles and Harold Bloom. New York: Oxford University Press, 1965.

Bloom, Harold. *Wallace Stevens: The Poems of Our Climate.* Ithaca: Cornell University Press, 1977.

Bornstein, George. *Transformations of Romanticism in Yeats, Eliot, and Stevens.* Chicago: University of Chicago Press, 1976.

Carroll, Joseph. *Wallace Stevens' Supreme Fiction: A New Romanticism.* Baton Rouge: Louisiana State University Press, 1987.

Vendler, Helen. "Stevens and Keats's 'To Autumn.'" *Close Reading: The Reader,* ed. Frank Lentricchia and Andrew DuBois. Durham: Duke University Press, 2003.

STEVENS AND PHILOSOPHY

Bevis, William W. *Mind of Winter: Wallace Stevens, Meditation, and Literature.* Pittsburgh: University of Pittsburgh Press, 1989.

Critchley, Simon. *Things Merely Are: Philosophy in the Poetry of Wallace Stevens.* London: Routledge, 2005.

Doggett, Frank. *Stevens' Poetry of Thought.* Baltimore: Johns Hopkins Press, 1966.

Eeckhout, Bart. *Wallace Stevens and the Limits of Reading and Writing.* Columbia: University of Missouri Press, 2002.

Leggett, B. J. *Early Stevens: The Nietzschean Intertext.* Durham: Duke University Press, 1992.

Leonard, James S., and Christine E. Wharton. *The Fluent Mundo: Wallace Stevens and the Structure of Reality.* Athens: University of Georgia Press, 1988.

Miller, J. Hillis. "Stevens' Poetry of Being." *The Act of the Mind: Essays on the Poetry of Wallace Stevens,* ed. Roy Harvey Pearce and J. Hillis Miller. Baltimore: Johns Hopkins Press, 1965. 143–62.

Poirier, Richard. *Poetry and Pragmatism.* Cambridge: Harvard University Press, 1992.

STEVENS' SEASONAL CYCLES

Frye, Northrop. *Anatomy of Criticism: Four Essays.* Princeton: Princeton University Press, 1957.

Lensing, George S. *Wallace Stevens and the Seasons.* Baton Rouge: Louisiana State University Press, 2001.

Macksey, Richard A. "The Climates of Wallace Stevens." *The Act of the Mind: Essays on the Poetry of Wallace Stevens,* ed. Roy Harvey Pearce and J. Hillis Miller. Baltimore: Johns Hopkins Press, 1965. 185–223.

Riddel, Joseph N. *The Clairvoyant Eye: The Poetry and Poetics of Wallace Stevens.* Baton Rouge: Louisiana State University Press, 1965; reprinted 1991.

Sheehan, Donald. "Wallace Stevens' Theory of Metaphor." *Papers on Language and Literature* 2.1 (1966): 57–66.

STEVENS AND THE LYRIC SPEAKER

Beehler, Michael. "Penelope's Experience: Teaching the Ethical Lessons of Wallace Stevens." *Teaching Wallace Stevens: Practical Essays,* ed. John N. Serio and B. J. Leggett. Knoxville: University of Tennessee Press, 1994. 267–79.

Dolan, John. "'The Warmth I Had Forgotten': Stevens' Revision of 'First Warmth' and the Dramatization of the Interpersonal." *Wallace Stevens Journal* 21.2 (1997): 162–74.

Masel, Carolyn. "'Receding Shores That Never Touch with Inarticulate Pang': Stevens and the Language of Touch." *Wallace Stevens Journal* 26.1 (2002): 22–40.

Vendler, Helen. *Wallace Stevens: Words Chosen Out of Desire.* Knoxville: University of Tennessee Press, 1984; reprinted Cambridge, Mass.: Harvard University Press, 1986.

STEVENS AND LINGUISTIC STRUCTURE

Borroff, Marie. *Language and the Poet: Verbal Artistry in Frost, Stevens, and Moore.* Chicago: University of Chicago Press, 1979.

Brogan, Jacqueline Vaught. *Stevens and Simile: A Theory of Language.* Princeton: Princeton University Press, 1986.

Campbell, P. Michael, and John Dolan. "Teaching Stevens's Poetry Through Rhetorical Structure." *Teaching Wallace Stevens: Practical Essays,* ed. John N. Serio and B. J. Leggett. Knoxville: University of Tennessee Press, 1994. 119–28.

Cook, Eleanor. *Poetry, Word-Play, and Word-War in Wallace Stevens.* Princeton: Princeton University Press, 1988.

Gilbert, Roger. "Verbs of Mere Being: A Defense of Stevens' Style." *Wallace Stevens Journal* 28.2 (2004): 191–202.

Justice, Donald. "The Free-Verse Line in Stevens." *Platonic Scripts.* Ann Arbor: University of Michigan Press, 1984. 176–204.

Maeder, Beverly. *Wallace Stevens' Experimental Language: The Lion in the Lute.* New York: St. Martin's Press, 1999.

Miller, J. Hillis. *The Linguistic Moment: From Wordsworth to Stevens.* Princeton: Princeton University Press, 1985.

Rieke, Alison. *The Senses of Nonsense.* Iowa City: University of Iowa Press, 1992.

Vendler, Helen. *On Extended Wings: Wallace Stevens' Longer Poems.* Cambridge: Harvard University Press, 1969.

STEVENS AND PAINTING

Altieri, Charles. *Painterly Abstraction in Modernist American Poetry: The Contemporaneity of Modernism.* New York: Cambridge University Press, 1989.

Costello, Bonnie. "Effects of an Analogy: Wallace Stevens and Painting." *Wallace Stevens: The Poetics of Modernism,* ed. Albert Gelpi. New York: Cambridge University Press, 1985. 65–85.

Feinstein, Sascha. "Stanzas of Color: Wallace Stevens and Paul Klee." *Wallace Stevens Journal* 16.1 (1992): 64–81.

MacLeod, Glen. *Wallace Stevens and Modern Art: From the Armory Show to Abstract Expressionism.* New Haven: Yale University Press, 1993.

———. "The Influence of Wallace Stevens on Contemporary Artists." *Wallace Stevens Journal* 20.2 (1996): 139–80.

Qian, Zhaoming. *The Modernist Response to Chinese Art: Pound, Moore, Stevens.* Charlottesville: University of Virginia Press, 2003.

STEVENS AND THE FEMININE

Brogan, Jacqueline Vaught. *The Violence Within/The Violence Without: Wallace Stevens and the Emergence of a Revolutionary Poetics.* Athens: University of Georgia Press, 2003.

Fisher, Barbara M. *Wallace Stevens: The Intensest Rendezvous.* Charlottesville: University Press of Virginia, 1990.

Halliday, Mark. *Stevens and the Interpersonal.* Princeton: Princeton University Press, 1991.

Schaum, Melita, ed. *Wallace Stevens and the Feminine.* Tuscaloosa: University of Alabama Press, 1993.

STEVENS AND BELIEF

Jarraway, David R. *Wallace Stevens and the Question of Belief: Metaphysician in the Dark.* Baton Rouge: Louisiana State University Press, 1993.

McCann, Janet. "A Letter from Father Hanley on Stevens' Conversion to Catholicism." *Wallace Stevens Journal* 18.1 (1994): 3–5.

Murphy, Charles M. *Wallace Stevens: A Spiritual Poet in a Secular Age.* Mahwah, N. J.: Paulist Press, 1996.

Scott, Nathan A., Jr. *The Poetics of Belief: Studies in Coleridge, Arnold, Pater, Santayana, Stevens, and Heidegger.* Chapel Hill: University of North Carolina Press, 1985.

Taylor, Mark C. *Erring: A Postmodern A/Theology.* Chicago: University of Chicago Press, 1984.

Zizek, Slavoj. *On Belief.* Thinking in Action Series. New York: Routledge, 2001.

REFERENCE MATERIALS

Bates, Milton J. "Stevens' Books at the Huntington: An Annotated Checklist," parts I and II. *Wallace Stevens Journal* 2.3/4; 3.1/2 (1978; 1979): 45–61; 15–33, 70.

Brazeau, Peter. "Wallace Stevens at the University of Massachusetts: Checklist of an Archive." *Wallace Stevens Journal* 2 (1978): 50–54.

Cook, Eleanor. *A Reader's Guide to Wallace Stevens.* Princeton: Princeton University Press, 2007.

Doyle, Charles. *Wallace Stevens: The Critical Heritage.* The Critical Heritage Series. Boston: Routledge & Kegan Paul, 1985.

Edelstein, J. M. *Wallace Stevens: A Descriptive Bibliography.* Pittsburgh: University of Pittsburgh Press, 1973.

Moynihan, Robert. "Checklist: Second Purchase, Wallace Stevens Collection, Huntington Library." *Wallace Stevens Journal* 20.1 (1996): 76–103.

Serio, John N. *Wallace Stevens: An Annotated Secondary Bibliography.* Pittsburgh: University of Pittsburgh Press, 1994.

———. *Wallace Stevens Journal: The First Twenty-Five Years.* Potsdam, N.Y.: Wallace Stevens Society, 2002. Text-searchable CD-ROM.

Serio, John N., and Greg Foster. *Online Concordance to Wallace Stevens' Poetry.* http://www.wallacestevens.com/concordance/WSdb.cgi, 2004.

Sukenick, Ronald. *Wallace Stevens: Musing the Obscure: Readings, An Interpretation and a Guide to the Collected Poetry.* New York: New York University Press, 1967.

INDEX

CAMBRIDGE COMPANIONS TO LITERATURE